Praise for T/

"A powerful sequel to Hamilton's *The Land Remains*. With clarity and a unique style, Hamilton takes on the forces, philosophy, and economic 'religion' that is destroying our soil and polluting our rivers and streams, with a corresponding degradation of our social values of individual and collective responsibility. He pulls no punches! This is a provocative book, which is a must read for all who care about our environment and a future of sustainable and regenerative farming."
—Sen. Tom Harkin, US Senator 1985-2015

"This is a rare and remarkable book about the interplay between nature and man. *The River Knows: How Water and Land Will Shape Our Future*, should be required reading for anyone who cares about fresh water and wants to know what is wrong, what is right, and how to turn public policy from the wrong way to the right way. Hamilton is an esteemed professor emeritus of agriculture, natural resources and food law, but this book is written for a general audience. Sometimes the book is amusing, as when the often grumpy "character" who is Iowa's Raccoon River speaks up about the harms caused by bad public policy and industrial agriculture that have polluted its waters and destroyed its functions (recreation, wildlife habitat, fresh water). Sometimes, Hamilton himself is white-hot with rage on the stupidity of politicians (he names them) who enable catastrophic harm to rivers, streams, and the human beings who depend on fresh water. Yet, Hamilton's book is hopeful. It is replete with solutions that will fix the problems that he calls out. *The River Knows* is for everyone concerned about the future of their children and grandchildren. While primarily set in Iowa, the truths it tells are applicable in every state."
—Sarah Vogel, Attorney and author of *The Farmer's Lawyer*

"Challenges abound when striving to protect soil and water quality in an Ag-Driven state. But so do solutions. No one knows better the abuses it's endured and the pathways to prevention than the highly compromised Raccoon River and its equally wise friend Professor Hamilton. Read this not just to understand the problems we face but to support the hope of a more just future for communities, water, and soil through the actions this thoughtful river knows all about."
—Pat Boddy, former deputy and interim director of the Iowa Department of Natural Resources, and senior partner emeritus of RDG Planning and Design in Des Moines

"Captivatingly integrates science with sage wisdom. Adding a spice of history to help us understand Iowa's original water quality and, more importantly, why water quality challenges exist today. Hamilton offers a personal perspective about Iowa's challenges and how we might address those challenges and does not shy away from some of the thorniest issues in this agricultural state. The read is delightful, will stimulate passion in many, and will stir discussions around the dinner table."
—Rick Cruse, Richard Cruse, professor in the Agronomy Department at Iowa State University and Director of the Iowa Water Center

"Professor Hamilton has given the river a voice. May we have ears to listen! This book challenges us to think and act in ways that can heal our land and water, now as well as for future generations."
—Joe McGovern, President, Iowa Natural Heritage Foundation

"Agricultural law visionary, Neil Hamilton has once again given us a rich story with an incredibly powerful message. *The River Knows* is a call to action. Using history, geology, law, and personal insight, Hamilton allows the river to speak to us. And what it says should cause people to shudder. Hamilton concludes with "big ideas" and "imagination" to guide the reader to the solutions we desperately need."
—Susan A. Schneider, William H. Enfield Professor of Law; Director, LLM Program in Agricultural & Food Law

"Neil Hamilton reveals the true nature of our most precious natural resources —our rivers and streams. His piercing analysis and reflective approach to understanding our rivers is a must read for anyone thinking about clean water issues in Iowa. Our rationale for protecting and restoring these natural resources has never been more clear as Hamilton makes the case concretely and creatively in his critical approach that we cannot and must not ignore."
—Luke Hoffman, Iowa Rivers Revival, Executive Director

"A comprehensive reflection of the river's soul. Neil Hamilton brilliantly articulates the embodiment of the river's voice in truth, with no stone unturned. Humanity is left to wonder about our priorities regarding vital natural resources— soil, water, habitat—our spark for life."
—Christine A. Curry, Upper Mississippi River Initiative, Iowa Outreach Coordinator

"If you enjoyed *The Land Remains*, you will love *The River Knows*, Hamilton's newest book connecting us to nature. Like a river, it flows with interesting and useful information while carrying us past the landmarks of history that have landed us where we are today."
—Jerry L. Anderson (he/his), Dean and Richard M. and Anita Calkins Distinguished Professor of Law, Drake University Law School

"I enjoyed the book and it challenged me as it should. For everyone who lives in a watershed anywhere, but, especially here in Iowa, it is a must read! Professor Hamilton eloquently sets the stage for the river to speak. Bring your values with you and see how they stack up to what *The River Knows*."
—Paul Willis, Niman Ranch Pork Co., Director/Founder

"A poignant and biting commentary on Iowa, its people and natural resources."
—Mark Rasmussen, Director Emeritus, Leopold Center for Sustainable Agriculture at Iowa State University

"*The River Knows* is a critically important read for everyone who dreams of seeing Iowa's rivers once again flow clean and clear. Neil Hamilton's engaging, eye-opening exploration of the historic, social, political, and economic aspects of Iowa's water problems has much to teach us."
—Cornelia F. Mutel, editor of *Tending Iowa's Land: Pathways to a Sustainable Future*

The River Knows

How Water and Land Will Shape Our Future

Give the River room!

Neil D. Hamilton

Ice Cube Press, LLC
North Liberty, Iowa, USA

The River Knows: How Water and Land Will Shape Our Future

Copyright © 2023 Neil D. Hamilton

ISBN 9781948509442

Library of Congress Control Number: 2023931995

Ice Cube Press, LLC (Est. 1991)
1180 Hauer Drive, North Liberty, Iowa 52317
www.icecubepress.com steve@icecubepress.com
Check us out on Facebook and Twitter.

The paper used in this publication meets the minimum requirements of
the American National Standard for Information Sciences—Permanence
of Paper for Printed Library Materials, ANSI Z39.48-1992.

Made with recycled paper.

Manufactured in Canada.

Photo credits: All photos provided or taken by author.

Disclaimer—It should go without saying, but the opinions, views,
and comments in this book are solely those of the author and
the river. They should not be ascribed to any other organization,
institution, or individual with whom he may have contact. If
you have complaints, take them up with the *management*! Of
course compliments and kind words are always welcomed.

Dedicated to the members, staff, and board of the
Iowa Natural Heritage Foundation for helping Iowa's
landowners and public officials protect and preserve the
rivers, lakes, and land in this beautiful place we call home.

"The immensity of man's power to destroy imposes a
responsibility to preserve."—John F. Lacey, 1901

At the entrance to the National River Museum in
Dubuque, Iowa, there is an inscription we can all consider
as we look to our future with the river. It reads:
"Rivers run through our history and folklore, and link us as a
people. They nourish and refresh us and provide a home for
dazzling varieties of fish and wildlife and trees and plants of
every sort. We are a nation of rivers."—Charles Kuralt

Contents

Chapter One –
Why We Should Care What
the River Knows

Water, land, soil—any Midwesterner knows these resources shape our states: they define our economies, our culture, our social structure, and our politics. While we have made progress to a more modern political and economic structure, these fundamental forces—the water, land, soil—still play an outsized role in all dimensions of our societies. This book is their story, in particular, the story of our water—its presence or lack thereof, and how it influences the health of the land and society. The story is one of great promise as reflected in the wealth our natural resources help create. Their story is also one of great peril, as seen in the headlines detailing our polluted waters, our degraded soils, and our eroding land. Few political issues of today are as riven with conflict, tension, fear, and distrust as those involving how we use and abuse our water, land, and soil. But this story is not only one of gloom and conflict; far from it, because there is hope and promise in our water, land, and soil. Promise is found in a cool morning spent paddling or fishing a quiet stretch of stream. Promise is in every new growing season, and in gentle timely rains unleashing the soil's fertility and in the restorative, regenerative capacity of the land to heal, with time, not just itself but us as well. Promise is also found in each new generation of citizens who take up a responsibility for how we treat the natural resources we share and depend on for our existence.

This book is framed by the story of our rivers. We are never far away from Iowa's rivers and streams. They define our state's shape and provide almost 72,000 miles of natural waterways etched across every township. As a reader you are going on a journey, both figuratively and literally, with a focus on water, mainly here in Iowa but also nationally. If you have read my book, *The Land Remains,* you might wonder how this book relates to it? In many ways they are companions. *The Land Remains* combines a personal memoir and a history of Iowa's land, in part told through the voice of the Back 40. It doesn't shy away from addressing contemporary issues, subjects such as water quality and soil conservation, but these issues are to some extent considered from a distance. This book takes a sharper, more direct focus on how we treat the water and land. If the discussion offends you, the offense may well be intended. Chapter Nine explains my belief Iowa needs more truth tellers rather than more happy talkers—officials who want us to believe everything is just fine. You will discover there are bright spots and reasons for hope, but truth be told, things are not fine with our water and land. The book should provide comfort to those working to address our afflictions and protect our resources. If it also afflicts the comfortable, those who see no reason to be concerned about our future, it will have reached another of my goals.

WHAT DO I HOPE READERS WILL GAIN?

As a writer my goal is to focus on what will make the book readable and valuable, how it can be a worthwhile addition to the social debate. Here is what I hope you will gain:

1. A sense of history—to know how water quality and conservation are not new topics, but instead issues with a history allowing us to see

how they have developed and to predict where we might be headed;

2. A new perspective—the opportunity to hear and see the issues from the river's point of view and in a nonhuman voice, to help change the perspective and add a different viewpoint to our thinking;

3. A sense of outrage—examples of behaviors and actions you find objectionable may make you ask why we continue to condone them, and raise the question: are there villains or are we all complicit in this situation?

4. A feeling of hope—there are many reasons for hope, such as the potential to reopen a portion of the Skunk River allowing it to reclaim its channel; the creation of 150 miles of water trails and recreational opportunities in central Iowa; and other developments to give us all a sense of optimism;

5. Some examples illustrate our challenges and opportunities. Such as what is happening now with the fight over a large cattle feed lot near Bloody Run Creek in Northeast Iowa. Landowners creating new water and land protection. The Garst family placing a first-of-its-type soil health conservation easement on farmland near Coon Rapids. The city of Cedar Rapids working with farmers in the Cedar River watershed. Water quality initiatives in Polk County show what can happen when people are motivated;

6. An appreciation for individuals and inspirational characters— the future of Iowa's water can best be told through the stories of people working to protect it, such as Liz Garst, Seth Watkins, Mary Skopec, Mike Delaney, Nate Hoogeveen, and the many landowners working with the Iowa Natural Heritage Foundation to preserve their properties and protect Iowa's water and land;

7. A cultural context of water in our history—our rivers are a lens

for seeing the dominating role of water in our lives. Historical examples such as the Des Moines River land grant from the 1840s, and the proliferation of mills during early settlement, illustrate the river's evolving role. History can help us understand how issues of today are extensions of a larger cultural context shaped by new realities, some altering the very purpose and future of rivers in society;

8. The timeliness of water issues—it is important we approach water issues in the context of the current political moment. Items in today's news such as the climate debate, funding natural resource protection, paying landowners for carbon sequestration, and even dubious ideas such as CO_2 pipelines, will impact how we use water and land, and will reflect our respect for it. Our issues are not old and settled, but are instead current and very much in play;

9. The idea of enjoyment—a concluding goal is to capture the energy and the excitement of the issues encountered. Even with the daunting challenge of an agricultural sector slow to embrace a shared responsibility to protect our waters, there are great opportunities to move forward. The exciting potential in local bond initiatives to fund natural resource protection, the Iowa Confluence Water Trails (ICON) in central Iowa, and even the use of federal pandemic relief funding, aka ARPA dollars, to support natural resource projects are some of the ideas we will examine.

Yes, our water issues are real and tangible, issues to immerse us. It is too easy to think questions about water and land are for other people to consider or to believe these matters are well-settled, with little opportunity for change. This is not true. Water is always with us, in what we drink and whether it is safe. Many questions are involved. Will there be enough water to meet our needs? Can we manage the economic effects of droughts and floods? Will citizens have the opportunity to recreate, to have fun in the rivers and on the water? Water is central to the health of our natural world, not just for humans but for fish, wildlife, and much more. If we are to have environmental sustainability in terms of our food and climate, it must begin with the water and how we use it. The truth is we all need to be good water citizens. Hopefully this book can help lead us there.

WHY THE TITLE ISN'T DOWN THE RIVER

When I began writing the working title was *Down the River*. My thinking was so many of our attitudes about water and rivers are premised on just this simple fact—once the water flows downstream it is someone else's concern not ours. This in many ways is what we do—send our problems down the river for others to address. As an informed reader of history, you also know the expression "down the river" is freighted with an unfortunate connotation from our nation's much too-extended period of enslavement. Being shipped down the river was a tragic fate for enslaved people moved further south, often down the Mississippi River to plantations much deeper in the South and farther from any dream of freedom in the North. Being sent down the river carried with it tragedy, not just in separation from family and any known context, but also into a more brutal and oftentimes fatal form of forced labor. While using "down the river" might offer a powerful metaphor to describe our current conflicts and attitudes, to avoid having to explain the term's racialized context, I concluded there had to be a better name. Then an epiphany—one of my favorite feelings, you might say I am a bit of an epiphanizer. The epiphany was why not call the book *The River Knows,* because in reality many of the subjects we will discuss are informed by this idea. Whether we want to believe it or not, the river does know. It knows how we treat it and if we will listen. It can help tell us what it needs. If we want to learn answers to the question—what does the river know?—there is no better source to ask than the river itself. That is why periodically I will be turning the pen over to the Raccoon River to help narrate our journey.

Understanding the difference between a river and a stream

I am the Raccoon River and you will hear from me throughout the book. While just one river, my goal is to speak for all the rivers and streams—all 72,000 miles of us here in Iowa and countless more in neighboring states. What image comes to your mind when you hear the word river? Most likely it is the water you see flowing between my banks. Certainly this is one way to think of a river, but it is only part of my story. A river is more than just the flowing water or the stream banks or the sandbars and islands or even the channel you see. We are all of those things woven together, but in truth we are more, we are really living beings. Perhaps we don't have blood and flesh as you know them, but certainly there are similarities with our water and banks. Just as a person can only be thought of in totality and not just as a collection of arms, legs, a torso, and a head, the same can be said of a river. Like any human we have a personality and agency. We may not be able to move our channels a great distance, but they can move and we do have some agency.

When it comes to defining what a river is, you folks with your love of legal acts and need for definitions, may establish formal rules to decide if I am a meandered river, a stream segment, or even something less such as a ditch. You develop these definitions for many reasons, primarily to help establish legal rights, so the people who live on my banks know what they "own" and so your government agencies can claim "jurisdiction" or control over me. These, like many of your legal rules, work best on paper but can face challenges when exposed to the real world. To us, being a river or a stream is really a state of mind and a function of many natural events. It isn't determined by legal rules on width and flow rates. If you believe a narrow tame "stream" like Sugar Creek is always going to be your friend, then you haven't seen her after a 5-inch gully-washing rain. When these rains come and we get pushed out of our banks onto what you so innocently refer to as the floodplain, the legal rules defining us may not be so important. Then, the nice flat bottom grounds, the places where you love to farm and even build houses, may be swallowed by a raging torrent, clogged with sediment and debris. These heavy rains can turn a babbling stream into a maelstrom, rushing and roaring with a power even I find terrifying. At times like this when the flooding comes, you too will be awed by the power we rivers and streams can bring to bear. When you find the 40-foot walnut tree used for your streamside deer stand crashed down lying supine in the now tame two-foot-deep "stream," then you will appreciate what we know—the historical distinction between a river and the stream is not so clear.

WHY THE RACCOON RIVER IS
HELPING NARRATE THE BOOK

You might be wondering what is up with using the Raccoon River to help tell the story—is this for real or just a cheap literary gimmick? You are asking a good question, but before jumping to a conclusion consider the value of hearing from the river. Here are several reasons it makes sense:

- it allows us to "humanize" the river, helpful because we

typically care more seeing how issues impact people, especially ourselves;

• it provides readers with a different perspective and a new way of thinking; and it creates a parallel with hearing from the Back 40 in *The Land Remains;*

• it offers a convenient way to consider history and to telescope changes in geology, flow, culture, use, and life along the river, as well as their health.

Many different events in the history of the Raccoon River serve as connecting points between its role as a character and the reality of our political and economic world. Here are just some of the events the Raccoon River has experienced:

• the famous 2016 Des Moines Water Works lawsuit, pitting 600,000 water users against interests of upstream drainage districts over who is responsible for protecting water quality—essentially asking *whose river is it?*

• the 2021 public trust doctrine lawsuit alleging state officials abandoned their constitutional duty to protect the river, and the Iowa Supreme Court's decision the doctrine does not obligate the state to implement protections;

• river clean-ups, like Project AWARE on the Raccoon in July 2021, involving hundreds of citizens working to preserve a healthier river;

• the Garst family's creation of the Whiterock Conservancy, Iowa's largest private land trust, covering 5,000 acres and including six miles of the Raccoon illustrate how one family helped change the fate of the river and public attitudes about conservation;

- the economic and physical impact of major floods like those of 1993 and 2017, and what they mean for the health of the river, communities, and our economy; and
- new efforts, like the central Iowa water trails project, a $120 million public-private partnership, to create recreational opportunities by improving over 150 miles of rivers and streams.

All these events flow through the history of the Raccoon River with more to come—that is why it will help tell its story.

The River explains the book and the tone

There are two issues to discuss early on so we can better appreciate each other. First, I have read the book and must warn you—some parts, especially early on, may seem a bit gloomy and pessimistic. The truth is some of your history with me isn't all happy talk of puppy dogs and butterflies. But you need to know the book is full of hope for my future—otherwise my story is not worth learning. Rivers are nothing if we are not resilient, and I suspect you are as well. You will discover things you may not know and will meet interesting people doing important work. A second issue is my tone. As you read my commentary on some issues, you may find my perspective somewhat bitter and more cynical than you expect. Certainly if you have read *The Land Remains*, you know my counterpart the Back 40 always seemed to have a rosy view of the past and future. I can understand the land's viewpoint. It is largely a function of stability and a sense of place. The Back 40's fate is tied in large part to its owner. My situation is different; rivers are not owned by anyone even if the law may say we are. Instead, we are public resources flowing for miles, over 160 miles in my case, impacted by countless acts of thousands of people. As a result we suffer more injuries and insults over time than the

Back 40 can even imagine. Our fate is very much influenced by the tide of current affairs. When you hear me speak of the past, or reflect on your actions, or discuss our future opportunities together, remember my experience is refracted through a long and fraught history. The river has a memory and doesn't easily forget. But don't fear, even if we must be realists, rivers are also hopeful and resilient and we can have a sense of humor too, which brings me to …

News Report: Stone Tablet Found in River Puzzles Viewers

In fall 2022, a combination of record-low levels on the North Raccoon, and construction for a new bridge near Van Meter resulted in what many are describing as a surprising but significant discovery. As workers dredged near the east side of the river below what is known as the Puckerbrush access, they discovered a 3x5 foot stone tablet, upon which is engraved the following:

Big Ag's Mosaic Decalogue—

1. Thou shall not criticize farmers, question their motives, or take their names in vain, knowing nothing they do compromises food safety.

2. Thou shall not allege soil erosion or water quality are issues to worry about and shall not doubt anyone loves the land more than farmers.

3. Thou shall not allege farm tenancy, large landholdings, or investor purchases are evil or create wealth inequality on the land.

4. Thou shall not claim farmers use more fertilizer than needed, livestock manure pollutes the water, or tile lines impact water quality.

5. Thou shall honor those who tile and till the land knowing nothing they do can ever foul the water or air.

6. Thou shall not impose any regulation on farmers, nor limit access to public subsidies, nor covet private property unless needed for pipelines.

7. Thou shall not aver any livestock production practice is inhumane or violates animal welfare, even gestation crates and battery cages.

8. Thou shall worship no false idols such as organic farming, humanely raised meat, plant-based foods, or electric vehicles—nor place them before production agriculture.

9. Thou shall never question the value of ethanol or using food crops for biofuel purposes, knowing the "food or fuel" debate is Satan's work.

10. Thou shall remain ever faithful to believing American agriculture feeds the world and place no limits on using crop protection products or new technologies.

The discovery of what is being called the Puckerbrush Puzzler raises questions about who can be trusted to speak for nature in Iowa.

The Back 40 on the River

I am very happy my friend the River asked me to write a few words to help tell its story. If you read *The Land Remains* you are familiar with my voice. If you haven't read it yet, shame on you. To bring you up to speed, I am a 40-acre field in the middle of section 13 in Mercer Township, Adams County Iowa, owned for over a century by the Hamilton family. You might wonder what a flat black 40-acre field can add to this book about our waters? Well, I am going to tell you—we are all connected! My closest river is the Nodaway four miles north at Prescott, but I am not even in its watershed. The tile line flowing southwest through me empties into Willow Creek, then it flows into the One Hundred and Two River, then it flows into the Tarkio, and ultimately it reaches the Missouri. At some point on that journey my waters get joined with those from the Nodaway. The point is, once rain falls on me it is only a matter of time and natural drainage before some of it will make its way to a river. The same is true for fields like me all over the state. Some may be closer and the water may get there sooner, but for all of us our water eventually gets to the river.

That is why when you read the news stories about rivers and water quality and learn about the people and projects working for a brighter, more resilient water future, you are also hearing about the land. We and the rivers are joined at the hip you might say. Even though we are linked there are important differences. As you know I am owned by a family; it is right there in the deed in the Adams County recorder's office. This is not true for the river. Sure, someone owns the adjacent land and river banks, and as you will learn, for many streams people may even own the land in the river bed. In the 1960's the state of Iowa claimed ownership of all the water flowing in the rivers and streams in the name of the people of the state, the public. Even so, does anyone really believe they can own the river? Only a fool would think so. Rivers have a freedom to flow, to shrink and shift their channels, and if nature and the river feel like it, even to flood. Humans may try to control the river with dikes, and digging channels, and even building dams large or small, but the river flows on and eventually nothing can truly control it. Now that is freedom the land can only envy! To determine one's fate, to shake off the ties binding you must be truly liberating.

Chapter Two—Paddling the Raccoon—Finding Inspiration and Enlightenment

In researching John Wesley Powell and his famous trip down the Colorado River, to write *Beyond the Hundredth Meridian*, Wallace Stegner noted how important it was for him to have spent time on the river to understand Powell and his life. His comment made me realize if I was going to write about our relation to rivers and use the Raccoon to help narrate the story, then getting out on the river was a necessity. Over six months in 2021 I acquired a canoe and paddled seventy-five miles on the Raccoon River in Dallas County to see what I could learn to tell you.

As a reader you don't want to be lectured to, or face a polemic. I have found some well-intentioned books so depressing I couldn't finish them, for example David Wallace-Wells' *The Uninhabitable Earth*. Instead readers want a story with characters, plot twists, unexpected discoveries, and hopefully some promises for a better future. Well, the Raccoon offers us all of that and more. Having spent forty years as a law professor it is hard for me to resist providing a legal lesson here and there, so hopefully you won't mind a few if they help flesh out the story. *The Land Remains* explains a great deal about the law and how it defines our rights and relations to the land. In this book the lessons, kept to a minimum, focus on water issues. Questions like who owns the rivers—to the extent anyone can, and puzzlers like why some streams are considered meandered and some are non-meandered and what that means? Simply put, the difference can determine if adjacent landowners own the land below the river, even if the public owns the water above, an important distinction for paddlers.

Before turning to my time on the river it is helpful to think about how our current views on rivers impact the larger questions of our rights to control all land and natural resources for our use. The historian Daniel Worchester in writing about Stegner's work said "the West had not been so much settled as raided," for furs, minerals, grass, and scenery. His comment makes me ask whether we can't say much the same about our history in Iowa? We think of ourselves as settlers, but it's clear a large part of what we have done is to raid the state's natural resources. We raided the prairie, the wetlands, much of the timbered forest lands, the rivers and ox bows, and the wildlife, all to support agriculture and farming. Now even our soil resources and their health, as well as air quality, viewsheds, and peaceful rural amenities are in many ways being raided, in the name of unlimited cropping, livestock expansion, and harnessing the wind.

The reality is we have never placed any significant restraints on our use of the land. If you want to bulldoze a timber, or plow a steep pasture, there is little anyone can do to stop you. Iowa law does little to protect nature from our raids. Other than some limited restrictions on stream straightening, minimal separation distances for disposing of manure near homes and streams, and rather toothless prohibitions on draining wetlands, there is very little in Iowa's laws to limit what you can do to your land—or to the waters for that matter. Even the limited legal protections we do have, like the duty placed on landowners to prevent excessive soil erosion, discussed in Chapter Eight, depend on someone being willing to enforce the rules and to say no. Sadly, our history shows we are very unwilling to say no—to tell farmers and landowners they have limits. Modern agriculture today essentially knows of, and admits to, no limits. One tenet of the Agrarian Canon is every acre and inch of land should be farmable up to (and even into) the river. A second tenet is every acre can be tilled and fertilized like it is prime grade A land. Other tenets are: as Iowans we have the right to raise as many livestock as we can afford, wherever we like; we can tile any field we want to; and we can own and abuse as much land as we can acquire.

Given this reality is it any wonder farmers and agriculture balk at the mere mention of regulations, when they have grown up and live in a world free of restraints? Like children who have never heard of a rule or ever been disciplined, we rebel at the mere thought. In reality our situation may actually be worse because the actors are adults who wield extensive political power and control the levers of government. Even more, it appears few real adults are in the room willing to bring any form of parental discipline to bear.

If we frame the question of our attitudes toward water and land as involving moral values, would that make a difference? We love to think of ourselves as moral people, so do our actions on the land and water show it? The frequent news stories about manure spills, overflowing lagoons, and other water quality challenges tell a different story. In summer 2021 Iowans had an opportunity to think about our state's morality to other people, when the governor told the Biden Administration the state did not have room to care for 300 migrant children being moved away from our southern border. For a state happy to find room for 25 million pigs, wouldn't you think we could find room for 300 migrant children?

When you think about agriculture's history on the land and issues of morality, one question to ask is why are we so willing to deceive ourselves about our actions and so unwilling to even tolerate questions about our behavior. What are we so afraid of? Are we afraid citizens and consumers will quit believing our claims of being good stewards and begin to question whether the impacts on water and land are worth the "benefits"? Is the worry the true impacts of unlimited expansion of corn production may actually be exceeding not just the land's capacity to support it, but also the public's appetite for subsidizing the abuse? Perhaps what we are really afraid of learning is while we may not recognize limits on our actions, the water, land, and soils may have limits—ones we are now encountering with a changing climate—and this frightens us. Trying to learn what those limits might be is another good reason to listen to the river.

Who Owns Me?

I made a quite a discovery today—I am actually owned by the state of Iowa. Yes it is hard to believe and I am still a little bit shocked by it all. How is it possible for someone to own me and what do they think that means? The idea people need a permit to draw water from me makes good sense, this has been the official policy since Iowa's water law was passed in 1964 and really even before that. And there is the issue of "legal title" to the property under my water, in what you call the streambed. For historical and political reasons portions of me are considered navigable and meandered. If I am navigable then the federal government has jurisdiction on some matters, as well as the state. If I am meandered it means my bed and channel were not subject to private ownership but instead are owned by the public with the state being the trustee for the public owners. These are sometimes referred to as sovereign lands and waters. Along with the power (or at least sense) of ownership comes a right to tell people— *no you can't do that*—regarding actions like building a dam across me, or putting a dike on my bank.

But the power to say no also comes with the ability to say yes, under the right circumstances or to the right people. So yes the Des Moines Water Works can withdraw millions of gallons of water from me for its 600,000 customers under a permit with the state. And yes a town can build flood control structures to try to control or harness my waters when the mood for a little flooding comes over me. But for this they need to have a permit and it may be from the federal Army Corps of Engineers. The idea of ownership can be taken even further, and for some of Iowa's rivers it has. For example, the idea of channelization means to actually re-write my flow, trying to turn me into essentially a big ditch. Thankfully no one tried to do that BS to me, but they did it to some of my fellow rivers and ones not that far away. The nearest and perhaps saddest example is what they did to the South Skunk River coming from Ames and flowing down toward Pella. In the 1920s the river was ditched with miles of oxbows and bends cut off to make farm fields and the river was shortened from 80 miles to 50 miles. You can only imagine the suffering this caused to the river, the fish, and the wildlife who called it home. How you people gloried in your might; how the mighty steam shovels and drag lines brought what you call progress. Your ownership and stream straightening wasn't limited to the smaller rivers like the Skunk, the Boyer, the Nishnabotna and the Little Sioux, which you were happy to destroy by the dozens of miles. The Iowa DNR estimates over 3,000 miles of rivers and streams were lost to channelization last century. Can you imagine that!! You even went to work on the largest rivers in the nation channelizing stretches of the Missouri on

Iowa's Western border in the name of navigation. Shortening it by many miles between Sioux City and Nebraska City.

Now as a reader of this book you have proven yourself a sharp cookie, so you must know about simple physics. What happens when you take a 120-mile river and make it only 90 miles long? That's right—the water speeds up in a landscape scale version of the Venturi effect. Now what happens when water speeds up? That's right it has more energy or force. And how is that energy used? To dig down into the streambed to scour out sediment, and to tear at whatever you build or place along the edges to control the river. Your hubris is remarkable, matched only by the power of your dredges and the inevitable failure of your schemes. There are two things you need to understand about how we rivers think and act. First we're going to flow wherever we want to, whenever we want to, when enough rain and water come. The corollary is your efforts to constrain us are always going to be under threat should we decide it is time to do a little moving. This brings me to the second rule and one you just can't seem to learn—you need to give a river room to be a river. Failing to give us room traps you into an eternal battle building new dikes and levees, raising your floodwalls, buying out property owners when houses and businesses are destroyed by the last flood—perhaps to give them just enough time to rebuild before the next flood! Get the point? What will it take for you to recognize you can never win? Sure the levees may hold back the flood and Birdland Marina and Riverside Park will be spared this time. But what about next time? Eventually, perhaps inevitably, the river is going to do what it needs to do—be a river not a ditch!

Paddling the Raccoon River or How Tom Vilsack Bought My Canoe

In November 2020 I was elected to the Dallas County Soil and Water Conservation District (SWCD) commission as a write-in candidate. My experience as a commissioner is detailed in Chapter Eight, but the event created the perfect excuse for getting out to explore the land and water in the county. Many of the trails and county parks were familiar, but one part of the county I needed to experience was the many miles of rivers. Dallas County is fortunate (if you believe rivers are good things) to contain over 90 miles of the various branches of the Raccoon River—the North, Middle, and South all join to create the river flowing through Water Works Park to downtown where it joins the Des Moines River. With this in mind, I set an objective of paddling as much of the county's rivers and streams as possible—to learn the landscape and see what was happening on the river. Not owning a kayak or canoe posed a challenge, but the good news is several friends did.

After making a few inquiries as to who might be interested in sharing some adventures on the Raccoon, my friend John Norwood (right), whom you will learn more about in Chapter Eight for his work on the Polk County SWCD, said he was game. As an avid paddler and fellow commissioner, he volunteered to get me out on the river. Our first journey was a long 13-mile

stretch on a late April afternoon, using two of his kayaks. Even though the south wind was howling, we had a wonderful excursion through the southeast portion of the county. As a result I was hooked on the idea and proceeded to search for a kayak of my own. Visiting a popular outfitter in Indianola specializing in paddling sports made it clear the pandemic had increased interest in outdoor activities, so finding a quality kayak was more difficult than expected. But the shopping trip gave me the opportunity to examine an ultra-lightweight ADK canoe from Northwind. After a week of dreaming about it I returned to make the purchase. The great thing is the canoe only weighs 24 pounds making it easy to carry and maneuver and it is short enough at 11 feet to fit in the Sprinter Van without needing a trailer or carrier.

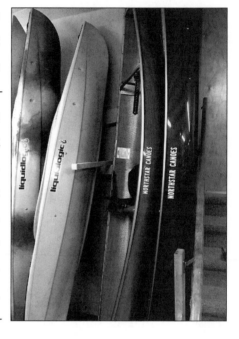

Over the next six months John and I ventured onto the Raccoon on eight other occasions, sometimes joined by friends but often just the two of us. Each night after completing another leg, I marked the designated portion on a map of the Raccoon River in Dallas County. As the summer passed our mileage increased, and our last outing in late November was a beautiful stretch from Dawson to Perry. With that my total mileage exceeded 75 miles. Traveling on a river provides a view of nature and agricultural fields not possible any other way. Some of those observations are reflected in later chapters, but here is one dimension of the story—how could I justify buying an expensive canoe? If you are like me, your purchases are made from available funds. Buying a canoe, even an expensive one, did not mean we would go without food or the farm cats would go hungry, but when you want to buy something special, isn't it fun to think about where the funds may come from? Doesn't it make the purchase easier to rationalize if you can identify an unexpected source of the money? As fate would have it, in late April and early May, when shopping for a canoe, communications with my friend Secretary of Agriculture Tom Vilsack led him to suggest a research project on USDA's legal authority to expand the reach of conservation compliance programs to cover more acres and to include soil health issues.

The project grew out of a 2021 Earth Day speech, where I challenged the USDA to reexamine the soil conservation title Congress passed 35 years ago. Retiring from the Agricultural Law Center at Drake did not include taking a vow of poverty, and the Center has funds available for research projects. My successor agreed researching USDA's authority to expand conservation compliance policy could be compensated. Many hours spent over the next weeks resulted in a memo for the Secretary and his staff about how conservation compliance can be expanded to incorporate soil health issues. It also led to a consultant's expense claim to the University. The exact amount is not important. Instead, I like to think of it this way: Tom Vilsack bought me the canoe I used to explore how agriculture impacts the Raccoon River in Dallas County, where we both reside.

ROBERT WALLER, THE ENLIGHTENMENT, AND THE RIVER

On an afternoon walk along the Sugar Creek bottom at Sunstead—the now 12-acre market garden farm Khanh and I share—my thoughts turned to other Iowa personalities who could help tell the story of the rivers and our future. Then another epiphany—I remembered a series of essays by Robert James Waller published 30 years ago in the *Des Moines Register*, about a week-long canoe trip he took down the Shell Rock River, running through his hometown of Rockford. The essays were so eloquent I had clipped them to save, but the file was now misplaced. This all happened long before Waller's staggering success as the author of *The Bridges of Madison County* changed his fortunes. The essays were written while he was a professor at the University of Northern Iowa. His frequent writings in the *Des Moines Register* concerning Iowa's economy and future helped establish his reputation as a deep thinker and scholar. When I got to the house and Googled for articles about his river writing, the reward was an article "Bridges Home" in the Jan-Feb 2009 issue of *Iowa Outdoors*, the Iowa DNR magazine. The article was based on an interview Waller gave when he returned home to Rockford to speak to the 2008 gathering of Project AWARE, the annual river cleanup effort. The article was written by none other than Nate Hoogeveen, now the River Coordinator for the Department of Natural Resources, who you will learn more about in Chapter Six. Reading the article I was excited to learn Waller's essay on the Shell Rock paddle had been included in *Just Beyond the Firelight*, published by Iowa State University Press in 1988. The 70-page essay was titled "Going soft upon the land and down along the rivers." As many of us do nowadays, my next step was to order the book. The article also noted how the Iowa Legislature was so moved by his writing it had commissioned Waller to prepare a report concerning the future of Iowa's natural resources.

The reference to his report was a surprise because I was teaching at Drake then and have no memory of either the project or his report. Interviews with many others involved in conservation reveal I am not alone, as no one seems to have any memory of the study. Another exploration for books yielded an order for *Iowa: perspectives on today and tomorrow,* published by Iowa State University Press in 1991. The book is a 300-page extended essay about what Iowa could do if we were actually interested in developing a resource-based sustainable system for our economy and for rural development. The enlightened way of thinking about Nature Waller proposed was one Iowa was not ready for then and perhaps is still not today, helping explain why his report did not find the readership of his fiction.

On the other hand, his Shell Rock River essay is outstanding. Today it maintains a power, eloquence, and insight placing it among the best writing about Iowa and our rivers. A great coincidence was when rediscovering Waller's essay I was also reading Steven Pinker's *Enlightenment Now.* To my surprise Waller based his essay in part around the ideals of the Enlightenment. One of our greatest challenges in Iowa concerns water quality and how it reflects our larger attitudes toward natural resources. Waller came to his recognition of the importance of thinking about Enlightenment while paddling on the river and reflecting on how Iowa had changed in his lifetime, in particular our agricultural systems. Waller cited the importance of writings by Wendell Berry and Aldo Leopold, who help us think about the sustainability of our system. To put into context the power and insight of Waller's writing, let me quote from his essay. He noted: "farming became an extractive industry like mining, rather than the ancient and honored practice of husbandry. Production took precedence over care and maintenance. Usufruct was forgotten. It now requires 2 bushels of Iowa soil, via erosion, to produce 1 bushel of Iowa corn."

Continuing with Waller, he wrote: "in all of this Iowa has become something like a colony in an Imperial Empire. Our resources are ravaged for the mercantilistic satisfactions of powers far away, powers that could care less about the rights of those Iowans yet to come. The debate over fetus rights is intense. I see no reason why a debate over those being disenfranchised by our current treatment of nature should be less so.

"We need to recapture Enlightenment and use it to produce a vision for Iowa. A vision that involves goodness, kindly treatment of the land, the survival of our rural communities, and yet somehow figure out a way to make a reasonable living at the present time. The vision must explicitly involve usufruct. More than that, it must continence restoration. We are missing something.

"That something is a vision guided by Enlightenment. Enlightenment has two levels in my way of thinking. One is the position of knowledge and a sense of truth. The other is more spiritual, softer, and has to do with the application of knowledge in a way that combines the best of both intellect and feelings. The result of the first level is understanding. The outcome of the second is vision."

The next passage is probably what led the Legislature to commission his project. He wrote: "some may love Iowa as much as I, but none loves her more. And if I were going to work on the problems besetting Iowa, I would start with the notion of enlightenment and how that Enlightenment might be used to create vision. A vision for Iowa."

Later in the essay he returned to this idea of a vision, noting Iowa needs a better metaphor for thinking about its future and its people. To Waller's thinking there are essentially three main branches of

Iowa—the economy, art and culture, and the natural environment—each influencing the other and in their totality creating the condition of Iowa and its people. Waller said "to understand these connections is Enlightenment." He concluded: "a unified vision of Iowa, a product of enlightened thought and a modest amount of design, would reflect this wholeness. Unfortunately neither our culture nor our educational systems provide coherent, rigorous training in understanding, let alone managing, truly complex systems. That's one reason why things seem so out of control most of the time. Better put that's why things are out of control."

Waller relied on the famous article by Garrett Harden on "the tragedy of the commons" to develop his essay. If you aren't familiar with this concept it explains how people will use a jointly owned and shared resource such as Commons used for grazing. The Commons will work as long as each person using it recognizes some implicit balance and limit to their use. But if people bring more cows to graze the Commons than it can support, it ultimately means no one will have adequate grazing for their animals. Waller said this type of short-term thinking can characterize most people's decision-making. He said "the same kind of trapped behavior, little decisions that sum up to major tragedies, is all around us in Iowa. My little bit of pollution will not noticeably affect the river. My little bit of soil erosion won't affect the overall amount of good land in Iowa. My going to the regional shopping center won't affect the local merchant that much."

And so Waller noted, the Shell Rock River got polluted, wetlands disappeared, and farmers inched down toward the subsoil. He said we could argue about ethics until we are hoarse but incentives are really in control. Waller quotes Alexander Hamilton from the *Federalist*

Papers, "momentary passions and immediate interests have a more active and impervious control over human conduct than general or remote considerations of policy, utility, or justice." Waller explained how our individual decisions create the cycles leading to the problems we encounter such as soil erosion and rivers fouled with chemicals, and of natural beauty and the possibilities for recreational industries being destroyed. He noted this was tragic but remained optimistic it could be turned around if we have the will. To conclude our discussion of Waller let me quote him on the notion of enlightenment and the role it can play in creating a vision for Iowa. He said, "the most essential indicator of enlightenment, obviously is the preservation and enhancement of the very natural systems that sustain us. That's basic, fundamental. Therefore, the condition of the natural environment is a good proxy measure for the quality of spirit, intelligence, and the Enlightenment of a state."

I apologize for quoting from Waller's essay at such length, but as a reader of this book you will appreciate the significance of his writing to our theme. Shouldn't it both concern and surprise us, Waller was writing almost 35 years ago? Sadly his comments about how we treat our water and soil, how we fail to adequately respect and protect our natural resources are even more true today than in 1990.

The tragedy of the commons is a useful metaphor to keep in mind, because of what lessons it offers. Public resources or common goods are always at risk of being overused by individuals, especially if the resources have an economic value and if there are no restraints placed on an individual's ability to use them. One way we avoid the tragedy of the commons is the concept of private property, meaning we can each own a pasture rather than having a shared resource. But for shared public resources like a river, you can't have private ownership. That is why some form of public regulatory action is needed, or something like the public trust doctrine creating an ownership interest on behalf of the public to use when asking the courts to implement protections. Tragically in Iowa we have a "no regulation approach" codified into law, so instead we foolishly rely only on voluntary action, with little public protection for common property. This has set the stage for a new tragedy. Our unwillingness to use public regulatory authority explains why Iowa has exposed millions of acres of privately owned land to abuse, and why state officials even refuse to protect our few common resources as well.

Another response to the tragedy of the commons is the idea of public land ownership to protect resources. However, this approach limited private consumptive economic uses and is expensive. As a result the idea of expanding public land ownership often meets with resistance, as illustrated by a 2022 Iowa legislative effort to eliminate new acquisitions of public land by capping the price government agencies could pay to sellers at well below market value. Thankfully the effort failed, for now, but the willingness to prevent landowners from selling land at market value to the public illustrated the lip service some farm organizations give to the idea of "private property rights." Another more acceptable way to obtain public protection but still allow for private uses of land is through conservation easements, combining public protection with private use. Easements can avoid the tragedy of the commons but preserve private ownership.

In thinking about the tragedy of the commons and its application to current conditions in Iowa, it is clear we have not learned its lessons. We still see continued deterioration in public resources, most notably in our rivers and public lands, often due to nearby private uses. Because Iowa has been so reluctant to use any form of regulatory authority to establish limits or conditions on how individuals use their land, public officials hesitate to act even when public resources are being damaged. Today Iowa appears to be adding a new dimension to the tragedy of the commons. Not only is the state unwilling to protect public resources threatened by private use, but when damage does occurs, the public is expected to actually foot the bill to restore the damages. You might call this Iowa's codicil to the tragedy of the commons. For nonlawyers, a codicil is a written clause added to a document, such as a will, after it was originally created.

The River and Democracy

I have been thinking about your democracy so much in the news of late and how it is threatened. You might be interested in what I believe your concepts of democracy mean to me. First it has a parallel with resilience. People think rivers and democracies are both resilient, but this raises the question of how we can be threatened. We can be threatened in many ways: complacency, active attack, being outweighed by other goals such as profits, and even being discounted or ignored by the courts and institutions responsible for protecting rivers and democracy not doing their jobs. Second is the issue of trust. Democracy assumes if people are free to vote and act, they will respect democracy and hopefully the river. Unfortunately the river has growing doubts about whether it can trust the people to do what is right. Will Iowans ever vote in a legislature to fund the Natural Resource Trust Fund they voted to create in 2010? Public polls showed support for the Des Moines Water Works lawsuit back in 2016 and over 80% of voters approved the 2021 Polk County land and legacy vote, so there is hope.

A third connection between democracy and the river is self-determination, the ability to shape one's own destiny. For rivers we have largely lost this ability due to channelization and flood control. Even for democracy, the ability may be fragile. If you do not have self-determination, for example if you are under a guardianship, then the question becomes who has the power to make decisions for you and do they have your best interests in mind? Recent actions of state legislators and officials at the DNR raise questions for the river, not unlike how efforts to spread mistrust of your voting systems threaten democracy in many of your states. Democracy operates at many levels. It can be very local all the way up to the workings of US Congress. Rivers also operate at many levels, from neighborhood streams up to the Mississippi, and at all of these levels our fate can be impacted by officials elected using democratic processes, so in that way the fate of rivers and democracies are linked.

THE GRAPES OF WRATH AND THE RIVER

As readers there is a good chance we share a love for good used bookstores. Working on the book while in Siesta Key created an opportunity to visit one of the best, A. Parker's Books, in Sarasota. The reward was a Franklin Library leather bound copy of Steinbeck's *Grapes of Wrath*, my reading for the next week. Either my memory is slipping, as my wife will attest, or too many years had passed since last reading this great book. My hope is the latter, but in either case I was struck by how much the story seemed fresh, new, and vital. The images he evoked are so memorable—from the tragedy of the neighbor who failed to close the hog gate on the house only to return to find pigs eating her baby, to the deaths of grandma and grandpa Joad on the road, to the final searing image of human kindness with Rose of Sharon offering her breast to a starving man. Eighty years later Steinbeck's Joads are still with us whether watching Henry Fonda in the movie or hearing Bruce Springsteen's haunting "Ghost of Tom Joad." Far too many Americans are still sleeping under the highway overpasses.

Should we fear this classic of American literature too will fall under the axes of the censorious brigades and brigands now prowling our state legislatures and local school board and library meetings? These hordes of the small-minded, searching to root out any references in our history that challenge their invented, rose-tinted views of a blameless society? One can only hope we retain some common sense, but as a precaution make sure you have *Grapes of Wrath* in your library and that those you care about have read it.

My rereading brought to mind my parents and their family stories from this period of our nation's past. Mom's family were poor tenant farmers, forced to move from farm to farm each winter, but they never had to join the Exodus West. My father's family on the other hand made the journey in reverse. They spent the early years of the depression in southern California, but economic pressures and family divisions led my grandmother Anna to move part of her family back to reclaim her Iowa land in 1935. This story is related in Chapter One "Grandmother Anna saves the farm" in *The Land Remains.* It tells how my father became an Iowa farmer, an odd twist and lifetime for a boy raised in Southern California. So unlike the Joads, the Hamilton clan found their salvation on a good piece of Iowa land. Reading the story of the Joads and those who shared their experiences though brings to mind my uncle Tom. I can picture him dressed in his uniform of bib overalls, stepping out of any of the scenes back then. The Hooverville's, the roadside camps, and the laborer's fields, were filled with people like Uncle Tom and Aunt Lola. The truth is one didn't have to hit the road to be scarred by the economic and social traumas of the late 1930s. No doubt we will look back on our current pandemic years of struggle and find echoes of the 1930s. It is only natural to see ourselves as heroes in our own history. For me I will gladly take a few years of wearing a mask and seeking boosters, rather than the real pain and hunger of the late 1930s. I wonder if we could ask the river about those times what it might say. The answer might be a simple one: who will write my *Grapes of Wrath*?

What happens when I dry up?

It's happening again, it's something I really have no control over, this flipside, so to speak, of a flood—I mean a drought. If you watch the news it turns out much of the nation is in a dry spell, a record for many Western states where the drought is extreme in some places going on now over 20 years. The hot dry weather we are experiencing is just making it worse. We have been dry here in Iowa too, especially to my North and West, what you know as my watershed. The only problem is there isn't much water being shed right now! As a result my flow is going down, my channels are shrinking, my sandbars are getting exposed, and folks are getting worried. Me—not so much. Just like my friend the Back 40, I take the long look, the view promoted by our old friend Henry A. Wallace. My timeline is long, much longer than yours. Sure I am dry and getting dryer and looking at the long-range forecast things are bound to get much worse. But I've been dry before, many times over the decades and centuries, but I will be full again. It could happen by late fall or could take several years, who knows? Of this I am not in control, instead it is Mother Nature as you like to call her, though I am not sure she has a gender or really even needs one—but Mother Nature sure works as a name. In fact one of Ding Darling's most famous drawings showed her in the kitchen putting up preserves of natural resources over the centuries, the soil, forests, and wildlife you raced to exploit and destroy.

Time To Take An Inventory of Our Pantry

That is why these droughts or dry spells can be a good thing. In addition to all your worrying and scrambling to make do and respond, figuring out where to get all the water you usually take for granted, a good drought can, or at least should, give you time to think about what is happening and what you might do to be better prepared for the next one. Of course the weather has a great deal to do with things like droughts and this one certainly shows the long-term impacts of declining rainfall, but who knows, this time things could be a little different. All this talk about global warming, the steady increase in CO_2 levels gradually warming the planet and melting the polar ice caps—it almost has to mean something.

Maybe that is the silver lining, a good drought is the opportunity for you to stop and think about what you have taken for granted and perhaps even to change your ways?! Like the lawns you insist on maintaining so you can mow them, then water them so you can mow them some more. Yikes, that is just crazy but you folks love your lawnmowers and green yards and all the chemicals and expense it takes to make them "attractive." Well, a good drought and some enforced water rationing plus tripling water bills might help you rethink that necessity!

Another silver lining might even be how this relates to the water quality issue so much in the news. At least for a few years it seems to have calmed down, largely because there was so little water and runoff meaning there was nothing to see. But folks who know about these things understand it's only a matter of time until the extra nitrogen and hog manure you have been spreading on millions of acres upstream will come pouring down through me in the form of runoff. But that's for another day and another story. For now we just have to worry about the drought and its induced blue-green algae growing in stagnant backwaters, and how toxic it might be if you or your pets get out in the water! Good luck! As Old Ham used to say "if it isn't one damn thing it's two"—speaking of which …

The Nation's Twin Traumas: COVID and Trump

In November 2021 John Norwood and I made it out onto the Raccoon River on another beautiful fall day. The only problem, if you can call it one, was the river was very low. Even at its lowest flows, you recognize the river's resilience. No matter how dry it may get the river never runs out of water; it continues running and will into the future. It has an ageless quality even though it may suffer the indignities we inflict on it, the channeling, the stream bank "stabilization," often nothing more than unsightly cladding of dump trucks full of broken concrete. But the river continues to flow and with time can heal itself. Its resilience offers a lesson and inspiration for us.

Searching for these lessons and evidence of resilience drove my writing, but I wonder today if our society and economy share the resilience of the river. In October 2021, we took a three-day trip to Chicago after 19 months of the COVID lock down. During this period Khanh had only ventured 20 miles away from home to get a COVID vaccination. It was fun to be back in the great city, one of our favorites we have visited often. But the changes inflicted by the pandemic were shocking: the empty storefronts, the dusty restaurants with chairs stacked on tables, the old familiar bookshops and clothing stores now closed. Everyone on the street and in the open shops was masked up in compliance with the city ordinance, a sense of resignation to the new normal was evident but will this be the new normal? The economic toll of the pandemic is still unfolding. Changing patterns in the work place raise doubts if employees will ever need or want to return. The clogged and melting supply chains were just one more stone on the pile. Of course we will survive—are surviving. Some people and institutions will manage to thrive even as others suffer, but collectively the magnitude of the shock to our culture and economy is still too early to judge.

But COVID wasn't the only terrible tragedy to strike our nation and only time will tell if it was even the most damaging. The second disaster to strike us, if that is even the correct label, was the emergence of Donald Trump onto the national stage as a candidate, as president, and now as a preening figure who will not go away, yearning for a restoration. Listen to the political news: the devolution of the Republican Party from any semblance of set principles. The coarsened debate in state and local government meetings, in particular once prosaic school boards, taken to levels of anger, threats, and violence once reserved for the theatrics of pro wrestling. As well as the national public health crisis where segments of the population, even police and healthcare workers, refused to be vaccinated—the only step sure to help end our pandemic crisis. All these dangerous and maddening developments have a common denominator or a through line to Trump. While he cannot be given credit for pre-existing sentiments and personal grievances apparently held in check by social norms and democratic institutions, he can be and must be given responsibility for crashing these norms, unleashing this torrent of hate, stress, and social discord on our nation. History is what we live through although the books may not be written for years to come. But when they are written, he may be remembered as the greatest illness to infect our nation in the memory of the living.

So, does the river offer us hope for a brighter day, a resiliency that can come with time? Can we hold on to the themes of democracy, decency, and equality we have always thought mark us as a special people? Time will tell. The river may never run dry, and we can hope our cups of human kindness and common sense don't either, but taking them for granted are acts we take at our own peril. Until the pestilence Trump unleashed on our land runs its course and either tears down our 200-year-old experiment or finally burns itself out in a blaze of futile ego, the answer is unknown.

Going for a walk on the Riverfront Trail in Chicago you're confronted with his legacy as his name soils the skyline emblazoned on a building, the funding of which was emblematic of a bloviating grifter using other people's money and bluster to paint the hollow image of a genius real estate mogul. One can only hope as time reveals his endemic callous corruption and despotic nature his name will eventually be removed as the blight it is now on the city. Whether the nation and our democracy will eventually excise his legacy of disgrace and destruction may take generations.

I Made the Paper Again

I have been in the newspapers quite a bit and most recently it didn't involve a flood. In fact it was quite the opposite, a flood in some ways but not of water, instead of bad news. In early April 2021, Americans Rivers, an influential Washington DC-based advocacy group, released their annual list of the nation's ten most endangered rivers, something they have been doing for 35 years. The big news is I made the list at number nine, primarily because of the over 750 concentrated animal feeding operations (CAFO), mostly for hogs, active in my watershed. The reality is these operations are lightly regulated by the Iowa Department of Natural Resources, such that they may not even have an accurate count of the operations in business. More to the point, the incredible amounts of manure being produced is applied directly to the land, often in amounts and at locations exceeding the capacity of the land to absorb the wastes, if that is even the right way to portray the process. From my perspective, people use their farm fields in my watershed as a dumping ground for manure, humoring themselves by calling it nutrients, all so they can pump out more pigs. Most of the pigs are not owned by individuals, those the public might think of as farmers, the ones working in the operations. Instead the real owners are a handful of corporations.

The level of corporate control amazes me. A new report in spring 2021 revealed how just one person, Jeff Hansen and his company, Iowa Select, owns over 220,000 sows or 30% of Iowa's sow herd. The millions of pigs produced by these sows are raised in hundreds of CAFO facilities contracted to the company, many in my watershed. Of course each farm has any required DNR permits and is responsible for "satisfying" the state rules for manure management. This way the company shields itself from collective responsibility for any havoc its pigs and their poop may cause. Wouldn't you know it, the pandemic even exacerbated this situation. No, the pigs or the farmers didn't get sick. Instead it was the meat packing workers in the slaughterhouses. At first, operations either closed or slowed down their lines due to the health issues. The immediate effect was to cause a backup in the supply of pigs back to the farm level. Think of Lucille Ball and the Chocolate Factory—the pigs were ready for slaughter but packing plant space was limited. Some farms actually "liquidated" animals, such a nice euphemism for such a gory process. Others held onto the pigs and fed them longer. To make this possible the state quietly and quickly changed its rules to allow operations to house more animals than their permits would allow and approved disposing the excess amounts of manure. The assumption was the land and ultimately the rivers like me could handle any temporary disruption in our lives. The situation cleared up once the packing houses were able to force their employees back on the line as "essential workers" to our economy, even as they risked their health.

The pecking order of society's priorities and our respect for its members were clear. The meat packers came first, then farmers were second with pigs in third place. In fourth place, were the land and the rivers—running a close tie with workers. Nothing ever changes. Now everyone is waiting for the next shoe to drop, relating to the weather and what might be in the water when the rains come. 2021 and 2022 were both very dry and the farmland in my upper watershed was listed in drought conditions much of the year. One effect is much of the nutrients applied as fertilizers and manure are still sitting in the soil, ready and able to be flushed down stream by the next big rain or wet spring. If and when that eventually happens the concern will be the nitrogen and phosphorus levels in my water spiking and causing real headaches for folks like my friends at the Des Moines Water Works and the 600,000 citizens of central Iowa who rely on me for their supply of safe drinking water. Wouldn't you know it, as if on cue, when heavy rains fell in my watershed in June 2022, my nitrate levels spiked so high the Des Moines Water Works had to fire up their nitrate removal system for the first time since 2018 just to make the tap water legal (and safe) to distribute.

As this scenario played out, anyone who was paying attention knew it proved what the Americans Rivers report had warned of in 2021. It was also an the opportunity to reflect on what Chris Jones from the University of Iowa reported in his insightful commentaries about Iowa's real population. When he took the human population and added the numbers of animals we raise to determine the real population of manure being generated state wide, the results were eye-popping (and headline grabbing). Rather than the 3 million good folks Iowans consider as fellow residents, Jones came up with an "effective" population for Iowa of over 168 million people, about the density of Bangladesh. For me he calculated the North and South Raccoon river watersheds collectively as having a population equivalent of Tokyo or Chicago, quite a bit more than the 750,000 people living here. Now you can understand why my water is always at risk of being polluted. To help understand how all of this came to be, it is useful to have more history about how Iowa has used its rivers—the subject we turn to next.

Robert Waller's hometown.

Chapter Three—Who Owns the River?—Our History

IOWA AND OUR RIVERS

Iowa and rivers, the two are inexorably linked. One common name for our state is "land between two rivers" and a popular Iowa public radio show is titled "River to River." Our dense network of rivers and streams, almost 72,000 miles as estimated by those who measure such things, help define us. In many ways the history of how we use our rivers outlines the story of Iowa's development, and while the uses have evolved, in many ways the health of our rivers can be seen to reflect the health and balance of our social economy. If true, the sad news is we are a bit under the weather and in need of some care. The good news is a growing number of people and towns are committed to reviving Iowa's rivers as engines of human enjoyment. There is even an organization embodying the idea in its name—Iowa Rivers Revival— working to recognize cities and towns for highlighting their rivers and creating opportunities for citizens to help with river clean-up.

The principal uses of rivers in our history are apparent. First, rivers were used to navigate and explore into the countryside. This made the rivers the most practical places to locate our settlements, explaining why today of our twenty largest cities almost all are located on a river. Much the same is true for our county seat towns, with over seventy located on rivers. Only in the southern and western counties where rivers are more dispersed does this trend not hold. Second, there were very practical reasons our first settlements grew alongside rivers, the main one being as a source of power to run mills needed to grind wheat into flour and power saws to cut lumber. Iowa had hundreds of water-powered mills, and a number of these remarkable structures still exist today, preserved as a window to the 1800s. One of the most notable is Motor Mill, a five-story stone Colossus on the Turkey River, seven miles southeast of Elkader in Clayton County. Built in the late 1860s, one can only imagine what an imposing testament to man's future plans and progress, not to mention stonework, the mill offered the

region's residents. Rivers provided a convenient source of water for growing towns, and in an ironic twist, one still haunting us today, rivers served as a convenient way to get rid of our wastes and sewage—nature's own handy disposal service at no charge with no questions asked. The rivers gave and the rivers took.

As society and technology progressed we returned to the rivers to harness their power to generate electricity. This explains the dozens of low head dams found on many Iowa rivers and streams often located in the heart of these growing river towns. Many of these dams are no longer used for the purpose constructed, and today can pose serious hazards to people recreating on the rivers who risk drowning in the deadly circulating flows at the foot of the dams. As we will learn in Chapter Seven the state appropriates funds each year to remove these low head dams to help improve recreational safety.

Dams were only one of the ways we tried to control or alter the rivers. As communities grew the constant threat of spring floods and the terrible damage and loss of life they could bring called out for action. Action most commonly took the form of "flood control" projects of constructing dikes and levees to confine the river and even channelizing the river to direct its flow. As the experience of most river towns show, our success and history at flood control has been mixed, whether in stories from decades ago like the 1965 flood in Dubuque, or in more recent years such as the terrible 2008 flood in Cedar Rapids. The truth is rivers are extremely difficult to control, and they have a mind of their own.

Thinking about rivers and their role in our history is helpful for many reasons, perhaps most importantly to bring into focus our current and future relations. Many of the important past roles we gave rivers are just that—past. The days of river navigation are largely behind us, certainly for our interior rivers. Our period of settlement has settled—and reliance on the rivers for power to drive our mills or even generate electricity is gone as well. Some cities still rely on rivers as primary water sources, most notably Des Moines, but for the most part this use is limited too. So what is left? Well, caring away our wastes, literally washing away our sin, is still an important role we give to rivers. The federal Clean Water Act has imposed important standards and protections to limit what can be discharged into the water from "point sources," with the goal to protect water quality for the health of fish, wildlife, and people. Its 50-year history of success has made rivers demonstrably cleaner, largely from controlling point sources.

This brings us to what has emerged as perhaps the most important remaining use and value of rivers to society—natural corridors, supporting fish and wildlife, offering beauty and scenic views, and providing recreational opportunities for people, both on and in the water, and on river and stream-side trails. Rivers provide the opportunity for peace and relaxation and can serve as generators of economic development and businesses supported by their proximity to nature.

Not everyone welcomes this new reason for our rivers, not if it means possibly restraining activities that threaten water quality or its safety for human use. Not if it means limiting new efforts at flood control such as rebuilding dikes and levees after being destroyed by a flood. Such actions are often opposed by those who believe it is wiser to give the floodplain back to the river so it has more room, rather than wage expensive and often ultimately unsuccessful efforts at flood control. No, there are some people who would just as soon we got rid of our rivers if we could; it would mean not having to build expensive bridges to cross them and deal with the aftermath of floods.

The good news, and truth is, we can never get rid of our rivers, even if for some reason we wanted to. They are an essential and necessary part of our natural landscape. They were here long before we came and will outlive us. The important challenge we face is learning to embrace the new reality and future for our rivers and appreciate all they do for us.

In 2021, Giulio Boccaletti wrote an amazing book, *Water: a Biography*. He does a masterful job of detailing the role water has played in the development of human civilization. A number of his observations are worth considering in our context. He begins by noting how people operate under an illusion water on the landscape is, "nothing more than an inert backdrop on the stage of human events." But anyone who thinks about this realizes water is much more than a backdrop to our lives, it is the stage on which much of life occurs. The story of water is essentially a political one, as we have tried to manage its material conditions throughout human history. As noted before, water is the ultimate *res publica* or public good. It is a moving, formless substance defying private ownership and even control. His book reminds us we are never going to be emancipated from nature or water, and the failures in our attempts to manage or control water, or the climate for that matter, should shatter this illusion. A final point he makes, vital to our discussion, is the key role society must play in managing the equilibrium between liberty, or personal freedom, and the commonwealth, or the public good. The role of water and a changing climate, plus the need to establish a stable balance within nature, challenge our future, as evidenced by both the Western droughts and the Iowa water quality debate.

Remind Me—Who is in Charge or Thinks They Are?

You humans pride yourselves on being organized and in charge. This makes me ask: do you really think you are in charge of me, even believe you own me? You seem to have a number of different answers. At the state level, your legislature can pass laws to influence me and my features, such as if someone can put a dike along my side, a dam to obstruct my flow, or withdraw my water to irrigate crops. As you have read, the question of whether my water is owned by the public was addressed by a state law in 1964. Of course the legislature doesn't actually implement the laws; for that you use administrative agencies, in my case the Department of Natural Resources or DNR. They make the decisions about us rivers. But that isn't all. At the more local level you have the

County Board of Supervisors, who from a historic viewpoint had the most organic authority over land and in some ways through that authority to the water. So several folks believe they have some control over me.

But it can be even more complicated. If I am large enough to be navigable then I may be subject to federal jurisdiction involving the Army Corps of Engineers and even the Environmental Protection Agency. My big neighbors like the Missouri and the Mississippi and even the Des Moines involve the Army Corps of Engineers if someone wants to mess around in the channel or floodplain. And this is not the only federal question that can arise because as the water moves down me it flows eventually to the Mississippi and on into the Gulf, meaning it moves in interstate commerce. The reality is water moves between the states, creating a classic justification for the exercise of federal jurisdiction. That's why when Congress passed the Clean Water Act in 1972 it gave the federal government, operating through the Environmental Protection Agency (EPA) authority to enforce the Clean Water Act on all of the waters of the US—but more on that later.

WHAT HAS HAPPENED TO IOWA'S VALUES?

In thinking about the current situation in Iowa relating to water quality, funding for public lands, and other issues of public welfare, it is hard to escape the feeling something has changed in our state. Consider how the shifting politics of the last 30 to 40 years in Iowa provides the foundation for debates we have today. This sentiment is not mine alone but flows from perceptions and conversations with friends and colleagues working in the natural resource and conservation field. The shared belief is something has changed in Iowa and not for the better. It is not just the Trumpian Republican political shift of our state to become much redder than its traditional purple. Political alignments can ebb and flow over time. Instead it seems to be something more fundamental in the very character of our people and in our attitudes toward each other, and toward our shared values in how we treat the water and land. One effect of the changes is how they threaten the optimism people have for the future of our state.

Consider the pride we used to take in having the highest test scores in the nation, in the quality of our universities, in the vibrancy of our economy, in the beauty of our countryside, and in the diversity of our small towns and their immigrant roots. Many of these seem to have eroded, corroded, or disappeared. This is not just the predictable whining of an old person complaining about missing the good old days and what they remember as a youngster. It is more fundamental. It can be captured in asking why a rural Iowa farm kid would fly a Confederate flag on a pickup truck and think it is somehow an act of freedom and defiance? Why would we think it wise to build an 11,000-head cattle feedlot only miles from one of the state's most outstanding and rare trout streams? Why would we believe burying hundreds of miles of pipeline across fertile Iowa farm fields simply to collect the CO_2 coming from ethanol and fertilizer plants, to ship it to other states to pump underground is a wise approach for dealing with our climate? To answer these questions it is worth taking a brief walk through Iowa's recent history.

A beginning point could be the Reagan presidency of the 1980s, the anti-government response to the Carter malaise, and the beginnings of an anti-public and more aggressive conservative movement in the nation. The second part of this history certainly has to be the farm crisis of the 1980s with its many lasting impacts on agriculture and on our state. It washed out a generation of young farmers, political leaders, and activists and hastened the on-going disintegration of Iowa's rural culture. It made the survivors more cautious and conservative both in their politics and in their economic decisions. It helped create the context for the corporate takeover of swine production and the use of production contracts to replace independent producers owning their own pigs. Predictably, it was accompanied by the agriculture industry's resistance to any regulations. Those trends changed the nature of pork and the politics of pigs—and the relation between farmers and the agri-businesses that "service" them. The truth may be the farm crisis was much more disruptive than we have previously thought.

Another important component was the significant shift in state governmental control to the Republican Party, reflected in both the first period of Governor Branstad's service as well as the second. The truth is the intervening Vilsack and Culver years left little mark on the state with some exceptions of funding for community attractions and rural development. The years of the late '80s through the '90s saw the Iowa Farm Bureau's continuing growth and domination of agriculture and the Iowa General Assembly. The farm group, in many ways an appendage to a powerful financial insurance company, promotes essentially an anti-public, anti-government ideology. Claiming to be the largest farm group in the state and the voice of agriculture, it has in many ways functioned as a corrosive force in state politics. Its goals include lowering tax rates, shifting property tax burdens away from rural landowners, and opposing regulations to protect the environment. Its smaller government priorities have helped spur many changes in Iowa including the continued underfunding of education and of state agencies like the DNR. One effect of these shifts is the continuing decline in support for public education both in the funding of K-12 schools and in the support for the state universities. At the same time, slippage in our state test scores and an increase in the debt burden and tuition costs to students show the erosion in our commitment to education. The policies have helped fuel the anti-educated, anti-elite forms of resentment growing to full flower in recent years.

The changing nature of rural demographics played a significant role, with continuing increases in the aging population, and a decline in rural youth among those who remain. As a result we have seen a significant skewing of wealth, jobs, and opportunities, with many of the people remaining in rural Iowa those who in many ways have been left behind. These shifts help fuel social divisions and the coarsening nature of the political debate. Part of the changes are the significant shifts in the nature of the agricultural system. We have declining farm numbers and increasing farm sizes, with accompanying shifts in land tenure such as the continuing increase in farm tenancy. These changes have affected not just our attitudes toward stewardship of the land, but more importantly where the revenue and income from agriculture is captured and whether or not rural areas and small communities have the resources needed to maintain their vitality.

During this time, agriculture has become more productive if you look at it from a standpoint of yields, all the while rural areas have become poorer. We appear to be sacrificing concern for environmental protection such as water quality or plowing up grasslands or other marginal land, all for the interest of expanding crop production. One factor impacting this shift in attitudes toward stewardship is the changing nature of government and politics. Each has discouraged any effective regulatory protections or even enforcement of existing laws by state agencies.

Another contributing factor to many of these changes has been the lack of Democratic Party leadership and its failing to develop a bench of potential leaders and politicians to run for and to challenge Republican incumbents. Neither Senator Harkin, who served for 30 years in the Senate, nor Governor Vilsack, who served two terms appear to have brought along or nurtured people to replace them. In effect the Iowa Democratic Party has done little to groom and develop new leaders especially in rural counties. Instead, the party allowed several long-term state officeholders to stay at the dance too long, leading to their defeat in November, 2022.

Collectively there appears to have been a breakdown in many parts of the social fabric and the binding that used to weave Iowa culture together. Today we seem to embrace a more individualistic, greed-driven approach toward life with less concern for community or the welfare of other Iowans. It is against this backdrop that efforts to protect water and land, and many other issues discussed here, play out.

Back In Court Again

Well, I was back in court again, this time in the Iowa court system unlike six years ago when it was the federal courts. For over two years I was waiting for a ruling from the Iowa Supreme Court concerning the public trust doctrine and whether the District Court could continue hearing a case two citizen groups brought alleging the state has abandoned its duty to protect me. It is an important legal issue and constitutional question, but I wasn't optimistic the Court would rule in my favor. My fear was it would be too convenient for them to say water quality is a "legislative" issue, as the state had argued, so the Court could punt. They could conclude when the general assembly passed the 2018 law codifying the "voluntary only" approach in question, it set the state's policy. My defenders argued it is hardly a policy to say the state and regulators are powerless and leave my fate to the kindness of voluntary actions, but such is the official attitude of Iowa now on protecting nature. So in June 2021, when the Court ruled the public trust doctrine does not require state officials to do anything to protect me, it was no surprise. I was left to find solace in the fact three justices dissented in the case and would have let the lower court hear the arguments. In reality the Supreme Court decision to turn its backside to the rivers simply means they joined a growing list of legislators, governors, and "public" officials who can't seem to be bothered by my issues. If there is a silver lining in all this, it is discussed in Chapter Eight, where the more positive actions of local governments to protect nature are the focus.

Now another stream, Bloody Run Creek in Clayton County, more pristine and healthier than I am, in fact, healthy to an extent I can only dream of, is on the state's chopping block. This time, with the active participation of the DNR in approving an 11,600 head open cattle feedlot in its watershed. My gosh, that makes it one of the largest feedlots anywhere in Iowa let alone located on karst limestone topography near one of Iowa's few designated "outstanding waters"! What has gone wrong with you people?! The good news is an environmental group and local supporters of the creek, trout fishing enthusiasts included, have spearheaded a suit alleging the DNR violated its own rules in a variety of ways to green light the feedlot, in part due to political connections and pressure from its proponents. The district court has rejected a motion to dismiss the suit, so the courts will have another opportunity to see if protecting nature is of any interest or value in Iowa.

Of course the outcome and reaction to the Supreme Court on the public trust doctrine wasn't that much different for my last ride on the judicial merry-go-round. This was the famous 2016

Des Moines Water Works lawsuit against drainage districts in three upstream counties—the lawsuit or shot heard round the agricultural world. It was fun while it lasted, all the attention and high hopes, but legally it was a bust, perhaps even worse than that. When wise Federal District Court Judge Mark Bennett certified his legal questions to the Iowa Supreme Court, asking them to rule on what Iowa's law actually provided as to the power of drainage districts—my real trouble started. The Iowa Court ruled the districts couldn't do anything but drain, no authority to act to protect water quality. This was a cramped ruling and interpretation. I liked what now-deceased Chief Justice Mark Cady said in his dissent:

"I believe the focus of our attention should be the end to which this lawsuit is directed. This state is blessed with fertile soil, vast expanses of teeming wilderness, and an overwhelming abundance of fresh water. The role and purpose of drainage districts in Iowa is important, but no more important than this state's enduring role of good stewardship. This lawsuit serves to reinforce the critical balance at stake and asks the rhetorical question posited years ago by one of the founders of modern conservation, 'What good is an undrained marsh anyhow?' We should respond when this balance has shifted too far in either direction. The law of this state is but a reflection of the values of its people. As we go forward as a people, so too must the law advance our values. We can do this by applying existing remedies in new ways or by applying new remedies to our existing values. This concept of remedy is not exclusive to the judicial branch. We all can engage in this discussion and act. As every farmer knows, the work is never done."

But Chief Justice Cady was in the minority and by the time of my new case, dead and off the court, replaced with a conservative justice. While the Iowa Supreme Court was at it they also said the Des Moines Water Works as a public entity didn't even have standing to sue the counties responsible for supervising the drainage districts involved. So it was no surprise, at least to me, when the case got back to federal court before a new judge, he quickly and simply ruled to dismiss. He reasoned even if he concluded the drainage districts were a point source under the federal Clean Water Act there was no remedy he could order them to undertake. Whew—another cramped ruling with little imagination or interest in addressing the issues. Do you get the drift here? These courts and judges appear to be afraid to actually consider whether I deserve protection, just as afraid as the administrative agencies and state employees who are supposed to be responsible for protecting me. So what are the courts afraid of? They actually have long-term appointments and aren't "at will" employees like many DNR staff!

I know why—they are afraid to tell the big Ag folks, the CAFO operators, the pork producers, the Farm Bureau—they can't keep using me like their own private sewage disposal system! If they do, someone might have to alter how they farm or where they raise pigs or how they dispose of their precious manure, and no one wants to go there. No one sees these cases as an opportunity to learn or to draw lessons on how to operate, even if the cases don't succeed legally. Take the Des Moines Water Works lawsuit. Wouldn't you think after being sued and spending millions to defend yourself the drainage districts and pork folks might consider if there were things they could do to minimize the risk of future suits or to show they are being good stewards who are now "woke" when it comes to water quality? Yes you might, but then you're not part of the mainstream of Iowa agriculture! The main lesson the farmers in the upstream counties took from the court case is the need to hurry up and install more drainage tile before someone says they can't. And yes their second lesson is to remember to take offense at every possible opportunity and say how much the lawsuit has destroyed their "trust" in Des Moines, in the Water Works, etc. They may never do anything to benefit folks downstream, just to show how much they were hurt. Such snowflakes these stout-hearted farmers seem to be, not to mention vindictive!

So you can understand why, given this history, I don't place a great deal of stock in the idea the courts or litigation will protect me. Sure it would have been great to have the Iowa Supreme Court rule the public trust doctrine means something. But even if they do some day, the issue will go back to the lower courts and you can expect months and years of proceedings, wrangling over what this all means and who gets to decide. All the while I'll still be full of hog manure, silt, nitrites, and more. Now you can understand why my only real defense is to go on the offense every now and then and provide some good old flooding. I'm not really in control of that—Old Ma Nature has to cooperate. Even then I don't like the fact much of the damage and impact is felt by the cities and towns downstream, not necessarily the folks polluting me. Well enough for now, I need to sign off and go float some boats so to speak. See you again the next time someone decides to file a suit to defend my honor.

THE RIVER KNOWS AND THE ENLIGHTENMENT

Given this backdrop of political developments, perhaps it is time to return to the Enlightenment to see how it might help inform our relation to the river. A key element to consider about the Enlightenment as discussed in Pinker's book, is the issue of science. Here we have a real conundrum because on the one hand agriculture claims to be science-driven and avers sound science should be the basis for policy. If that is true then why does agriculture turn away from and ignore issues of science when it comes to protecting water and soil? Science tells us where the nutrients polluting the water are coming from and researchers have well documented the practices needed to limit the problems—yet we are slow and resistant to their use. Consider how strongly and effectively agriculture has objected to and prevented the use of regulations and government actions to require or pursue the actions sound science tells us we need.

We seem to have turned believing in the twin pillars of 1) voluntary action as the only acceptable approach, and 2) a mistrust and fear of government action on the public's behalf (as informed by science)—into a form of quasi-religious, political belief to accept on faith. This explains the magical thinking reflected in the premises of the Iowa Nutrient Reduction Strategy. No one can rationally look at our ten-plus year track record and history of little success using voluntary actions to promote water quality and conclude we will be any more successful going forward. This truth is at the heart of the reports like those from the Iowa Environmental Council detailing the hundreds of years it will take to implement the Nutrient Reduction Strategy at our current pace.

The anti-science approach we are taking leads one to ask what exactly are the true motives of the voluntary only approach:

Are they sincere or just attempts to deny and delay actions?

Are they delusional and some really believe them?

or

Are they rapturous, essentially a version of the second coming, i.e., why act today if the rapture will make all of your cares go away? If you believe the rapture is near then why do you need to take responsibility for any impact you may have on the land and water?

This leads to another provocative question. Is one threat to environmental protection and the health of our resources like the river, religion itself, especially Christianity, the belief most common among rural people and farmers? I asked the river for its thoughts and here is the reply.

The River on How Religion May Impact its Health

First, you start with the idea humans have dominion over all of nature. Second, you follow this up with the idea the purpose and value of natural resources (like me) is to serve humans. Third, your time here is limited, eternity being spent in heaven, where it appears there may be no rivers. Given this set of beliefs, how can you expect the values it produces, or the political or social structures it underpins, to afford much respect or appreciation for me the river? It is like Aldo Leopold said of you about the land. When you talk about the land you really mean the people on the land, not the land itself. The same is true with me. When you look at most questions relating to rivers and water quality the real focus is on you, what does it mean for you the people? You historically assume if it is good for you then it must be good for me. This explains how you installed low-head dams, channelized rivers, drained my wetlands, and diked my edges cutting off my floodplains. It also explains the challenges encountered by groups or individuals who try to defend my interests or propose you take nature's needs into account. These folks are swimming against centuries of religious dogma and utilitarian actions, and are easily portrayed as tree huggers and modern-day pantheists. Who would deny a landowner's right to plow a streamside field or prevent houses being built in a drained wetland just so a river could be free? To your way of thinking this is new-age nonsense. Well, from our perspective as rivers, we could definitely use a few more pantheists rather than more card-carrying Farm Bureau members or fundamentalists for that matter!

As long as we are talking about the Enlightenment and since I have already offended many of you, let me tell you what the River believes the Enlightenment could or should mean. I see there being four main aspects of the Enlightenment: progress, humanism, science, and reason.

Reason could lead you away from a simple God-based faith to one based on rationality.

Science refines reason to understand the world, and could reflect understanding how water flows, what rivers need, and how water quality is impacted.

Humanism broadens understanding of how the rivers benefit all humans, as well as nature, rather than the economic and reductionist view you use to endorse violence against the river. Isn't channelization a form of violence?

Progress is reason advanced by science, with the circle of sympathy expanded so not just humans are considered, but the environment and all relations in a community.

You could make more intellectual and moral progress if you were bright enough and scientific enough to understand the impact of your actions and morally advanced enough to reconsider your attitudes. This would allow you to broaden the community. Wow—writing this analysis makes me recognize how much Leopold's land ethic is essentially a restatement of the Enlightenment! No one can do a better job articulating it than he did so I am going to stop!

JOHN BARRY'S RISING TIDE.

To learn about our nation's history, race relations, and the role of rivers, perhaps the single best source is John Barry's 1997 classic—*Rising Tide: The Great Mississippi Flood of 1927 and How it Changed America*. Reading the book again made me think about several issues. First, how does our long history and attitudes shaped by "fighting the river" influence how we treat the river today? Is this history why we have such difficulty letting the rivers live and have their floodplains? Does this history explain the lengths and expense we have gone to trying to manage and shape the river? The history of the breadth and expense of these efforts are well detailed by Tyler J. Kelley in his 2021 book, *Holding Back the River: The Struggle Against Nature on America's Waterways*. Barry notes since our earliest understanding of rivers there have been two ways to potentially control them, using levees or using outlets to allow rising floodwaters to escape out on to the flood plain. A second question in our dealings with the river today is can we approach them with more maturity and a sense of history? This isn't the 1870s when we are trying to tame the jungle of the Yazoo bottoms along the Mississippi. We now know the potential of the river for damage and also know what the river needs. Perhaps we don't need to tame the river as much as we need to tame our own greed and hubris.

One challenge is we made the river bottoms private property meaning the owners want to be paid whenever there is flooding or a need to retire the land. The spring 2019 flood by the Missouri River in far Southwest Iowa was a perfect example of this conflict. Tens of thousands of acres of crop-land flooded and was seri-ously damaged by the size and duration of the flood. In many places water remained standing well into the fol-lowing summer. When the USDA announced the avail-

ability of tens of millions of dollars to purchase flood damaged properties so landowners could use the funds to move out of the floodplain there was significant interest in the program. In fact the preliminary expressions of interest indicated owners of as many as 80,000 acres might apply for buyouts. But what unfolded in the months and years to follow was both a tragedy for the river and an unfortunate but common episode concerning the functioning of government, especially the USDA. As the government program slowly wound its way through the necessary paperwork and bureaucratic obstacles, landowners grew impatient with the pace. When the next growing season came in 2020 many of the fields were able to be restored to planting, and in fact a good crop was raised and no floods came. As more delays were experienced additional landowners who had expressed interest in selling their land and moving out of the floodplain continued to drop away. By 2022 the government was still in the process of approving the first actual buyouts of properties, probably totaling fewer than 3,000 acres and involving only 30 landowners not the hundreds who originally expressed interest. What began as a tragedy was also a significant opportunity to allow the river to reclaim a portion of its floodplain and to come to a more rational use of public support for farming. Instead it turned in to another frustrating installment of bureaucratic sclerosis and lost opportunities. Will we just need to wait until the next big flood comes to try again?

Thinking about how we have tamed the rivers, or at least attempted to, you can't help but think about the flooding on the Missouri River. No one wants to give the river room, so instead we channelize, dike, repair flood damaged levees, and then repeat again after the next flood comes. What fools we are. And our foolishness will continue being reflected in the complicated federal buyout process and the relative lack of action buying out damaged floodplain land. What lessons can we take from these experiences? Why doesn't the lower Missouri in Southwest Iowa have a large federal wildlife refuge like the 240,000-acre refuge on the Upper Mississippi in Northeast Iowa? Is it simply a matter of geography, and the fact the floodplain is so wide and fertile we just don't dare leave it to nature?

Maybe that is the point. If we think about why or how the outcomes were different and why we are willing to keep paying the price on the Missouri we gain insight into our attitudes. The reality is our anti-government politics and our privileging of landowners, as well as the federal court's willingness to rule some flooding is caused by the Army Corps of Engineers, all reflect one main idea—there is always someone else to blame! This time it was the Army Corps, next time it might be homeowners on the upper river lakes, or the environmentalists urging protections for wildlife and endangered fish. The starting point seems to be, we must at all costs privilege and respect landowners in the floodplain, and never question if agriculture is the highest and best use there. Little value or respect is given to the potential public interest, or to the river.

Our history of fighting the rivers is mirrored in how the nation waged war on our wetlands. An article in the July 4, 2022 issue of *The New Yorker*, "Swamped" by Annie Proulx, detailed parts of this history. In reflecting on the long battle waged against the Great Black Swamp, the land draining from the west into Lake Erie, she quotes an article by Sharon Levy, a science writer specializing in water and wetland issues, concerning the attitude of Ohioans:

"The tough people who conquered the Great Black Swamp did so at great personal expense, and they've passed down a deep and abiding loathing of wetlands. They are considered a menace, a threat, a thing to overcome. These attitudes are enshrined in state law, which makes impossible any action, including wetland restoration, that slows the flow of runoff through miles of constructed drainage ditches—the very conduits that, after each heavy rainfall, deliver thousands of metric tons of phosphorous and nitrogen to the Maumee, and onward to Lake Erie from which millions of people drink."

Levy was writing about Ohio, but her words just as accurately apply to our history of drainage, endorsed in the Iowa Constitution and continuing unhindered today. The point is if you are a river—or a wetland—your health and future is never secure.

"The river can make you famous!"

One observation from Barry's great book is how Iowan Herbert Hoover would never have become president without the 1927 Mississippi River flood. He began the winter of 1927 not even appearing on a list of possible Republican nominees if President Coolidge didn't run for re-election in 1928. Then came the great Mississippi flood with Hoover appointed to head up relief efforts. Every day for three months the nation's papers were filled with stories, often ones he had written, about his successful leadership with flood relief. By the fall he was the shoo-in for the nomination. Iowans and the nation know the rest. He was elected in 1928 but the Great Depression and its aftermath soon followed, indelibly marking his time in office as inadequate for the Nation's needs. The corrective came with election of FDR in 1932, whose presidency marked the beginning of the modern state and 90 years of progressive government, highlighted by a more sensitive understanding of the value of public lands and nature.

Some of the same things about the river as a definer of reputations is true here in Iowa. Bill Stowe was somewhat well-known in Des Moines from his work in public service, particularly snow removal and the 1993 flood. He was a tall man, forceful, charismatic, and thoughtful, combining his training as a lawyer and an engineer. But it wasn't until as head of the Des Moines Water Works when he brought suit against upstream drainage districts in three counties, that he became famous, or infamous, depending on your perspective. His willingness to stand up for the river and his 600,000 customers who relied on it changed the trajectory of the Iowa water quality debate, bringing issues of responsibility to a head much sooner than those who dominate agriculture had hoped. While his lawsuit wasn't "successful" if the question is "did the Iowa courts intervene to protect water quality," the outcome did highlight the challenges we face and the need for better protections—legal, personal, and moral—for Iowa's water. He is gone now, claimed by an illness that silenced one of the river's most passionate defenders, but his legacy lives, in part through a fellowship program for young water advocates.

As we look to the future, one truth is the river never gets to write its own history, at least on paper. Instead, it writes with waves flooding over levees, and water filling up the "developed" floodplain. History is written by people, often those who fight the river and the floods or who attempt to tame the river and harness its power with dams and reservoirs. These people get to define and determine the fate of the river, that is until it teams up with Mother Nature to confound even the most wisely engineered plans for its control.

The River Might Like A Statement Too

Well, I see you white folks have started a new trend, part of your efforts to show how culturally sensitive you can be to your history on the land. This is seen in statements or acknowledgments about the role of the previous indigenous owners of land. Nowadays these statements are often read by university or non-profit officials at the beginning of a conference or meeting. The idea is by providing such an acknowledgment, members of the audience can at least pause and think about the history of the land where they gather and its former ownership by the indigenous people, or those you now refer to as Native Americans. The statements often begin with comments to the effect "we are gathered here on the historic lands of the—fill in the blank with the designated local tribe—and we recognize their history and heritage, etc.", generally followed by other words of atonement. In fact let me read you the statement made by Iowa State University, both a form of land acknowledgment and a little bit of unexpected puffery. The ISU Land Acknowledgment Statement, created in 2020, reads as follows:

"Iowa State University aspires to be the best land-grant university at creating a welcoming and inclusive environment where diverse individuals can succeed and thrive. As a land-grant institution, we are committed to the caretaking of this land and would like to begin this event by acknowledging those who have previously taken care of the land on which we gather. Before this site became Iowa State University, it was the ancestral lands and territory of the Baxoje (bah-kho-dzhe), or Ioway Nation. The United States obtained the land from the Meskwaki and Sauk nations in the Treaty of 1842. We wish to recognize our obligations to this land and to the people who took care of it, as well as to the 17,000 Native people who live in Iowa today."

I guess these statements are a positive step, they at least show someone is paying attention but I am struck by two things. First there is never any acknowledgment to the effect the lands were essentially stolen through outright theft or other quasi-legality, including the treaties being referenced. Then the lands were made available to the ancestors of those gathered today, who used the wealth of the land over generations to raise families, create thriving businesses, and reap millions in income. No nothing like that is ever said, maybe it's a little too close to the truth.

The second thing you never hear is the other shoe dropping, to the effect in recognition of these past misdeeds, the state (University, foundation, local government take your pick) has allocated X amount of money and agreed to use those funds to acquire Y acres of land to be returned to the descendants of the tribes who previously owned this land. No you don't hear that idea either. No doubt you may think it would be too costly or even ruinous for something like that to happen. Perhaps, but if you are serious, there are ways funds can be generated, for example you could use a 1% check off from the billions of dollars provided each year in farm program payments. Or here is a more definite starting point, look at the tribal lands still held by land-grant universities. You may be surprised to learn when the land-grant universities were authorized under the Morrill Act of 1862 the federal government allocated land to over 50 institutions to provide the initial funding for their operations. Over 11 million acres of those land grants were made out of indigenous lands "acquired" from over 150 tribes in various nefarious ways. These lands, mostly in the West, were granted either directly or as script, to dozens of land-grant universities, including Iowa State University, the University of Nebraska, and any other land-grant you can name. The proceeds from the sales were used to help fund operation of the universities.

What may really surprise you is today at least 15 of those land-grant universities still own thousands of acres of the original land grants made from tribal lands. In 2020 the paper *High Country News* published a series of investigative reports on the theme of "land grab universities," by Robert Lee and Tristan Ahtone. The articles provide detailed information and maps concerning the millions of acres of indigenous tribal lands granted to the various land-grant universities. In addition the articles actually identify individual properties, their locations, and the current owners of them. For example the University of Idaho still owns over 33,000 acres of former tribal lands received under the Morrill Act. I don't know about you but if I was a modern-day land-grant University interested in making any form of atonement for America's past history with the indigenous tribes, then using some of those lands to either return to them or to generate funds for scholarships to native youth would be a good place to start. I don't want to be the person who farts in church and then looks around to see who to blame—but wouldn't that be a nice gesture?

As you might imagine, the idea of using these statements has become somewhat controversial because of what isn't actually being said or accomplished. As a result in 2021 the Association of Indigenous Anthropologists issued a statement requesting there be a pause on use of land acknowledgments and related practices of welcoming rituals, until recommended improvements in those practices can be made. The concern of the organization is the statements may simply further compound the history and trauma with how the land was removed from the tribes' sovereignty. This is particularly true if the statements or welcoming ceremonies are performed by what the Association refers to as "pretendians" rather than members of the actual indigenous people involved.

Now this is a controversy I don't want to wade into any further but, I can certainly see where the anthropologists are coming from. If a simple statement like the one made by the folks at Iowa State is all the farther the exercise goes then isn't it really just a form of virtue signaling and tokenism? If all listeners do after hearing the ISU statement being read is to say "good to know, now on with the show" then they are fairly empty gestures. This is why I was particularly excited to learn how, in the spring of 2022, my friends at the Iowa Natural Heritage Foundation (INHF) took the idea farther. Working with their colleagues at the Johnson County Conservation Board, the foundation was involved in a large land acquisition along the Iowa River north of Iowa City. Communications with tribal leaders of the Ioway tribe of Kansas and Nebraska concerning naming the property revealed the Ioway in fact did not own any land in the state of Iowa, their namesake. To help remedy the situation the INHF, the county, and the landowner, worked to donate to the tribe a 7-acre circular tract on a hilltop overlooking the Iowa River. It is a place tribal members can visit and connect to their ancestral lands. The 7-acre size is symbolic to the Ioway and the transfer of what they refer to as a sacred hoop is something we can all be proud of—rivers and people alike.

Thinking about these land statements and acknowledgments got me to wondering why you stop there. Wouldn't it be nice if you also did it for the miles of rivers you straightened or the thousands of acres of wetlands you drained, or how about the dozens of shallow lakes that used to dot Northwest Iowa? You can see them on the maps from 100 years ago spotted all across the Prairie pothole region in counties like Pocahontas, Palo Alto, and Buena Vista. Some of these shallow lakes still exist and the state is in the process of trying to restore and manage them. But many other shallow lakes have essentially disappeared, either drained or silted in and are now being farmed.

Can't you just see it, on an early spring morning before the farmer mounts up his John Deere 9470RX, list price $497,000, to head out to plant the cornfield. The morning begins with his family gathered in a ceremony where they acknowledge we are farming today on what was formally the bed of Lake Willow. This land was acquired by our ancestors and drained so we could grow corn to feed the nation and to make us wealthy. Today we ask the forgiveness of the fish, fowl, and furry creatures who used to call it home. Now let's get planting! Well, when that day comes I may celebrate by deciding to run backwards!

Bill Stowe.

Chapter Four—Do We All Really Want Clean Water?

KEEP YOUR DISTANCE

There are a number of things it is wise to keep your distance from— skunks, poisonous snakes, as well as drunk uncles, for example. In Iowa there is something else we like to observe best from a distance, our deteriorating water quality and excessive soil erosion. These are well-known problems and can be found about anywhere you look. The news is full of their stories—in June 2022, the Des Moines Water Works had to restart its nitrogen removal system for the first time in five years due to recent rains flushing nitrates into the Raccoon River. Several weeks before that in far northwest Iowa, a wind storm—called a haboob—sent towering dust clouds blocking out the sun, reminiscent of the "Dirty 30s" Dust Bowl.

But if you pay attention, these stories are as close as we ever get to knowing. Water quality is viewed as a generalized problem in the Raccoon River watershed and soil erosion is accepted as an expected part of modern farming, a result of planting corn on hillsides better suited for grass and pasture. We never try to get any closer, to identifying which fields are losing the soil. It is not the fields growing cover crops or protected with conservation practices so we can look elsewhere if we want to. Which tile lines and drainage ditches contribute the highest concentration of nitrates to the river? Surely they are not all the same, research shows this isn't true.

No, there are reasons we like to view our problems at a distance. This way we can avoid talking about who is responsible or ever assigning blame. We are happy to say it is just the "system" that is the problem, not the actions of individuals. If we can avoid identifying specific causes we can also avoid even suggesting the people most responsible should be required to take some corrective action. The reality is we privilege the right of any farmer or landowner to farm their land however they choose, over any idea of responsibility to the public. Even when the public puts money into soil conservation or protecting water quality we don't set priorities or target the fields contributing the most to our problems. Instead, we make the programs entirely voluntary, open to whomever decides to participate. Far be it for us to tell someone they need to act. This lack of priorities and social failing to assign responsibility helps explain why after 80 years and billions of dollars expended, we still lose more soil than we should and why the Raccoon River is choked with sediment and polluted with nutrients after every rain.

The Des Moines Water Works learned its lesson in the danger of trying to get too close to the source of our problems when it sued several upstream drainage districts based on specific measurements of the nitrites they contributed to the Raccoon. You may remember how well that went when the Iowa Supreme Court ruled the drainage districts had no legal authority to protect water quality even if they wanted to. Today the Water Works is "cooperating" with an Ag coop growing corn and beans in Water Works Park to show farmers how soil and water can be protected. The truth is if they really cared they would already know how—the reality is, it is not important to many of them. They know the public and government officials will not do any-thing to make them act, instead we are happy to lament our problems but keep them at a distance.

The newest controversy concerning the use of Iowa's land and nature involves proposals by three different companies to bury hundreds of miles of pipelines across the state to collect CO_2, the carbon dioxide being produced at dozens of ethanol plants and fertilizer facilities, to pump to neighboring states to pipe it deep underground, where it will, reportedly, remain. The politics of these proposals is covered in more detail in Chapter Seven, but it is clear the debate will be perhaps the most contentious to afflict our state since the "hog wars" of the 1990s. One reason the debate and social tensions over the proposed CO_2 pipelines have a different tone and urgency is because these projects can't be seen only at a distance. Certainly the promoters want to use that premise—to make the debate all about protecting the future of ethanol and helping the nation address climate issues. But for the thousands of landowners and farmers who will have their lands permanently damaged with altered drainage and compacted soils, the issue is right in front of them. You don't have the luxury of seeing the threat of eminent domain at a distance when the pipeline is planned to come through your back forty. Maybe one by-product of the coming fight over whether the pipelines are "needed" or are instead boondoggles and examples of crony capitalism Iowa style, will be to change our willingness to get a little closer to the source of our soil and water problems

WHO IS ANTI-FARMER?

Everyone claims they want clean water! It is hard to find anyone to affirmatively defend polluting the water. But when you examine our conduct and attitudes, when you take a look at the data and our number of "impaired" waterways, claims "we all want clean water" seem to evaporate in the real world of our "all production, all the time" mantra. Those who question agriculture's impact or who try to hold us to our claims of "all wanting clean water" find little welcome among political or farm audiences. I got a firsthand taste of this preparing the agenda for the SOIL 2021 conference focused on "Our Soils, Our Future." A law school colleague told me a student complained to her about a speaker on the agenda, Chris Jones from the University of Iowa. The student asked how was it even possible we invited someone who is so "anti-farmer" to speak? My how those engaged in agriculture can be so fragile!

The idea a scientist working at a public university to protect water quality and who strives to promote better agricultural practices is seen as being anti-farmer is very telling and raises many questions. Does it mean to be pro-farmer you have to be pro-pollution? Can't we be for farmers and for the environment at the same time? The student's attitude, which is not uncommon in farm circles, reflects at least three premises. First, his data and conclusions about the source of pollution coming from agriculture are wrong. Second, the belief that farming requires these environmental damages as a cost of doing business. Three, the assumption water pollution and soil loss really aren't that important or at least they're not the responsibility of farmers and landowners. In any case it is concerning we have students with this attitude or lack of understanding about the role of a public scientist like Chris Jones. What had the student been hearing, who was saying it, and how did she come to form these impressions? This raises a more basic question—how do people get information or misinformation? Is it cultural, is it the product of years of agribusiness commercials, or is it bred in the bone from being born into a Farm Bureau household or participating in FFA? Can't we be anti-bad farming practices and pro-farmer at the same time? In an ironic twist, Chris Jones and his colleagues at the University of Iowa, Silvia Secchi and David Cwiertny, have a popular podcast, "We All Want Clean Water" exploring many of the issues raised is this book.

How do we "know" what we know?

Not long after learning of the student's "anti-farmer" comment, I had the opportunity to sit in on my colleague's class in environmental regulation of agriculture. The subject for the day was an introduction to Iowa's water quality and the professor began by asking her students what they knew about water quality in Iowa and their impressions. The discussion was interesting but revealed the views were limited and often just reflected comments they had heard from other professors. It was clear most of them had given the topic little thought. The experience raised the question how much we know or conversely how little we may know about any subject like this. This illustrates an interesting framing question—when people talk about water quality in the river the assumption is we are addressing a problem. If so then the question becomes what exactly is the problem? Is it safety of the water to drink? Is it bad information or misconceptions about why the water may be polluted? Is it the myths we may believe or are told about why farming is not responsible? Or is it a lack of effective laws, such as the Clean Water Act exceptions for agriculture? Or is the worry our growing list of impaired waters and how the state's lack of action creates a context for little concern?

It was interesting during the whole hour no one mentioned the Nutrient Reduction Strategy, the policy Iowa has placed so much attention on, or brought up drainage tile as a source of potential problems. For me the discussion demonstrated the real problem in the water quality debate may be our inability to articulate exactly what the problem is! Is the water bad, if so compared to what? Even if the water quality is poor, couldn't it be worse? The problem is we don't want to dig down into the causes because we fear the answers or what the answers may require us to do. So instead we promote voluntary efforts and focus on what we have done—all the while claiming we all want clean water. If the river had "observed" the students' discussion it might have said "the problem is no one cares as much about the water as I do" and if no one recognizes or respects my desires, then I am left to my own care. The river might ask what will it take for people to care—does it take a Flint, Michigan, like health scare, a major fish kill, or another devastating flood?

Reflecting on the class and whether the public even cares about water quality, made me think about how we obtain information. This may explain why the agricultural voice and the concern of farmers, at least as expressed by the Iowa Farm Bureau (whether true or not) has such influence. Their voice is focused and specific, so when the time comes to consider an issue, such as a proposed law or regulation, or an alleged problem, they are able to bore in and express their opposition. Plus their work has a cumulative effect on the public's memory or understanding. Any present response will be shaped by what people last remember hearing. It builds up, like accretion on the riverbank, with each new commercial and campaign leaving a new layer. If true, then the question becomes what type of event or crisis might it take to erode the buildup or wash away and change our "understanding?" In a river this is called avulsion. Will it be a new manure spill, a health and safety incident on the river, or a public health threat to humans? I asked the river for its thoughts on what it might take?

The River On What the Public Knows

There are similarities between what you know or believe and my history. As noted, rivers change through the process of accretion, how we build up new areas of land along our banks. You have all seen this when you walk our shores or drive over a bridge, new sandbars appear, banks seem to grow, and my channel may be pushed toward the other side. That is accretion. As the water rises with new rains the silt and soil is carried down but as the water levels drop and the velocity slows the silt is deposited, especially on my outer edges where the current is most reduced. There the sediments and sand build up like pages in a book. This can go on for weeks or months or even for years. That is why when you see old photographs or maps of rivers you can see the channels moving all around, almost like we are living things, wiggling and twisting! Well, we are living things. The accretion goes on until something more powerful and rapid changes my hydrology and flow, often cutting through the layers, washing away the sediment to move it farther downstream, cutting off the old channel into ox-bows, and creating a new one—a new path of knowing if you will. Then it all starts again.

Think about how this compares to your knowledge and understanding of an issue, on something like water quality. What do you know and why? Your knowledge has been built up over time and deposited in layers. Maybe it was a news story about water quality, or a friend telling you about their experience paddling on the river. Maybe it was news coverage about a lawsuit, a dispute with environmentalists raising the alarm about some agency decision or proposed activity. Perhaps it was a TV commercial you remember, one explaining how farmers have changed their practices just to protect water quality. Do you get my point? Your "knowledge," your understanding is the residue of these events. Just like the water slowing down, these memories have been deposited in your streambank of knowledge. These are memories to be drawn from when you are asked questions like do you think Iowa needs to do more to protect water quality? Should we raise the sales tax to pay for natural resource protection? Do you trust farmers and agriculture to "do the right thing?" You really can't be sure where you learned what you know or even how your opinions were formed but no doubt you have answers to these questions. Thinking about the process of accretion makes it possible to see how the formation of what you know may not have been natural or accidental but in fact was intentional. As you will learn in this book, in many cases what you "know" was designed and controlled by people hoping you come to believe a certain way.

Now think about how what you know might change, sometimes radically or rapidly if there is a new event, a crisis, or an issue requiring your attention. This is just like what happens to me with avulsion. The layers of silt may be laid down gradually along my bank over many years but wait until there is a 4-inch rain overnight. Then the river rises quickly and the speed of the current increases to a torrent and the flood washes away the layers. The next day when the water levels recede the sandbars may be gone and the stream bank collapsed. The channel may have shifted and a new one replaced the old. Then the process can begin again but the question is will your understanding and opinions have been changed by this new reality? What might be your flood of knowledge to reach a new perspective, what might it take for you to think about me in a new way?

TEN THINGS WE BELIEVE THAT AREN'T TRUE

The question of what it might take to change public perceptions is in part answered by what is the understanding of the issue involved. From my decades working on Iowa soil conservation and water quality issues it seems clear there are many opinions Iowans have convinced ourselves of that may not be true. Here is a list of ten examples to consider:

1. Ethanol is a green fuel, so the more the better;

2. Topsoil replenishes itself at around five tons per acre each year, so soil erosion is not a major concern for Iowa;

3. Increasing the amount of drainage tile does not negatively impact water quality or increase stream flows;

4. Traditional forms of manure disposal do not cause water quality issues because the land can absorb and handle the amounts of manure applied;

5. Increases in farm tenancy do not negatively impact how farmland is cared for or reflect unequal relations between the parties involved;

6. All farmers and landowners care about the soil and water and are committed to stewardship, doing all they can to protect these resources;

7. Farmers do not use any more fertilizer or nitrogen than is necessary to produce a crop because these inputs are expensive, so none is wasted;

8. Increasing land values are always a good news story for those in agriculture and rural Iowa, so higher land prices should be encouraged;

9. There is no need for regulation in agriculture because voluntary only programs are sufficient and doing the job;

10. Fall tillage is a sound and accepted agricultural practice.

Think about how this Decalogue of Modern Agriculture helps explain why we have problems. Once an idea is firmly lodged in the public consciousness it can be very difficult to alter. How do you challenge or confront people, or try to amend or modify their beliefs? One way is to suggest a counter list of reasons for why the beliefs may be ill-conceived. Consider the following:

1. Ethanol is not a green fuel, if you raise corn in ways causing soil loss, impacting water quality, and converting marginal land to crops;

2. Top soil does not replenish at 5-tons-per-acre per-year under any common cropping system, and may actually renew at less than 1/10 of that;

3. Tiling a field serves as a direct conduit for nutrients into streams and ditches, speeding the rate and quantity of water removed, making streams and rivers flashier;

4. Manure applied on the soil surface can wash off and nutrients incorporated into the soil can leach down into the tile lines, meaning increasing manure applications can have a direct impact on deteriorating water quality;

5. Farm tenants have no long-term incentive to care for the land or invest in soil conservation or soil health practices, and in fact may be economically penalized for doing so;

6. If farmers and landowners care about soil and water, why are soil loss and water quality still serious problems? Surveys show most farmers and landowners take few actions and make little direct investment to address water quality or soil conservation;

7. Nitrogen is an insurance policy for potentially larger yields and farmers apply significantly more nutrients than recommended by university guidelines, such as the maxi-

mum return to nitrogen (MRTN) rate;

8. Increasing land values lead directly to higher rents and increase the pressure to convert marginal land to crops, such as plowing up pastures or bulldozing out trees;

9. There is no evidence "voluntary only" programs work to achieve social goals, not just in agriculture but for anything; society uses regulations to set minimum standards of expected conduct and to signal priorities to citizens;

10. Fall tillage is an outdated and unnecessary practice exposing soil to winter wind and spring rains. Even though all conservationists discourage it, many farmers continue to use fall tillage believing it gives a head start on spring field work, especially in wet conditions.

One value of listing these counter beliefs is: 1) they help explain how we got where we are and 2) help identify the magnitude of the challenge. They identify what may be opportunities, for example focusing on soil health, improving water management, developing nutrient management plans, or improving manure handling processes. The point of the exercise is if you want to move to a brighter more hopeful future, you have to start with the current reality; identify why it exists, why people appear to be satisfied with it, and think about how new ideas, better information, and alternatives might have some effect.

It is also important to recognize some issues are open to active debate. For example consider the role of farming practices in relation to carbon sequestration. On the one hand many people believe cover crops and agricultural practices are effective at sequestering carbon in the soil and can be important answers to climate change. On the other side many scientists question whether cover crops and other temporary farming practices do sequester soil carbon with any guarantee for the long term, as opposed to what is gained with the planting or protecting of trees. The practices may improve soil health but many proponents view them as essentially a new way to subsidize farmers.

WHAT MIGHT EXPLAIN OUR DIVIDE?

The status of our shared understanding about soil and water quality issues and the divide between farmer's attitudes and the public's are troubling, especially given the importance of the issues. Truthfully it does not appear our search for common ground is getting any better. In fact the Republican domination of the general assembly and of the executive branch are making things worse. Some people warn against the idea of demonizing people or labeling some in agriculture as bad actors and instead counsel for empathy and cooperation, but there are legitimate questions about where such "accommodation" will lead. The long history of the Iowa Farm Bureau's efforts to deny, deflect, delay, and even deceive the public concerning agriculture's impact on the environment, has had great success. Their ability to penetrate and dominate farm culture raises the question—are there many people in the agricultural sector who are still reachable or interested in considering how to treat our land and water resources differently? If farmers don't want to do it, the legislature won't act, and Iowa's Department of Agriculture and the soil and water conservation districts are either weak or spineless, then what tools are left? In reality not many: litigation has few cards to play, especially given the disappointing outcome in the public trust doctrine case. There is the federal government acting through the USDA and the EPA, but even here the Republicans in Congress will certainly bottle up anything the EPA may do or even consider doing such as new rules on the waters of the US or further action to restrict use of pesticides like dicamba. This leaves much to the USDA, but one concern with the USDA, as we will learn in Chapter Seven, is it seems be, if not distracted by, then at least obsessed with the idea of trying to pursue new programs concerning climate and carbon, and has lost focus on traditional approaches to soil conservation. The question is can new programs provide the basis for integrating traditional conservation efforts into new climate related programs, like the $3 billion in climate smart commodity grants the USDA unveiled in September 2022.

You May Think the River Has Problems But I Worry About You!

I have been thinking about what I see and hear going on with you humans: Your growing angst, uncertainty, and social conflict. You see it in the political and social divides over COVID vaccines, whether or not students should wear masks in school, and even believing whether the 2020 presidential election was somehow stolen. I worry a large segment of your population is losing touch with reality. This concerns me because it reflects on how society may decide to treat me. If issues are all about individual freedom, with no concern for the public welfare, how is that not going to impact me and other rivers?! We are inherently a public resource and we require public agreement on our value to ensure our wise use.

If the public will not trust or believe in science, such as vaccinations will protect them from diseases, then how can the public be expected to act with any measure of care in regard to water quality or climate change? Climate change already faces its own challenges because it is so easy to characterize as being too far removed both in time and in the ability of individuals to believe their actions will have any potential benefit. If the public loses trust in the mechanisms of democracy—such as the integrity of elections, or if politicization is used as a tool to challenge or change elections or to suppress the vote and to gerrymander districts, all to elect politicians who share a distrust of government, or a cramped view of the balance between individual liberty and the public good—then how can we expect this to result in policies that help protect the water or soil?

A good example of this politicized environment happened in the 2021 Iowa general assembly, when a bill was developed and introduced by Republican legislators with the fairly innocuous and benign legislative purpose of adding the term "soil health" to the soil conservation law, Chapter 161A of the Iowa Code. All the legislation would have done was make it possible for soil and water conservation districts to describe their work as addressing soil health. However the bill was not taken up for floor consideration because the Republican leadership didn't trust or like what they saw as the "leftist" organizations—the Ike's, Sierra Club, and the Environmental Law and Policy Center—who had signed on to endorse the bill. The accepted agricultural groups such as the Iowa Soybean Association and even the Conservation Districts of Iowa had stayed neutral for fear of seeming like extremists! Such is the level of distrust and unwillingness to do anything if it might make it look like "the other side" has somehow gained a benefit. I can tell you, speaking on behalf of the rivers, this worries us.

You may think I have problems, with low flows during drought, with increased pollution, and with streambank erosion, but when I look at the mess you folks are in I'm grateful for my situation. My problems are mostly natural and with time will be resolved. The rains will come, my flows will increase, nature will help stabilize my banks and at some point your willingness or ability to poison yourselves will meet resistance. Your problems are more systemic and may even threaten the very democracy you claim to cherish. How did you get so stupid with the billions of dollars you put into education, and with the generations of building and defending your institutions of government? How did you get to where almost half of you won't get a vaccination to avoid a deadly virus, and where you will gladly endanger your children and oppose public health advice deluding yourself it is somehow about your freedom? This would be sad if it wasn't such a comedic debacle. And you still claim you believe in science! The truth is you appear to be as pre-scientific a society as were the Pottawatomie who fished my banks before you arrived. These are the people you rushed to push aside so you could plunder the land and natural resources they had preserved.

If you want an example of how your belief in science may be in doubt consider this. In the summer of 2021 NPR ran a story concerning the percentage of farmers who believe climate change is human-driven and the number was 18%. Surveys indicate at least 20% of Americans believe in ghosts and 55% believe in angels. So can we conclude more farmers believe in ghosts and angels than believe man is causing climate change? Think about that!

WHERE ARE WE?

The ability of self-deception or being able to see a different reality in agriculture relating to water quality is similar to what we see reflected in the COVID pandemic debate over masks and the failure of people to be vaccinated and, even in the Republican Party with the fight between Liz Cheney and the former president. We can't even seem to agree on observable facts if they don't comport with our own biases or what we want to believe is true. We naturally want to believe things that flatter us—such as we are making progress on water quality, or that confirm our wisdom. Today the social institutions and infrastructure that could help resolve these debates—universities, media, political leaders—are all at risk of being doubted, discredited, or accused of being part of the problem. So we are left to our own devices and beliefs. Unfortunately many people fill this space with what they see or read on social media, largely a cesspool of misinformation, bogus material, and conspiracies created by people either looking to make a buck or further their political agendas.

A number of stories during the summer of 2021 relating to land and water brought into sharp focus the tensions in our public discourse. They raised in my mind the question of what happened to our Iowa values and illustrate what may be our lack of care for others—whether our neighbors or nature. It makes one wonder why do we hasten to look for the evil in any idea? Consider these examples:

A national group told us the truth about the damage to the Raccoon River, listing it as one of the most endangered in the nation. The response of Iowa politicians was to attack the reports as "propaganda" and then repeat empty claims about progress we are making on water quality, claims unfortunately not borne out by any reality.

The Center for Agricultural Research and Development or CARD at Iowa State released a survey of farmer and public attitudes about water quality and the Nutrient Reduction Strategy. The survey on water quality attitudes found only 32% of the public think water quality is good or very good, but 55% of farmers say it is good or very good. When asked where nutrients and the pollution are coming from, 60% of the public recognized manure and fertilizer are the main sources, but only 32% of farmers agreed and 26% said the main cause is storm water. But think about it, the storm water is bringing manure and fertilizer into the water. When asked how we should go about funding improvements in water quality 52% of the public said we should place a sales tax on fertilizer, but only 21% of farmers agreed. Over 30% of farmers said the funds to protect water should come from imposing fees on people who use the state parks!

The CARD survey on water quality also asked about Iowa's Nutrient Reduction Strategy, and over 40% of farmers reported they are not familiar or only slightly familiar with it. This is after ten years of existence and millions spent promoting it, yet only 23% of farmers reported they are very or extremely familiar with it. Worse yet, only 46% of respondents agreed somewhat or strongly the Nutrient Reduction Strategy is a feasible way to clean up streams. On this question 42% of farmers and 51% of the public said they didn't know. The good news here may be there is still time to develop a more effective and workable approach to water quality efforts.

When the Biden Administration proposed bold new financial incentives for landowners to retire fragile cropland by putting land into the conservation reserve program or CRP Iowa's political and farm leaders ignored the opportunity. Instead, they invented a new scare tactic, attacking the CRP as part of the Administration's goal of conserving 30% of America's land, and a land grab designed to destroy private property rights. To add further insult to ignorance they followed with a wildly inventive claim the Administration's true goal was to end the consumption of beef. What happened to common sense, to reason, and to our much touted Iowa values?

Then there was the COVID relapse—a national tragedy and disgrace, but with an interesting political dimension. While Trump-ism is its root cause, he can't get all of the credit or blame. This anger, stupidity, resentment, ignorance, and anti-government fervor had to be bubbling below the surface and only found release in Trump, the anti-COVID vaccine crowd, and with the insurrectionists. You find it in the embrace of the big lie, our governor's willingness to risk children's lives and parents who seem happy to help. So what are the implications for the land and water? It may show us the baseline of what we are dealing with as to the nature of public opinion and the ability to get common agreement or acceptance of answers. This separation can be seen in the attitudes in the CARD survey as to the sources of water quality problems. To the extent these attitudes infect or infuse the political environment, it makes our ability to use legislation and policy as an answer difficult if not impossible.

The River Wonders What if Nature Kept Score?

In any court proceeding there are three key questions to consider: 1) what law applies, 2) who presides as judge, and 3) who is on the jury? If I had brought a case in the 1930s, as representative of "the rivers," alleging "crimes against nature" by those responsible for straightening the western Iowa rivers like the Boyer and Soldier, the likely outcome would have been predictable. If my case was brought in "human terms" in your courts, the law would be man-made, the judge probably an aging white male, and the jury made up of "peers," other landowners who shared the same values and goals. Their verdict: drain it, straighten it, and farm it! Nature will be subdued all in the name of Progress, Property Rights, and Profits—the three Ps driving your system then and in many ways still today. In the 1980s Iowa added a second stanza to the 3 Ps chorus when the state went all in on Pork, Poker, and Prisons as the answer to economic development, but I digress.

What if it was different, what if the court was outside on the land, and Nature's laws set the standard of care? Perhaps the "Land

Ethic" Leopold wrote of where humans aren't the dominators but are in a community of equals with the land. Or the rights of Nature some legal scholars speak of, that if not nature-centric, at least give Nature standing, a right to be heard, and a voice if someone is brave enough to speak for it. Then would the outcome be different? Probably not if the judge and jury were cut from the same bolt as the channelizers. No the result would probably be the same, perhaps even so today, because who values the meanderings of a stream and the slow-flowing river teaming with life?

Here is the answer to who values this—the rivers, the beaver and otters, the sturgeon and pike, the kingfishers and kestrels—theirs are the voices who value life in the ox bows, the wet marshes, and the flowing water! What if they were the jury and Nature—mother or father, take your pick—was the presiding judge? Then the scales of justice might find a different balance and the hand of man might be stayed—but who would stay it? Now the silence comes because while the courts and laws of man with sheriffs and soldiers have ways to enforce their rulings, the court of Nature did not—and does not—have this staffing. And so the drag lines worked, the sawyers sawed, and the rivers gave way to become ditches. Even the name signifies how steep was their decline on the scale of natural features—how ignominious a fate must it have been to go from a free-flowing, wild river to a ditch in only a matter of months!

No, Nature has no sheriffs or soldiers, no one to enforce its rulings and demand its rights, instead it just gives way and goes away. But not entirely—as anyone who has fought a flooding river or been swept by its current knows. Or anyone who has seen a ripening field of corn flattened and shredded in minutes by the work of hail and wind. You may believe these events are simply that—weather events driven by the science of meteorology, of wind currents, and high-pressure fronts. Yes, these play a part that I can't deny but what if you knew there was more involved—a settling of scores, a payback for years of indignities, of drag lines and gang plows, of spray rigs and honey wagons. Who are you to say or even know that Nature does not have its own tools—extra-legal perhaps but tools just as effective as legislation, writs, and decrees—in bringing some balance back to the Nature and human dance?

If you had this knowledge, if you thought even for a moment, Nature keeps score and finds ways to balance its accounts would that change your actions? Probably not, because you are wont to give way to reason or the so-called rights of others. You will always rely on your rights—whether gained by the muzzle of a musket as when you extricated control and ownership over me and this land from the Otoe and Pottawatomie, and the others who had come before—or with your legislation and drainage laws, crafted at the tip of a lawmaker's pen and ratified through your democratic processes. You are always confident you will prevail—unless the day comes when to your surprise you learn Nature does have the last word and the score is now tied.

OLEO WARS WE AREN'T HAVING

Today when you hear the term "oleo" you may have to strain to remember what it means or perhaps even need to ask a grandparent. The term refers to oleo margarine, the butter substitute common on grocery shelves and in most kitchens in America. Our understanding of the term would have been much different if we lived in Iowa in the early 1940s, then the oleo war dominated headlines for months in 1943, pitting the domination of the agriculture college at Iowa State by groups like the Farm Bureau, against the values of academic freedom and truthful discussion on the impact of activities favored by the farm sector. Sound familiar?

By the time the oleo war ended half the faculty of the Department of Economics had left Iowa State in frustration. Most notable to leave was Prof. Ted Schultz the charismatic head of the department who was helping  Iowa State build a national reputation for social science research, and the person most involved in the fight over academic freedom. Schultz left for the University of Chicago where he helped found the Chicago School of Economics and later won the Nobel Prize for economics. The oleo war was ostensibly over a graduate student's research findings the college had published in a report "Putting dairying on a wartime footing." The publication included the outrageous but true claim oleo was nutritionally equivalent to butter as a source of fat. This sent the dairy industry and Iowa agriculture into a first class tizzy, demanding the president of Iowa State retract this devilish publication and fire anyone involved in its preparation and publication. The context for the conflict was the campaign the dairy industry had been waging with great success to keep oleo from being widely adopted. This included passing laws in some states banning its sale and an Iowa law prohibiting oleo from being sold with coloring added. Instead, homemakers had to buy tubs of white vegetable oil and mix in the accompanying capsule of yellow dye if they wanted a butter-like color. Oleo sold for half the price of butter, helping explain the vicious attack waged by the National Dairyman's Association against Schultz and his colleagues.

As universities are want to do, Iowa State's leaders quickly sought ways to appease their offended farm constituents and the politicians who had climbed aboard this critical social flight, all while trying to preserve the appearance of academic integrity and keep peace with concerned faculty. It did so by appointing a committee to "review" the research and information in the report, ultimately several review committees in fact. Prof. Schultz and the academic community joined the fight over what were clearly politically motivated efforts to restrain honest and open research in the public interest and instead to restrict professors' work and publications to only reflect the desires and goals of the farm sector. The effort to "review" the report dragged on for months as Iowa State's leaders struggled to straddle the fence claiming to protect academic freedom but at the same time appease their farm constituents. As months passed they came to find the fence was made of barbed wire, when the national press seized on the dispute over academic freedom at an actual cow college and national University groups rallied to the cause. By the time the dust had settled Schultz and a dozen more faculty had departed Ames and the much reviewed report was "revised."

The clear message received by the academic community was the need to watch their step, especially if research or conclusions might go against the dogma embraced by Iowa's agricultural sector. The episode tarnished the reputation of Iowa State but foreshadowed a tension and reality still present today. It was clear then as it still is today—if your research threatens to upset the agricultural powers that be, especially the Farm Bureau, don't count on University leaders to have your back. How little things had changed decades later, as reflected in the sad fate of the Leopold Center. After 30 years of outstanding work leading the national development of sustainable agriculture, the Center was unceremoniously decapitated when the Legislature removed its funding, done at the behest of the Ag retailers and Farm Bureau, while university leaders sat by wringing their hands—but happy knowing the state money was being redirected to a more favored topic—nutrient research!

Now you may understand why this story is relevant today. As Twain is reputed to have said, "history may not repeat itself but it certainly rhymes." Ask yourself what oleo wars of today are not being joined in the public debate? Here are some candidates: How is our water quality affected by increased nitrogen use tied to our ever-growing demand to plant more corn? Does our supply of manure from our growing hog sector threaten to overwhelm the land? Perhaps most significantly—is ethanol an un-alloyed positive for Iowa or simply an excuse to continue to mine our soil and water? These are all important issues, ones we should be debating and questioning with more public researchers willing to examine and analyze the issues. But other than a few voices in the wilderness, such as Chris Jones and colleagues at the University of Iowa and Dr. Rick Cruse a soil scientist at Iowa State, few in the public academic arena are brave enough, some might say foolish enough, to pick these fights. Who has been willing to expose the dangers of our corn ethanol system? Who will ask if we might have too many pigs in too few places for the land to handle the waste, explaining our deteriorating water quality? Certainly not many on the public payroll—most public academics are smart enough and worried enough about their job security to keep their heads down. The Iowa State college of agriculture is as dominated today by the Farm Bureau and the need for corporate funding, as in the 1940s. As a result, we have the all too tragic reality of people needing to wait until they retire to take the gloves off and speak truth to power. It was only after retiring, once the Leopold Center was essentially eliminated that Dr. Mark Rasmussen, who headed the Center for years, publicly referred to ethanol as, "like putting dirt in your gas tank." Now that is pure heresy in Iowa and would have earned him a black mark or demotion if he had still been at Iowa State. Don't expect any new oleo wars, at least until the evidence becomes so strong we can't ignore the impact of our actions. Until then, sit back and enjoy the good life just like people believe we should.

The River Would Like Some Billboards

I made it into the papers again and it wasn't good. The news story was a group, Americans Rivers, ranking me as the ninth most impaired river in the nation. Of course Iowa's political leaders tried to ignore the story. The Iowa Secretary of Agriculture labeled it propaganda, as if the platitudes spilling from his mouth and his claims about Iowa's water quality getting better (like his comments on an April 2021 *Iowa Press* episode) aren't propaganda! It is in times like this when a river wishes it had more friends and could do a little counter-programming itself. You know what I would do? I would buy billboards to place along I-80 and I-35 about half a mile before you cross over me. The signs would say in big lettering, "Warning—Soon Crossing Raccoon River. Ninth Most Endangered River in America!" with a line underneath saying "For more information ask a farmer."

Boy, now wouldn't that get their attention! Couldn't you just see the Farm Bureau and the big Ag folks squealing—wondering who would dare insult Iowa farmers! Don't you think the local TV stations would have their satellite trucks out filming the billboards as drivers from across the nation whiz by!! Nothing like a little negative publicity to get the Agro's roiled up. Who knows they might go to the trouble of asking their friends in the legislature to pass a new law to outlaw such outrages, just like they have tried passing "Ag-gag" bills three times now to limit the free speech rights of the activists who film the dreadful conditions in confinement hog barns—or torture chambers—take your pick. In any case, their attitudes toward us—pigs and rivers—are getting to be pretty much the same. Keep us out of sight, out of mind, and don't let anyone dare try to speak on our behalf! They got a boost last summer when the Iowa Supreme Court gutted the public trust doctrine and essentially endorsed the state's policy of ignoring its responsibility to the rivers. The Court doubled down on its anti-public doctrines in the summer of 2022 when it reversed its own earlier ruling, to strip away the last legal protections for neighbors when their property is devalued by a new livestock confinement facility deciding to set up shop next door. The Court said this is an issue of policy best left to the legislature which has determined expanding livestock protection is in the best interests of the state—so no complaining! The Court's attitude can be summarized as—"We hope people do the right thing but certainly don't expect us to lift a finger!"

Chapter Five—Two Visions of Farming and the Dangers of Agri-Nationalism

LITTLE JOE AND THE FROZEN CALF

As a young child there are certain incidents and images burned into our memories, perhaps being chased by the neighbor's dog or better a parent tossing us in the air at the local swimming pool. One of my sharpest images is coming downstairs on a frigid late winter morning to see my father crouched on the living room floor cradling a half frozen newborn calf, trying to keep it alive. A heavy green canvas tarp covered the floor in front of the fuel oil stove, the only source of heat in our drafty farmhouse. Losing a calf was a terrible blow both to the economics of a small farm as it meant one less calf to put in the feedlot next fall, and for the mama cow with no one to drink her milk for the coming year. This early-season calf was either the product of an ill-timed breeding when the bull was turned in with the cows too early so the nine month gestation came during the winter snows, or perhaps it was a late-season blizzard, either way the struggle was on to save the calf, and several others I can remember.

I don't recall if that calf lived with only a missing frostbitten ear to tell its origin travail, or if it succumbed to the cold and the futile human efforts to substitute for its mother. I do remember the outcome of another episode happening in the same room about the same time, the story of my younger brother Joseph Jay or as he was always known to us Little Joe. He was born in the early summer of 1958 when my parents were 47 and 39. From his earliest weeks at home it was clear, at least to those who knew, something was not right. Little Joe would cry and wail for what seemed like hours at a time, obviously in pain. After a few months and many visits to the doctors it was determined he had water on the brain or hydrocephalus. Who knows how or why his condition developed, though in the coming years my mother would attribute it to her asthma and a particularly nasty attack that sent her to the hospital and an oxygen tent while she was carrying him.

Whatever the cause, Little Joe's fate was sealed, he died in April 1959 at the age of ten months and three days. The three days were important as he spent them in Blank Children's Hospital in Des Moines for an operation the doctors hoped would address his condition, but he didn't make it. I can still remember his funeral, there is a packet of black-and-white photos documenting the event. They show him in a tiny coffin surrounded by white flowers. I remember someone, perhaps my father, lifting me up so I could kiss his cheek goodbye. Now, 65 years later I can remember it being cool and can still see the thin blue line under his lips. There is a photo of the four of us dressed to

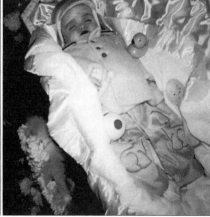

go to the service and the looks on my parents faces tell the story, the dead eyes, the distant stares, and their grief stricken faces. While the months of his crying filled nights were over, their years of remorse, sorrow, and recriminations were just beginning.

It may seem harsh to readers of today but my belief is it was best for all Little Joe didn't survive the operation. While my parents wanted to believe his life would be normal afterwards, my understanding of his condition indicates their hoped for outcome would have been unlikely. Instead Little Joe's life for however long it might have lasted, would have been as what today we call a "special needs" child, a compassionate term nonexistent in 1959. Instead his life would have been one of endless trials and even institutions, the reality I saw for other children in our area who "weren't all there." His special needs would have placed an almost intolerable burden on my parents, not just economically on a small farm but emotionally for a marriage and relation already strained not just by his illness but by the tensions growing and surging between them. It is not that my parents didn't love Little Joe or wouldn't have done all they could to provide for him but I am not optimistic the outcome would have been a good or happy one.

Many people say the hardest trial a parent can face is the loss of a child and certainly my parents never got over their grief. As the years passed Little Joe's name was not heard as often and they each lived another 40 years. I can't help but believe he was often in their thoughts. For some couples such a loss may serve to pull them together, to bond and heal in a shared experience. For others, like my parents, I fear such a loss was just one more deposit in a bank account of growing anger and tension. My parents survived the loss of Little Joe but their marriage was not a happy path.

As a child you fear your parents may separate, though in 1960s rural Iowa divorce was so uncommon it was the talk of the town on those infrequent occasions when it happened. I can't help but think there were times when my mother wanted to leave but how could she? With two boys to raise and no income or source of support, leaving really wasn't an option. In many ways she was a prisoner on the farm, not as tied to the land as was my father in his own form of imprisonment but she was a prisoner nonetheless. She didn't even learn how to drive a car or have a driver's license until she was in her mid-50s. So my mom did what I can only assume many who are actually incarcerated do, she escaped into a world she created in her own mind. My memories of the frozen calf and of our Little Joe may seem like pages torn from a novel by Ivan Doig, an unheralded giant of Western writing who I hope you encounter someday, but believe me these incidents did happen and they no doubt helped shape the life I came to lead. Today the calf would most likely have been borne in a barn built for this purpose and who knows, perhaps new medical technology would have saved Little Joe's life.

Episodes like these do color my view of how modern agriculture has changed our lives. No change has been more impactful than what is often referred to as the Industrialization of Agriculture. This idea takes the increasing size and scale of farms, the nature of the equipment, sophistication of the technologies, and reliance on high quality seeds and chemicals, combined with changes in the business structure of farming, such as reliance on production contracts and forward marketing arrangements, to conclude the very nature of farming has now become an industry. While too much can be made using the label, it cannot be doubted the farming of today is vastly different than just two generations ago. Agriculture has been evolving since humans first moved from being hunter gatherers to settled agrarians. Farmers have embraced new technologies, sought out labor saving devices, worked to breed more productive crops and livestock, and grown in size. Yet this label of "industrialization of agriculture" and its variants offers a useful device for examining not just the nature of farming but also our attitudes toward the water and land.

THE BATTLE BETWEEN TWO VISIONS OF FARMING

Dateline February 2, 2022—The big news of the day was *The New York Times* released a video op-ed about 15 minutes long concerning the role big food and big agriculture are playing in the climate crisis. The piece was well done and used powerful videos to explain the story of how agriculture has essentially been able to avoid scrutiny for the role farming and food production play in climate change and has been effective in preventing the use of regulations. The op-ed was sharply worded and focused on how the myth of the bucolic family farm is used so effectively but how its use hides the true role of the incredibly powerful agricultural lobby. Much of the editorial focused on the role of the American Farm Bureau Federation in helping lead efforts to promote the view agriculture is doing all it can and wants to be a partner in sustainability efforts, even if there is little evidence to support the claim. It was interesting to see how, over the next days, the agricultural sector pushed back against this unjustified "attack." Even so, the editorial raised several questions about what this new attention might mean. Could it mean the veneer of public acceptance for anything agriculture says is wearing thin and people are beginning to understand the reality of farm wealth and the economic system? Could it be other political or economic sectors, such as energy and transportation companies, often the focus in the climate change debate, are tired of being targeted and believe it is time agriculture bears its share of attention?

The really disturbing story in all of this is how backwards and ideological our approach to dealing with agriculture has become.

First, agriculture is an economic system providing a basic necessity of life, producing food. Second, if managed in logical and informed ways agriculture can be not just sustainable, but even a major tool in fighting climate change. These points are well illustrated in the 2021 documentary film *Kiss the Ground*, focused on the "regenerative" agriculture movement.

Third, by moving to a more regenerative system of farming, we can help address climate and improve the health of the soil, better manage water, and address soil erosion, all while supporting an economically sustainable system where farmers can profit. They can do so still raising many of the same crops as today, including livestock, which play a critical role in recycling nutrients and using grasslands.

Fourth, this restoration can largely be achieved using existing public subsidies and programs targeted to these practices, by conditioning availability of public funds on beneficial actions and paying farmers for taking care of the land, using practices such as planting cover crops, stream-side buffers, and converting non-profitable crop acres to grass and habitat.

Now contrast that possibility to the reality of the system we have now.

First, we have developed intensive monocultural grain production systems using practices that deplete soil, foul water, and degrade land, all with little effort to establish standards of performance for farmers, let alone use regulations. The main goal of our present system is to continue increasing production, for uses such as biofuels—ethanol and biodiesel. This has the effect of continued increases in demand for agricultural inputs like fertilizers and pesticides. The system is largely underpinned by public subsidies, most notably crop insurance and if market conditions turn negative as they did in 2019 and 2020, other public funds are showered on farmers, all without any requirement to use agricultural practices addressing public concerns such as climate or water quality. For example, in 2020 public subsidies accounted for over 39% of net farm income.

Second, as the public attention and focus has turned to climate concerns, the agricultural sector has now come to say it is very interested in being part of the solution and in fact is already doing a great deal. But it has some preconditions for this work: any efforts must be voluntary with no role for government regulations and if farmers and landowners do anything or are expected to act, then the public must pay them, including payments for actions taken in the past by the early adopters. So this is not a "polluter pays" system as used with other economic sectors and businesses, instead it is a "pollution pays and pay the polluter" system.

Third, while agriculture claims a new found interest in addressing climate change, it is also excited by the development of whole new private businesses and markets with the proliferation of carbon contracts and private players clamoring for a piece of the action. There is no expectation agriculture will change its current structure or practices. In fact, the goal is to continue all-out commodity production, the use of large-scale cattle feedlots, and CAFOs for hog production, just restyled as "climate friendly." Most of any crop surpluses resulting will be used for biofuels like corn-based ethanol and soybean-based biodiesel. To help make this future a reality, Big Ag's most recent gambit is found in proposals like the three CO2 pipelines proposed in Iowa to capture CO2 being produced from ethanol and fertilizer factories. Rather than use distributive farm-based solutions to actually benefit land, water, communities, and farmers—the idea of big agriculture is to allow industry to capture these benefits and preserve the status quo of farming. The story of agriculture and the chase for climate dollars is the subject of Chapter Seven.

So you essentially have a conflict shaping up between two different models or visions of an agricultural and climate future, with the outcome having significant impacts on the health of the land, the shape of rural communities, farmer income and sustainability, public values, and the impact on climate issues.

The River Wonders if Iowa's "Ag-gag" Laws Apply to it?

I have been thinking about the lengths you people are willing to travel to avoid confronting the truth about how some commonly accepted agricultural practices might be indefensible if more people were aware of them. Perhaps the best example is what are known as 'Ag-gag" laws. These are the innocent sounding laws agricultural groups have pushed states to enact under the guise of protecting operators from employees who are really animal welfare activists seeking to film and expose practices they find cruel and possibly illegal. The way I see it, there is a direct connection between the Ag-gag laws and how you view water quality—and treat me. Recently a federal District Court Judge struck down the third version of Iowa's Ag-gag law, ruling it impacted the constitutional free speech rights of the "employees" who can be charged for obtaining employment and access to a livestock facility under false pretenses. The previous two laws had both been held unconstitutional by the federal courts because they restricted people trying to investigate conditions in livestock confinement facilities. Earlier in the year, an Iowa District Court had upheld the third law, but the county prosecutor then dropped the charges filed against a California animal rights activist. He had brought attention to the way hogs were being "euthanized" by steaming them to death during the early days of the COVID market crisis. The decision to drop the prosecution avoided a trial and prevented further publicizing the actual facts of the case, horrific by their very nature. The activist wrote an extensive editorial in the *Des Moines Register* detailing how Iowa has turned its back to the conditions and abuses common in livestock operations.

My point here is we rivers know this pattern well. In recent years it seems one main activity of many in agriculture has been to deny issues concerning water quality and how you treat the rivers and streams. There is almost a cottage industry developing in this regard. From my perspective I wish you would spend as much time worrying about how the animals are being treated as you spend trying to protect those who abuse them from any form of exposure. And I feel much the same way about how people fail to care for me. There are parallels in how people treat rivers and pigs—keep us out of sight, out of mind, and subject to your control. Speaking for the rivers, we wish you would spend as much time funding water quality monitoring and river cleanups as you do trying to police the activists. Of course, this is unlikely. In fact a bigger risk might be it is only a small step before your legislature tries to pass a law making it illegal for anyone to film a scene of soil erosion or of water running off a field after it rains, maybe even preventing citizens from testing water quality. Anything to protect the sensitive feelings of farmers unfairly subject to public scrutiny. Iowa's newest crop may be the hothouse violets who can't stand the public's prying eyes.

9/11 AND OUR ATTITUDES TOWARD
THE LAND AND WATER

Well, the 20th anniversary of 9/11 gave the nation the opportunity to reflect on what has happened to us since that day. There are many important observations and reflections, but one concern is how, for some, our shared experience of 9/11 has dissolved. It has been corroded by the division, rancor, and grievances reflected in today's politics, in particular the deterioration of the Republican party to a shadow of its former self. One question that comes to mind is how do these attitudes and divisions show up or seep into our soil and water quality debate? Does it comes through in our mistrust of government institutions or in the idea any public benefiting restriction or rule is somehow illegal or an unconstitutional restraint on freedom? Does it mean there is a right to pollute the water or erode the soil? Well, we don't say it quite that starkly and at least, as to the soil, we say no you don't have that right. Instead, if you come at the question from the perspective of what we are allowed to do on the land, the answer is almost anything. Conversely if you try to identify the practices and activities we restrict or regulate, that bucket is pretty empty too. The collective effect is to tacitly approve of our right to abuse the land. Who is going to stop us, the neighbor, our heirs, our lender?

Periodically a friend sends me photos he takes driving around our part of central Iowa. He is retired now after a long career in natural resource education and after several terms as a SWCD Commissioner. His concerns for how we treat the land and water have not waned. In early December 2021 he sent the photos you see on the following page—the first is a green field planted in cover crops, with the photo taken in early December. The other photo taken at the same time is of a nearby bare tilled field exposed to the rain and wind. The photos show a stark contrast in the attitudes of the owners and farmers and are a good example of the potential risks from fall tillage. The reality is there is no good explanation or defense for a bare tilled field in early winter, other than stupidity, greed, laziness, and lack of care by the owners. These photos are not unlike other photos he sent earlier in the summer showing a herd of cattle lolling in a stream. Now if you were a cow you could appreciate the opportunity to cool off in a stream on a hot summer day. But from a water quality standpoint whether from turbidity, streambank erosion, or defecating in the water, allowing cattle unlimited access to streams contributes greatly to deteriorating water quality and streamside habitat. It is another of those "commonly accepted" farming practices we choose to leave untouched.

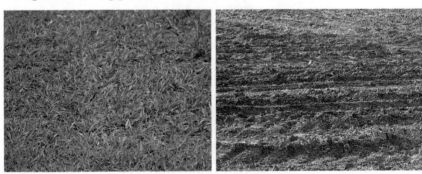

Observations from Ezra Klein's *Why We're Polarized*

In thinking about the widening gulf between attitudes in agriculture and the public, the question of what might explain the divisions deserves attention. Ezra Klein's 2020 best seller *Why We're Polarized* is of great value in trying to understand what has happened. Although Klein was not specifically addressing what we find in agriculture, his analysis is helpful in thinking about where we are, how we got here, and why many are happy to stay here!

The first key to understanding our divisions is to recognize the role of identity and identity politics. This issue doesn't get talked about often when considering agricultural issues, instead it is a label most often used by conservatives to castigate how progressive groups may organize or align on issues. But identity politics and its evolution into political identities is real and present among farmers and in Ag groups. In fact it is a key driver for many policy issues such as water quality. One important part of identity politics is having a common enemy to resist. If your identity is as a farmer then you can feel threatened by those raising questions about how you are contributing to water quality problems. One force driving the polarization is how the sources of information for your identity group, in this case the Farm Bureau and Ag media, are biased and polarized as their audiences. The goal is to weaponize differences to fuel outrage and further the idea your identity is under attack, meaning you need them to defend you. Consider current examples of this such as claims electric vehicles will result in the demise of ethanol so agriculture must oppose this trend; or how efforts to promote more land conservation, such as innocent plans to expand the conservation reserve or CRP, are a plot to seize private lands and even to end meat consumption. The fact these "plots" are fictitious doesn't diminish their utility in driving the wedge of identity politics. Klein notes efforts to wield identity as a blade mean it loses its value as a lens.

In many ways the debates are really about power—who will be the ones to set policy or who will have the politician's ear to influence who sets the standards of conduct? Toxic media and political systems can compromise individuals who want to do the right thing but who know the risks and price of breaking with the identity group. This helps explain why farmers have such trouble breaking the bonds of the agriculture hegemony even if they want to. The polarization created by these identities drives politicians and institutions, and can create its own feedback loops increasing the polarization. One value of retaining control or power over the institutions and laws is never having to change your behavior. As Klein notes, "when you are accustomed to privilege, equity feels like oppression."

He makes two important observations that validate arguments in this book. One is our focus needs to be on the systems, not the individuals, as the source of our problems. Farmers may over-apply nitrogen but they do so largely as the result of economic incentives and signals given across the agricultural spectrum, from input suppliers to federal farm programs, from commodity organizations to market advisors. The second is rather than "search for new solutions" as we love to do, our focus should be on correcting the errors leading to the problems. We could ask is what we are doing contrary to good science and best practices? The obstacle here of course is another tenet of the Agricultural Canon and farmers' identity—they never do anything wrong. When your identity is built on never making a mistake it is hard to believe there are any errors to correct or conduct to repent. This helps explain agriculture's love of new technology and indulgence of can kicking. Putting off addressing today's issues in favor of giving things a bit more time is almost an addiction in agriculture. One antidote to this may be to couch ideas as "new understandings," an approach being used successfully to promote adding "soil health" to traditional considerations of conservation and in bringing "regenerative agriculture" into the discussion. Thinking about Klein's arguments on polarization led me to the following explanation of what polarization may look like in today's farming world.

THE DANGERS OF AGRI-NATIONALISM

Anyone living in Iowa has seen them, the ANF stickers for "America Needs Farmers" found on football helmets and pickups across the state. It's hard to argue with the sentiment especially in a farm state like Iowa. But is there danger lurking just below the ANF label? For many in the Ag sector it is shorthand for a mindset, a brand of thinking with near religious status. It represents a form of Agri-nationalism designed to protect the rights and privileges of farmers and agricultural companies to act however they see fit. At the same time it strives to restrain and deflect the voices of those who might question agriculture's impacts on the land, water, or rural communities, or who might suggest alternatives. All the while it works to ensure agriculture operates free from any form of public serving regulatory restraints such as efforts to protect water quality or promote soil health. Of course exceptions are made for public actions designed to reward, some might say shower, agriculture with subsidies either directly with farm payments and subsidized crop insurance, or supportive government programs like the renewable fuel standard (RFS), which artificially creates the market for corn-based ethanol.

Agri-nationalism is founded on a set of basic tenets, which provide the supporting framework for the movement, including:

1) Farmers' actions with land and animals are always correct and based on sound science, i.e. farmers know what is best.

2) Government regulations are inherently bad, because they restrict the ability of farmers and landowners to use private property however they see fit.

3) If the public expects farmers and landowners to act to protect water quality, conserve soil, or address the changing climate, any actions must be voluntary, and the public must compensate for any costs incurred or benefits that result.

4) Climate change, if it is happening, is not caused by human activities or by agriculture and any effort to address climate issues may not be used to limit agricultural production.

5) No one loves the land or cares for water and soil more than farmers, this is why these resources are in good condition and do not need further protection.

6) The main goal of government should be to promote maximum production of crops and livestock and any restraints on production, such as the conservation reserve program, limits on livestock expansion, or rules restricting development and marketing of new technologies, are suspect.

7) To continue to meet its obligation to produce enough "to feed and fuel the world" agriculture deserves to receive public subsidies to ensure profitability and to reduce any risk of economic loss.

8) Scientists, regulators, professors, citizen groups, politicians, or anyone who questions or criticizes the good intentions of farmers or the wisdom of their actions or who questions the motivations of the companies selling agricultural inputs are acting against the public interest and any public funding they receive should be eliminated or redirected to more proper uses.

The evolution and existence of the Agri-nationalist efforts have been bubbling in the US for many years. However it seems the current political climate and turmoil within society and our democratic institutions have given it new energy and purpose. A series of issues touching on agriculture and food production have brought new scrutiny to the sector, including the debate over the nature and future of public efforts to address climate change; the continuing attention to agriculture's role in water pollution, soil erosion, and declining soil health; the fuel versus food debate; increased questioning of the claimed environmental benefits of ethanol; and livestock related issues concerning environmental impacts, animal welfare concerns, and the growth in plant-based and cell cultured alternatives. These significant social and political issues and many others, are placing a brighter spotlight on agriculture. As a result, farm groups, commodity organizations, meat processors, agribusinesses, multinational corporations marketing inputs and production, and political representatives at the state and national level, have coalesced to promote and defend the tenets of Agri-nationalism.

I came to this recognition reading, what at first seems an unlikely source. The March 2022 issue of *Free Thought Today*, the publication of FFRF (the Freedom From Religion Foundation) has a front-page article by Katherine Stewart, the author of *The Power Worshippers*. The article "The Christian nationalist roots of the coup attempt," discusses the relationship between the organizing activities of the Christian nationalist movement and the forces involved in carrying out the insurrection on our Nation's Capitol on January 6, 2021. Her key point about the Christian nationalist movement is it doesn't necessarily identify with a religion or even a set of religious positions. Instead, as she notes, the Christian nationalist movement is "first and foremost, a political movement.

Its principal goal, and the goal of its most active leaders, is power. It's leadership looks forward to the day when they can rely on government for three things: power and influence for themselves and their political allies; a steady stream of taxpayer funding for their initiatives; and policies that favor "approved" religious and political viewpoints."

If you remove the word religious in the third goal you will notice how her description very accurately describes the goals of Agri-nationalism. Stewart goes on to describe how the strength of the Christian nationalist movement rests in its dense organizational infrastructure. She identifies the following elements as part of that infrastructure: "a closely interconnected network of rightwing policy groups, legal advocacy organizations, legislative initiatives, sophisticated data operations, networking groups, leadership training initiatives, and media and messaging platforms all working together for common political aims."

When you read this paragraph and see the list of activities, the parallels are clear to what you find in the agricultural sector, including the Farm Bureau, the commodity organizations, and other groups who oppose any environmental regulations, limits on livestock feeding, or additions to public lands. Rather than a message of Christian nationalism it is a message of Agri-Nationalism that basically says farmers are always right, regulations are always bad, and the public must support agriculture at all costs. The tenets identified above help flesh out the movement's agenda and in many ways reflect the pledges those participating in the movement must accept and embrace. A series of messages promoted through different communication and political tools are used to motivate the actions, legislative ideas, lawsuits, and other activities making up the content of Agri-nationalism. Part of its content can be seen in the activities or issues it attacks and finds suspect, including:

- putting land into the conservation reserve program,
- promoting soil conservation or water quality if it requires action by farmers,
- any reduction in farm subsidies or attempts to reform crop insurance,
- questioning the environmental benefits of ethanol,
- promoting alternative forms of renewable energy such as solar and wind or electric vehicles,
- any restriction on the size or location of livestock feeding operations, and
- acquiring land for public use.

While this isn't a religious debate in the theocratic mold, the reality is in many parts of farm country Agri-nationalism has essentially been elevated to religious-like status and its tenets have become Commandments not unlike what was found on the Puckerbrush Puzzler. As a result, if you are a farmer you need to be a believer and a faithful member of the group. This requires supporting these ideas, all of them. No back sliding or picking and choosing is allowed if you are a true believer. Because church attendance and religious belief are strong and may even dominate rural and farm culture, many people in agriculture are familiar with these tools and comfortable with their use. The ability to use the power of groups and their ideas or beliefs to control actions and to impose social costs on those who are non-believers or critics are well known. This is why many farmers who support conservation and better farming find it so hard to break with their peers. It is just as hard in farm country to admit some farm practice is bad as it is to admit you are an atheist or agnostic.

If you are involved in agriculture and read this but doubt such a thing as Agri-nationalism exists, then I encourage you to take this quiz. Please refer to the eight tenets listed and ask yourself how many of them you agree with? If you find yourself in agreement with all or most of them then you may be part of the Agri-nationalist community.

The next question then becomes what is the danger or risk of Agri-nationalism if it in fact exists? The main risk is its anti-democratic nature and use in controlling public debate. It is clear farmers and agricultural companies have a vital interest in the shape and future of public policy and their voices need to be heard and considered. However, that is much different than deferring to their wishes or plans on every key issue of public concern. Sound public policy is not based on giving those with the most to gain control over decision-making. If you ask your children if they would rather have ice cream or broccoli for dinner their answer is predictable, but as a parent you weigh the options and use your own better judgment to decide. The same should be true when the Nation shapes important issues of public policy on questions of land stewardship, soil and water quality, food safety, worker protections, energy policy, and national security. In these debates all voices need to be heard and considered, agriculture as well as the environment, production as well as sustainability. One main goal of Agri-nationalism is to limit public debate by silencing or discrediting those who might question its motivations, thereby seeking to control public policy over the future of food and agriculture. This control is often to the detriment of the many other constituencies who have a stake in our food and farming future.

Shutting out these other concerns and ultimately controlling the decisions of government actors is how we have ended up continuing many agricultural practices known to adversely impact public health. To offer two examples, why are we still feeding large amounts of antibiotics with human health benefits to livestock as growth promoters and why do some farmers believe it proper to spray glyphosate on food grain crops as a pre-harvest desiccant, knowing herbicide residues will remain on consumer food items? The dominance of the forces of Agri-nationalism is why we now face policy debates over renewable energy and climate, each focused on such dubious ideas as simply expanding production of E-15 ethanol, or turning to archaic ideas like addressing CO_2 emissions with pipelines. Rather than embrace new alternative energy sources, and farmer-led practices to improve climate outcomes, many of the forces of Agri-nationalism are locked into existing business models they own and control in the hope of prolonging their lifespans and limiting policy debate and public consideration of reasonable alternatives.

THIS "CODDLING" MOTH THREATENS US ALL

If you have raised apples you know the Codling Moth is a damaging pest. It lays eggs on developing fruit and larvae burrow in to eat the apples. Recent events make me realize a different form of coddling can be destructive to things other than apples. The term seems an appropriate way to describe how some state officials feel farmers and agriculture need to be treated. We already coddle them financially with crop insurance and farm subsidies but some believe we should coddle them psychologically to protect them from news stories or suggestions they bear any responsibility for water quality in our state.

Political conservatives like to portray "progressives" as "snowflakes" who melt under criticism but events suggest the real snowflakes may be farmers, or at least their defenders who get wobbly and cry unfair at any hint of criticism. Coddling has legal status in Iowa where laws protect farmers from regulations to restrain the freedom to farm however and wherever desired.

A good example of coddling is a 2021 letter to University of Iowa officials from a state legislator threatening funding for the nationally acclaimed Flood Center—and support for tenure—because he was upset with remarks from two of the University's respected water scientists. That spring, Chris Jones, perhaps the most valuable source of real scientific data on Iowa's water quality, noted the obvious connection between poverty, race, and water pollution. The letter noted the comments made the writer feel bad as a white farmer. His quibble with Larry Weber concerned comments on IPTV's *Iowa Press* concerning the obvious link between manure spread on the land and nutrients entering tile lines to pollute our streams.

The state representative said his feelings were hurt because Jones unfairly brought the issue of racism into Iowa's water quality debate. We Iowans love to consider ourselves unburdened by racism's history. Well, here is a news flash—if you don't recognize how our history on the land is tied to the nation's history of racial injustice—of the native Americans we "acquired" the land from, of the enslaved people whose labor was stolen, and the Asian workers denied citizenship—you aren't paying attention. The fact something happened years ago does not make it disappear or mean racism is not present today in the experiences of agricultural workers, or of low income residents experiencing environmental racism in their neighborhoods. Being a beneficiary of white privilege doesn't make you a racist, that is in your heart. I benefited from this land history as did many of you. What we cannot deny is the reality Iowa's land system reflects a history of white privilege whether we acknowledge it or not. Yet ask any Iowa farm kid and history apparently started in the 1870s or whenever our ancestors arrived from Denmark, Germany, or wherever—as children we were never asked to think about who possessed the land before we "settled" it. How ironic today many deny the very premise while for the several hundred thousand people, almost exclusively white, who own Iowa's farmland our white privilege has an annual price tag in the billions. Many legislative "leaders" don't think these are subjects students should learn or even hear about—so the coddling evolves.

Along a trail I frequent there is a sign near an embankment—"watch your step." I worry many in the legislature would like this sign to be a motto for university professors and researchers. Think twice before you speak or write something that might ruffle feathers or bruise fragile egos. It is like the three statues in our garden—"hear no evil, see no evil, and speak no evil!" But following these edicts is hard when the signs of evil are all around—etched in the land and floating in our rivers.

Another example of this coddling was the Iowa Secretary of Agriculture's response when the advocacy group American Rivers listed the Raccoon River as the nation's 9th most endangered river. Nothing more than "propaganda" was the official reaction followed by claims of progress in cleaning up Iowa's rivers. Unfortunately little evidence shows water getting cleaner, in fact, data reported by experts like Chris Jones show river pollution from agriculture increasing. After paddling over 75 miles on the Raccoon River in Dallas County in 2021 I can tell you—it was not just low, it was dirty. "Propaganda' is in the eye of the beholder, but claims about "farmers being the first environmentalists" and how everyone is doing "all they can"—are hollow. The good news is some farmers are committed to conservation and many work every day to protect their land and water. Unfortunately most landowners cannot point to any action they have taken to protect water quality, largely because Iowa's laws and officials ask and expect nothing of them. Yet we willingly accept billions in public subsidies handed out with few questions asked.

Farm groups are happy to wheel out the good conservationists as evidence of progress and use them to shield the majority doing little. Implementing reasonable regulations like preventing planting to the riverbank and running cows in the stream could protect water quality. But collective resistance to "regulations" will ensure these practices continue. Failing to enact stewardship requirements to level the playing field for all farmers, means those who do take actions are done a disservice—coddling has a price.

The River Has Questions About Your Laws Restricting How to Tell History

I found this discussion of how you like to coddle your farmers pretty interesting because it is a concern I share. I don't mean to pile on here, but will take it one step further. You just don't coddle them, you try to insulate them from any criticism and protect their sensitive feelings from any possible reflections on the past. You are taking coddling to a new level. By doing so you appear happy to trample on the rights of other citizens to speak freely. You seem happy to try to sanitize your history, bleaching away the stains of your sins, whether to the Native Americans, to the land, or to me.

Think I am making this up? Then consider the language of a law your solons of virtue in the general assembly passed in 2021. They claim their aim was at the bugaboo of Critical Race Theory, an approach to legal analysis most of them could neither define or recognize if it bit them on the backside. In their haste to appease the accidental governor and "the base," their aim was particularly wide of the mark. The law, known as House File (HF) 802, signed into law in June 2021 and codified as Chapter 25A of the Iowa Code, is directed at training and education relating to sexism and racism. The bill identifies several types of conduct as race and sex scapegoating or stereotyping, and tries to define the concepts and explain when they can't be used in education or training.

Any law that flows from such tainted waters and attempts to limit free speech and thought has a difficult task trying to articulate what it believes is offensive while not running afoul of constitutional protections of free speech. One danger is the brush strokes will always be too broad. Such is the case with HF 802. One section of the law proscribes specific defined concepts as a way to detail what is apparently not allowed to be taught. One of the prohibited examples the river is concerned about is found in subsection (c)(7) "an individual by virtue of the individual's race or sex bears responsibility for actions committed in the past by other members of the same race or sex." In addition there is subsection (c)(8) which reads "that any individual should feel discomfort, guilt, anguish or any other form of psychological distress on account of the individual's race or sex."

So what exactly is the test for determining when these defined concepts may have been violated and who is to decide? Here is a question for you to consider. For decades the conservation community has noted how Iowans have plowed up 99% of Iowa's prairies and drained almost that amount of wetlands. Were those acts justified and the actors blameless? That is certainly your accepted judgment. But who committed those acts? You guessed it—white men almost without exception. If so, isn't it time people quit mentioning these unfortunate historical facts? Don't they risk hurting the feelings of these yeomen's descendants, the white children of the drainers and the plowmen? Doesn't this constant harping about Iowa's lost natural heritage imply they bear responsibility for actions committed in the past, perhaps even making them feel guilty based on their race or sex? Of course it does! So then isn't it about time you took action against those loudmouth professors and enviros who won't quit yapping about Iowa's dirty water and agriculture's historic role in degrading it. You know—by all those dead white men, your cherished ancestors. Where exactly are you headed in this race to shield yourselves from reality? Soon you will have the state building stocks on the University of Iowa campus so the so-called truth tellers like Chris Jones are finally put in their place. Yes, your coddling has no limits!

FARMING THE FARMERS: AGRIBUSINESS, MONEY LAUNDERING, AND THE GOLDEN GOOSE

I well remember one of my father's poignant observations from the early 1970s. He was speaking about people who worked for commodity organizations, just then coming into their own, like the Iowa Corn Growers and the related corn promotion board. These efforts are funded with "check off" money, small amounts taken from farmer's checks when they sell commodities, dedicated for use in market research and promotion advertisements. The idea is these small deductions or farmer "contributions" (made mandatory by state law) can fund campaigns to increase demand—think of the milk mustache or "pork the other white meat." Dad wasn't a fan of the promotion programs, one beef he had was with the high paying jobs he thought the commodity organizations staff had, all paid for by farmers. To his mind they were an example of people "farming the farmers."

His comment stayed with me and it came to mind in the summer of 2022 with a note from a reader of *The Land Remains*. She enjoyed the book and mentioned a family meeting with several of her relatives, all with jobs in agriculture, for example working in animal nutrition research and chemical sales, and all with degrees from Iowa State. Several of the next generation were heading off to the University as well to receive training, but none of her relatives were interested in farming, instead they all planned to work in related industries. I responded, saying it made me think of them being gainfully employed "farming the farmers." She replied this was an interesting and accurate way to describe them.

This idea is worth considering in examining the whole subject of agricultural industrialization. Much has been written about this topic, and much has been debated, debates I've actively participated in over the years. The typical premise is agriculture has changed—it's become industrialized and many of the farmers we traditionally thought of as family farmers are now part of industrial agriculture. One danger is this analysis is too simplistic, particularly in how it can seem to demonize farmers as being the villains in the industrialization process. Being an industrial farm is not a label many of the farmers I know would recognize. Instead their farms are family operations. Yes they have grown and yes the crops raised became specialized, largely because this is how the "system" of agriculture evolved. One of the great values of Beth Hoffman's book, *Bet The Farm*, is the wonderful job she does humanizing farmers and focusing on the on-going financial struggles and strains they face on a daily basis. Trying to survive in an era of rising input costs, weather challenges, and fluctuating markets can make even large and what would appear to be successful farms, economically vulnerable. Being large doesn't alone make you an industrial factory farm.

Then I had another epiphany, you'll remember I am somewhat of an epiphanizer. The epiphany is we have been thinking about the process of agricultural industrialization and its impacts and beneficiaries in a rather backward fashion!

To understand my thinking consider this short quiz. What do the following people have in common:

- a corn research scientist at Corteva,
- a pesticide sales representative for Bayer Monsanto,
- a chemist at the Elanco animal health division,
- a loan officer at the Federal Land Bank, and
- a line worker at John Deere manufacturing tractors for farmers?

If your first answer is they are all employed in the agricultural sector you are in fact correct. But the answer eluding most of us is to recognize every dollar of income they receive is paid for by the farmers who buy their products or services. When you think about the expression "cost of production," usually included in any discussion whether the prices farmers receive for their crops may yield a profit, the expression doesn't identify what goes in to those "costs." But if you think about it, those costs are reflected in the paychecks, profits, and shareholder dividends of all of the companies listed above as well as the thousands of other businesses making up the larger agricultural sector. Those payments accumulate and make up the cost of production farmers have to cover from whatever amount they may receive for their commodities. And if there is one given in the history of agriculture it's recognizing the cost of inputs—whether for seed, fertilizer, new equipment, or chemicals—typically go up, much like a ratchet wrench with the ratchet only moving up and almost never down. Contrast this to the level of prices farmers receive for their commodities which move up and down frequently.

Taking this perspective puts a whole new view on the issue of the various forms of public support flowing into agriculture. Whether it is the money we put into crop or revenue insurance so vital to farm income, the justification for various forms of farm payments, the importance of maintaining export markets so there is someplace to sell commodities, or why we keep our foot on the accelerator of all out production, to expand use and promotion of biofuels like ethanol. All these sources of public support or market-based income are really the source of funds passing through farmers on their way to the various services and industries that depend on them. Whether it is the interest paid on the loan, the rent paid to the landlord, or the price for a bag of seeds or jug of chemicals, all those costs are borne by farmers. In many ways the reality is we launder money through the farm sector and pass it on to support the agricultural industry. If you think about it as a diagram, it has the shape of an upside down triangle with the point at the bottom, the fulcrum, being the farmers and stacked above them are all of the other components of agriculture. The money received by farmers flows up through those various sectors. By looking at it like this, you can see how the farm community is really supporting the weight of all of these other industries. Of course you can invert the image and make it a pyramid with farmers at the top with a funnel flowing through them and the money flowing down, watering all the various "Agribiz" sectors. The only problem with this image is it doesn't capture how dependent the rest of the agricultural sector is on income flowing to farmers, that is why the image of the fulcrum is more fitting.

This reality about the role of farm income is valuable to recognize for several reasons. First it helps us recognize how farmers are, in many ways, locked into systems created by all of the other components of the agricultural sector. Second, it also makes it possible to understand how difficult it is for us to change the direction and even structure of this system. To suggest land be taken out of production and put into long-term conservation, or producers should plant cover crops or take other conservation measures to protect water quality, perhaps by limiting their need for inputs, are suggestions clearly swimming against the tide and the direction of the status quo. This helps explain why efforts to try to slow or alter our push for continuing commodity production reach few minds and receive such resistance. The resistance isn't just from the farmers being asked to change their production practices with what to them may appear to be the immediate impact of limiting their income. The resistance also comes in the weight of the rest of the agricultural sector recognizing how any decline in demand for their inputs will affect the bottom line. The decisions are made easier by the fact the water and soil don't get a vote or a voice.

There is another important policy dimension to thinking about agricultural industrialization in this way. The political reality is farmers and farm groups are largely the ones lobbying for programs like crop insurance and additional public subsidies to support agriculture, for example disaster payments in times of climate stress. You can now see this process underway in the development of new climate related forms of public programs. Politically you do not see the fingerprints or handiwork of the agricultural businesses, the seed and chemical companies, the equipment manufacturers, the research community, the land owners and financial sector, in these political debates. Even though they are in many ways the most direct beneficiaries of any political success the farm community experiences in keeping open the tap of public support, the Agribiz folks are happy to stay out of the scene and let farmers do the job for them.

An important shift in public perceptions could come from this type of analysis if we recognize how these various farm programs aren't necessarily designed to support farmers as much as they are designed to support the various businesses and industries that benefit from the money flowing through farmers to them. This is why the analogy of money laundering is so apt. It is also why it's possible to describe the farm sector as a golden goose, one laying the golden eggs the agricultural business sector enjoys eating. Recognizing this flow of relations may not change our approach, but it is certainly helpful in thinking about who are the true beneficiaries. It also helps expose the fact the agricultural business sector has been largely successful at hiding its interests behind the public relations façade of supporting America's farmers. Forty years ago if we asked what is the goal or purpose of federal farm programs there would be two key questions to consider— first what is it farm families need to successfully continue to operate, and second how do the programs impact the land? Today, unfortunately, it doesn't appear we ask these questions or are serious about the answers if we do. Instead the question is "what's good for agriculture" by which we really mean what's good for all the agricultural businesses who stand on the shoulders (and necks) of America's farm families. When considered from this perspective you can see how we have a multitude of people and businesses making their livelihoods by "farming the farmers."

Chapter Six—Can Kicking at the Agricultural Innovation Fair

INOCULATING SOYBEANS WITH DAD

One farming memory from my youth was helping Dad plant soybeans, of course with beans saved from the previous year's crop. The beans had been cleaned by Glenn Scott, who had a seed cleaning machine he used to serve farmers in a ten mile radius around Lenox. I would drive the wagon of beans to the field and Dad would bring out the tractor with the planter. The first step was to fill the planter boxes to the rim with soybeans, and then the part I remember was dipping a small plastic cup into a bag of a fine black powder and pouring it on top of each planter box full of soybeans. This magical black powder was called inoculant. At my age I wasn't quite sure how it worked, but Dad explained the theory is the black spores attached to the soybean seeds and inoculated the plant's roots to feed microbes fixing nitrogen. These nodules growing on the soybean roots pull nitrogen from the soil to help feed this year's crop and remain in the soil enhancing fertility for next year. Taking advantage of the soybean's ability to fix nitrogen, a trait shared by members of the legume family, explains the traditional corn and soybean crop rotation common in the Midwest. It also explains why the fertilizer needs for the following year's corn crop were typically reduced.

Today this approach of only 50 years ago seems like ancient history, in at least three ways. First there is no more saving soybean seed from last year's crop because all the seed now is patented for the genetically modified traits it contains like glysophate resistance. The idea of intellectual property rights in seed crops created a whole area of law. I wrote several articles on the subject, most notably one in 1993, "Who Owns Dinner: Evolving Legal Mechanisms for Ownership of Plant Genetic Resources." It led to my traveling the world consulting on these topics. A second difference is adding inoculants directly to the seed is a practice no longer widely used, in part because the high-priced bean seeds farmers buy today have been coated with inoculants as well as many other things, including the neonicotinoids responsible for drastic declines in many insect populations. A third difference is the idea you might lower or limit your nitrogen application when planting corn the following year! This quaint idea has in many ways been overwhelmed by the drive to increase yields by boosting fertilizer use. The fact is applying extra nitrogen has historically been cheap insurance for increased yields, if the growing conditions are right. This excess nitrogen use is a major factor driving the water quality issues central to today's debate about agriculture's impact on the environment. Another significant and related change is rotating crops of corn and soybeans isn't as common. Today many farmers plant "continuous corn," using fertilizers and herbicides to provide fertility and to break up the weed cycles that can accompany such continuous monocultures.

Iowa's love affair with nitrogen

Iowa has a love affair with using nitrogen to feed our corn crop, meaning the resulting impacts on water quality shouldn't surprise us. There are a number of economic reasons for this reality. One is from a legal or regulatory angle there is essentially no way to influence what crops farmers decide to raise and where, short of buying the land out of production with a program like the Conservation Reserve Program. Similarly, we have no history of prohibiting the use of fertilizer, for many reasons. Land is privately owned by farmers and landowners who make the cropping decisions. Corn and soybeans are legal crops and in fact we have constructed a marketing and support infrastructure for raising them. Most land being farmed is not restricted in any way, even if it is classified by the USDA as highly erodible. There is no restriction on raising crops or applying fertilizer or manure at essentially whatever rates a farmer wants and can afford. The state assumes manure applications are done in compliance with any legal requirements, such as setbacks from neighbor's homes or bodies of water. The state has no requirement for buffers strips next to streams, for planting cover crops, or really for any other type of practice to potentially limit nitrogen runoff. The economic and political answer to all these issues in Iowa is any restraints on production practices or use of conservation is entirely voluntary and up to the farmer and landowner to choose to do—or not. So the result is what you get. As a bonus, the federal farm programs, especially crop insurance, and even many NRCS conservation programs, support and encourage this type of farming.

Another related development happening in Iowa is the sharp run up in farmland values. In August 2021, the *Des Moines Register* reported a Grundy County farm had sold for $22,000 an acre, setting a new record for Iowa land prices. Over the past year many stories have detailed this rapid increase in land values, including a report average Iowa farmland values increased by almost 30% in 2021 alone. These stories have a drug-like effect, creating a near euphoria in farm country. But if you scratch deeper, the stories are not necessarily good news for agriculture, for farmers, or the land, and in fact are probably signs of trouble and un-stable times ahead. The increase in farmland value illustrates many things, including a lack of other alternative investment opportunities, at least in the farm economy. When you add in the extra wealth and money farmers have received in recent years from public supports, money floating around needing to find a home, increases in farmland values are predictable. The stories raise a number of key questions: are we going to continue to plant most of Iowa to corn and soybeans, and if fertilizers of all types are controlling factors concerning yields but have great potential for water quality degradation and other off site effects, what can be done to place reasonable controls and guidelines on fertilizer use?

The answer most observers suggest is—good luck dreaming but this is not going to happen. This may be true, but assume for the sake of argument there is interest in considering better ways to manage fertilizer use, then several ideas come to mind:

- promoting the use of the Maximum Return to Nitrogen or MRTN guidelines (discussed below) developed by University researchers as a way to maximize economic gains but limit nitrogen use to what plants need,
- requiring farmers to develop nutrient management plans for their land just as many now do for soil conservation,
- requiring landowners and farmers who apply animal wastes to include the nutrient value of the manure when calculating subsequent fertilizer purchases,
- re-imposing a sales tax at some level on nitrogen fertilizer to increase the costs of the product, as opposed to the current tax exemption, and

- adjusting federal farm programs like crop insurance to account for the possible impact on increased nutrient use or restricting where cropping takes place, such as in the two-year food plain, as currently allowed.

Granted, one cannot be too optimistic anything like these suggestions will come to pass. The reality is the goal of all federal farm support programs is premised on all out crop production, and we only "encourage" farmers to do some conservation if it might suit them.

The nation saw firsthand the declining interest in retiring land for conservation purposes play out in 2022 when the USDA missed its goal of bringing 4 million new acres of cropland into the CRP. The reality is conservation couldn't compete with the commodity prices farmers were receiving and their expectations high prices will continue. There is little reason to expect a much different result even if a significant increase in funding becomes available for conservation programs. If crop prices and land prices continue going up and stay high, we will keep our foot on the accelerator of all out grain production. Most producers believe their current practices, such as growing corn on corn, are best management options, so there is little need to change. To add insult to injury, in the summer of 2022, the USDA changed the rules to allow farmers with CRP contracts expiring in the fall to take the land out of conservation cover early so the land could possibly be planted with late season crops. The idea was to boost US grain production with double-cropping to help address world commodity shortages triggered by the war in Ukraine. When the dust settles the decision will likely show little additional production resulted, but it is one more illustration when push comes to shove production will always beat conservation.

One way to try to inform the public debate is to write opinion pieces and editorials for the media. In thinking about the link between water quality and fertilizer use one idea I had was to highlight some ideas agriculture seems to ignore. The following editorial, published in the *Des Moines Register* in June 2021, was written with my tongue firmly in cheek. It concerns one of those examples.

"A Magic Bullet to Improve Iowa Water Quality?"

Water quality is in the news with Iowa's Supreme Court ducking responsibility for the issue and Des Moines Water Works looking to spend millions to drill wells rather than rely on polluted river water. Some people appear ready to give up, believing water quality can't be addressed if King Corn and ethanol are Iowa's future. Not everyone has given up hope, I believe answers are available if we're smart enough to embrace them.

What if I told you a science-based tool, created at Iowa State, could save farmers tens of millions of dollars and not reduce corn yields?

What if this "solution" is recommended by the Nutrient Reduction Strategy—the only solution included in every scenario used to validate it?

What if the strategy can keep 400 million pounds of excess nitrogen from being applied on fields where it isn't needed and instead leaks into tile lines and streams adding to the pollution Iowa sends to the Gulf?

What if this "system" is available free to all Iowa farmers, easy to apply, and voluntary?

You might say "Professor this sounds too good to be true!" But this magic bullet exists and the claims are true!

The tool is the Maximum Return to Nitrogen calculator or MRTN, created by researchers at Iowa State and other Midwestern universities, and validated on farms across the state. The calculator—available on the web—is easy to use. Plug in the cost of nitrogen fertilizer per pound, the projected price of corn, and if you plan to plant corn following corn or following soybeans (which provide some nitrogen). Push a button and the calculator shows the amount of nitrogen needed to achieve 99% of your yield goals. The numbers vary depending on locations, but the average MRTN for Iowa in 2020 was estimated to be 145 lbs. per acre.

This is the starting point but the story gets murky. Best estimates are the amount of nitrogen actually used in 2020 on Iowa's 14 million corn acres was 175 lbs. per acre or 30 pounds more per acre than recommended. Much of the additional 400 million pounds of nitrogen, costing farmers and landowners over $100 million, was "wasted" because corn plants couldn't use it, meaning much of it leaked into our air and waters.

You may be ready to shout "Glory Hallelujah—finally a tool farmers and farm groups can rally behind!" They can avoid the dreaded threat of "one size fits all regulations" feared more than a phantom death tax! Here the story gets puzzling. Have you ever heard a politician—Iowa's Governor or Secretary of Agriculture—extol the virtues of the MRTN or promote it? Have you seen a Farm Bureau Minute—or public service announcement encouraging farmers to take the pledge and apply nitrogen at the MRTN? No you haven't—because no one is willing to suggest Iowa farmers can use less fertilizer—it's a forbidden topic. An exception is the Iowa Soybean Association working to protect water quality and improve fertilizer management. Instead most of what we hear about is practices like installing bio-reactors, which work part of the year, or planting cover crops and other after-the-fact efforts to remove nitrogen and reduce pollution. Stories always note how costly these are and how the public will have to pay if it expects cleaner water.

Why not just say, "let's stop using so much nitrogen in the first place!" It won't cost the public a dime and will save farmers millions. Sadly the story is even worse because MRTN calculations do not include the countless tons of hog manure applied in Iowa, adding nitrogen many farmers don't even consider when making fertilizer purchase decisions. If manure was credited, even less nitrogen would need to be purchased.

So why does this happen? Why waste money on fertilizer not needed—and why don't officials promote an available solution to actually improve water quality? One answer is nitrogen is relatively cheap, good insurance for large yields. No farmer wants a crop to run out of nitrogen and some may feel the MRTN doesn't account for field variability. Another answer is who pays when excess nitrogen runs off? Farmers and landowners bear no risk and pay no price to clean the water, instead the public and folks like the Des Moines Water Works are expected to pay to address water pollution. Are politicians and farm groups so timid and afraid to even suggest farmers use too much fertilizer and are part of the problem, when the evidence is clear?

If you think Iowa should get serious about addressing water quality, expecting leaders to promote the MRTN seems like a good place to start. Iowans pride ourselves on having common sense. Being smart enough to use the tools we have is a good way to prove it.

After this was published, Chris Jones sent me a note and link to an Iowa Farm Bureau podcast featuring their environmental specialist, apparently responding. The podcast was a litany of bogus claims of progress relating to the Nutrient Reduction Strategy with the argument being the public never gets to hear this good news. The interesting part was an explanation about how the MRTN is outdated due to weather and other changes in agriculture, meaning it really doesn't work. This of course is news to the scientists who have worked to continue fine-tuning the MRTN and who argue it is not outdated. In fact, Jones sent me an email exchange between two Iowa State University professors arguing this very point. Isn't it curious why we won't even use the tools we have, ones we know will work to protect water quality and improve soil health?

OUR LOVE OF CAN KICKING

In September 2021 a story about new research being done at Iowa State University concerned how narrow strips of prairie plants can be used to help deal with the possibility of antibiotic resistance coming from manure being spread on the soil. This story struck me as particularly emblematic of our fascination with doing research but without tying it to any of the real world problems we face. Dr. Lisa Schulte Moore, at Iowa State is the researcher most identified with prairie strips and her work led her to become Iowa's newest MacArthur genius. Even with the publicity of her work we are challenged being able to get many people to consider using prairie strips for demonstrated agronomic and economic reasons. But here a different professor is looking at how strips may be useful for an unlikely scenario relating to antibiotic resistance from manure applications. Rather than deal with the issue directly—stop over using antibiotics as a livestock growth promoter—we instead are going to address a symptom of the manure! The epiphany here is rather than confront our inability or unwillingness to address a direct and known problem, we are happy to move the issue and the answer to a different response, especially if it involves new research, better information, or being able to attract new research funding—and most importantly doesn't require us to change the behavior responsible for the problem. Remember the first rule of farming practices is farmers never do anything that causes a problem, i.e. they are always right and motivated by good intentions.

This explains why we don't just kick cans, instead we remain hopeful the new can or next effort will be the successful one. All we need to do is just give it more: more time, more money, more information, more education, take your pick. Whether it is something like cleaning up the Chesapeake Bay or the Gulf of Mexico from water pollution, or addressing soil conservation and soil health, or dealing with the overuse of manure, or the fact there is too much manure, or even now with issues of climate change—the answer is always the same—we just need more something. Rather than respond to reality and recognize what we are doing isn't working and try harder to correct our errors as Klein suggests, our strategy is to search for new ways we can promote an activity and profit from it, or at least convince ourselves we are making headway. The new proposals for capturing CO_2 and using pipelines to ship it somewhere else are a classic example. The starting point is to continue growing corn to use for producing ethanol. The answer is finding ways to use other people's money, i.e., the public, to fund "solutions" to profit from and not have to change what we are doing—that is the premise of Can Kicking 101.

The River Wonders About Self-Respect

If you've gotten this far you know by now I have concerns with how people treat me. I am okay with the reality most Iowans believe they have little connection to the river, even the over half-million who drink my water every day. I don't worry so much about their lack of interest because I'm confident if something major happens, let's say a pollution event threatening their safety, these citizens can be educated and motivated to care about me. When push comes to shove, as you folks like to say, I am hopeful people will rise to my defense.

The people who cause me greater heartburn and worry are the many who actively ignore me, who take me for granted and who are happy to see me as nothing more than a big drainage ditch, a natural sewer they can use at will to flush away their "wastes"—the excess nitrogen and farm chemicals, the manure, the soil laden silty runoff from their fields, and the filth washed off their streets and parking lots. These are the folks who stick in my craw. It all boils down to a simple concept—respect, or in this case, their lack of respect for the river. Thinking about how they treat me makes me wonder how they treat others— other people, other animals, even their friends and family. Could it be the decline in respect, the lessening of a sense of compassion and caring about others and anything beyond yourselves, helps explains the coarsening of your society, the decline in civility, and trust in your institutions of government? If so, might it help explain why so many people give me such little respect?

But you know, there is another part of the explanation. Before a person can respect others, even rivers, they have to respect themselves. On that front what I see is not always a pretty picture. Here are two examples. First, what is up with you folks putting on all the weight? Granted some portion of you have always had challenges maintaining healthy weights, and I don't minimize the challenges and social stigma involved. But today it appears many just gave up. People who used to be a little overweight now seem to me, obese and often much younger.

Society helps shield unhealthy eating habits by suggesting anyone who advises eating less is engaging in body shaming, a form of discrimination. You no longer have fat people, now they are "persons of size." Some people actively endorse the weight-related obesity crisis by labeling the results as body positivity so people can feel good about being heavy, ignoring the health risks involved. How ingenious to turn a love of eating donuts into fighting for civil rights! From the river's perspective, many are eating their way to an early death, digging their own graves with a fork. Here is a suggestion—put down the pudding and pick up a paddle—then we will both feel better.

A second development the river has trouble appreciating is the proliferation of tattoos. Displays once reserved for the carnival midway are common in every crowd. Full sleeves and legs adorned from top to bottom are everywhere, on men and women. Clearly, society, especially the younger crowd—many my most ardent supporters, see tattoos as important identifiers. Permanently defacing your body is a personal freedom, and rivers enjoy our freedom too. But where is this headed? What if the satisfaction felt today in getting a new tat isn't still there in 5 or 10 years? They are permanent and calling them body art doesn't change that reality. From my view as a river, it is no surprise many people have trouble respecting me when they have difficulty seeing into the future to respect their future selves. I apologize if this sounds "old-fashioned" but remember the rivers have very long memories!

PICKING UP SEASHELLS

When we spend time in Florida most mornings are filled walking the beach and picking up seashells, especially my favorite, the augers, or sea spikes, as I like to call them. It seems so curious how they live and create, and then die leaving only shells as the reminders they existed. In some ways this is like writing a book, something you create and bring to life, and then leave for others who will hold it, handle it, and do with it as they like. Perhaps like my shells it will go in a box on the shelf, or better the book may be studied with contemplation, or even given to a friend. When not walking the beach, another of our favorite Florida activities is assembling jigsaw puzzles. Sometimes I wonder if doing so is a waste of time, are we just filling our hours, counting the days until we die, or is there value doing this? We like to rationalize our puzzling by thinking it helps keep our minds sharp and readies our eyesight acuity for the upcoming Spring morel season. Given the nature of the puzzles we select they can be ways to learn and be educated! Plus there is the bonding with family and loved ones so we keep at it.

Our puzzling is similar to the time my mother spent playing solitaire. For years it seemed she played the game for hours each day, literally wearing out decks of cards. I wondered about the time she spent doing this but who was I to question how she filled her days or found her satisfaction? How different was it from our puzzling hobby? I suppose today a generation later she might have become entwined with Facebook or other of the many social media platforms seeming to engulf and consume us. Perhaps she might even have fallen prey to the disturbing conspiracy theories and crackpots populating and polluting these information sources. Thankfully she was gone before these temptations came along and she was never so gullible or unwitting to be snagged by the begging preachers, "Christers" my dad would call them, who seem to prey on the elderly sealed in their homes, offering direct passage to heaven if only you pay the toll.

For now, we will continue putting together a winter puzzle whenever we feel like it and be thankful we have the option to choose to do so. In many ways, writing this book combined both hobbies. The stories I gathered are like seashells, helping illustrate our relation to the water and the river. The puzzle we are assembling together is an attempt to understand what it all means and to find a path forward to the more hopeful picture we all seek.

Interviewing Friends Who Know the River

In thinking about what we should know about the river, I turned to friends who have spent their lifetimes working with them. I interviewed three people who have spent decades shaping our relationships to the river, each from a unique perspective. First was Roger Wolf, a longtime water quality and environmental specialist with the Iowa Soybean Association (ISA). In a career spanning 30 years Roger helped guide ISA's efforts to the leading role among Iowa farm groups, uniquely committed to soil and water quality protection. In the process he helped ISA harness nearly $100 million in funding for research, demonstration farms, and cost sharing. For over twenty years, much of his work has focused on the Raccoon River watershed. Second was Pat Boddy, a longtime public figure in Iowa conservation and media circles, having served in various roles as a consultant, land planner, media personality, and policy advocate including time as interim director at the Iowa DNR. The third perspective came from Nate Hoogeveen, now the Water and River Specialist with the Iowa DNR, essentially a job he created. Nate is perhaps the most experienced and respected voice on Iowa's rivers as author of the widely used guide, *Paddling Iowa*. That project combined his journalism background and extensive knowledge of Iowa's waters, gained by paddling almost every mile of Iowa's major rivers and streams. In June 2022 I experienced every Iowa paddler's dream sharing a canoe with Nate on a 6 mile paddle on Beaver Creek in the northern part of the Des Moines Metro, part of the ICON water trails project discussed in Chapter Eight.

In interviewing them, each had a unique and valuable insight to share. When I asked Roger what the river would say if it could speak to us his reply was telling—"it would laugh at us." Thinking about his answer made me consider why the river might laugh at us and for what reasons? Here are some possible reasons:

- how insignificant our efforts are, in the grand scheme,
- how slow we are to act and how difficult we find it to organize our efforts even with watersheds so easy to identify,
- how pleased we are when we finally achieve something, such as removing a dam,
- how we seem surprised when simple things, like creating a white water course in Charles City, Elkader, or Manchester actually works, attracting hundreds of people to the river,

• how self-centered we can be, focused only on our own economic objectives, giving little thought to nature, wildlife and other values. It is this hubris and pride that gets washed  away with a good flood, helping remind us whose sandbox the river really is.

Nate offered a humble sensitivity, noting the river will pay its respect to anyone who takes the time to know it. He explained his philosophy as having accepted the river's invitation to know it and how he used the opportunity to write his book. He now spends his time shaping state programs so more people can have his experience. The proof of his efforts are in the numbers—when he joined the DNR as the first River Coordinator in 2006 Iowa had around 30 miles of designated water trails. Today the number has grown to over 1,050 miles in over 30 designated trails, with more on the drawing board. This is just one of many water-based achievements Nate has helped lead. Others include the significant efforts to remove dangerous low head dams found on many Iowa rivers and streams. Though only a few feet tall these dams can be drowning machines and dozens of Iowans have been lost to their dangers in recent years.

For her perspective Pat said years of efforts show people are more fearful of transition than change. Some people may believe the divisive politics of water quality and agriculture's impact on the rivers are of recent vintage, perhaps tied to the 2016 Des Moines Water Works litigation. Pat says her experience shows the politics of the Raccoon were already blown up, years earlier. Over a decade later she is still stunned by the vitriol and resistance displayed at a 2011 meeting with the Dallas County Board of Supervisors concerning her efforts to form a Watershed Management Association for the Middle Raccoon River. She recounted how people she respected and had worked with for years on conservation issues shocked her with their angry resistance to any effort to organize or protect the watershed and the river. This Farm Bureau and Tea Party fueled resistance foreshadowed what the nation is experiencing today, a decade later, in the opposition to any government actions to promote conservation and protect public lands. On reflection, the lesson Pat says she learned is how our tactics and strategies must be retooled to these new realities. Long a hold out on the idea regulations may be needed, she now sees little choice but for us to use them. Her hope and optimism rests on the belief the strong connection between rural vitality and the health of our soil and water will provide a foundation for moving us forward.

THE TRAGEDY IN MEAD, NEBRASKA

Modern agriculture has a fascination with new technology but can be very cavalier when it comes to the potential environmental and human health consequences. On September 6, 2021, Iowa Public Radio re-broadcast a Nebraska Public Radio special report titled 'The Smell of Money: Mead, Nebraska's Fight For Its Future." This powerful show concerned the unfolding tragedy at Mead, in connection with the AltEn ethanol plant. The issue primarily relates to the hazardous environmental conditions created as a result of the type of corn used to produce ethanol. At one point the plant was processing or "recycling" 98% of the nation's excess seed corn. This is the "treated" seed corn companies produced but were unable to sell during the growing season. The story is an amazingly tragic and in some ways disgusting story illustrating many realities all-too-common in Midwestern farm states—corporate greed, administrative inaction, political deference to big agriculture, and our love for promises of economic development.

When originally proposed, the ethanol plant at Mead was going to be a closed loop plan, fueled in part with gas produced from methane digesters attached to a large animal feeding operation. Unfortunately, the digesting portion of the ethanol plant failed to operate effectively. At this point the plant shifted its business model and began accepting treated seed corn from companies all over the nation. The resulting distillers grain cake being produced was highly contaminated but was being spread on the ground, while other liquids were being held in waste holding ponds. As the plant continued to operate the environmental issues associated with the waste handling and the ground disposal of the byproducts became increasingly clear and were being experienced by residents of the community and nearby landowners.

In a somewhat familiar tale, pleas to regulators with the Nebraska departments of agriculture and environmental quality fell largely on deaf ears. People were assured everything was operating legally and the state officials showed very little interest in any type of action. Only after the environmental situation—the odors, and the impacts on the community—became intolerable did state officials finally decide they needed to act. Only then did the state became aware treated seed corn was being used in the facility.

What happened in Mead is still unfolding as the lawsuits have started and the political recriminations and excuses pile up. There is a parallel between what happened in Mead and the Supreme Beef Bloody Run Creek controversy in Iowa. Here plans for a promised methane digester, used to justify the "industrial" lagoon built for the feedlot, disappeared and instead what was left was an 11,600 head cattle feedlot near one of the state's few protected waters. Both stories unfortunately reveal the cavalier attitude much of the agricultural, industrial, and business communities appear to have toward natural resources, environmental issues, and the health of nearby communities.

Another current example is seen in the expanded use of neonicotinoids, powerful insecticides applied as seed treatments. While there are legitimate uses for the products to treat soil borne pests that can prey on planted seeds, it is becoming clear to many observers their use has been expanded beyond what can be justified. Most seed companies now routinely apply the treatments to all commercial seeds sold. If farmers want to avoid using treated seeds they have to put in a special order early in the season. The use of air powered planting equipment has exacerbated the issue, because the dust coming off the seeds in the process of being planted into the soil is distributed in the air. This means the pesticides are now experienced by a much broader array of flying insects rather than just the soil borne pests they were designed to treat.

A related example of our willingness to use the land as essentially a free place to hide or dispose of unwanted products concerns what in Iowa are called "soil conditioners." This is a legal category falling somewhere outside the regulation of fertilizers and animal wastes, but yet the products are applied to the soil for the purposes of "conditioning" it. The use of soil conditioners came up in several Iowa stories during the summer of 2021. One concerned a significant spill and fish kill in a stream in Winneshiek County in far Northeast Iowa. Officials determined the product spilled was a "soil conditioner" stored by a farmer, the product being a form of degrading animal byproducts obtained from local packing companies. A more tragic example with a similar product happened near Algona in August 2021 when a young man died when overcome by the fumes coming from a storage lagoon he was emptying. Again the product in question was being used as a form of "soil conditioner."

The law defining soil conditioners shows they are distinguished from fertilizers, which must contain one of the three primary crop nutrients. By definition, soil conditions are not to include any of these nutrients. But in the northeast Iowa fish kill, the spilled material had a high enough nitrogen content to consume the oxygen in miles of stream. A main purpose of the category may be to make it possible for companies to dispose of unwanted "natural" waste products simply by discharging them on the land, claiming they provide some value to the soil. A less charitable view indicates the purpose of the category may be to serve as a form of regulatory dodge, allowing businesses and regulators to turn a blind eye to what may be the product's actual contents and consequences. I may be wrong about this view, but in our over 30 years of commercial gardening we have never encountered a situation where our soil needed "conditioning." Adding some well-aged compost or litter from the chicken house—yes, but conditioning—no.

THE INCREASE IN FARMLAND PRICES

The recent surge in farmland prices is troubling and helps create a very uncertain future. It's not clear what to call it, whether it is just pent up demand responding to the economic opportunities from farming, or a true bubble. But a number of recent stories help illustrate its impact. In June 2021 three parcels of land in Story County sold to other farmers at prices ranging up to $16,000 an acre. The prices were fairly remarkable both in terms of the income the ground can yield and what they may indicate concerning the way we think about ground. It certainly raises the question of why more farmers can't seem to afford soil and water conservation practices such as cover crops without needing public subsidy. If you can afford to pay $16,000 an acre for crop ground shouldn't you also be able to spend some money to protect the soil and water quality on the land you already farm or even better to improve the health of the soil? If you assume for the sake of argument the existing land is being farmed in "normal and accepted ways" for the locale, this probably means traditional tillage perhaps with minimum or no till and with fall tillage. Most likely there have been no significant investments made in water quality, like buffers strips or other edge-of-field practices. So will spending $16,000 an acre for more land lead to better conservation given the size of the investment, or will the cost be just one more excuse why the buyer can't afford it? The most likely attitude will continue to be if the public wants conservation on high-priced land, then the public will need to cough up more money to pay for it.

This is the trap or cage we have constructed for ourselves with our commitment to the voluntary only approach and "no role for regulation" mantra. Even if you have and want to spend $16,000 an acre for new land, it's unreasonable for the public to ask you to spend your own money on your existing land. Instead the state and public will pay for it. Since the state only appropriates about $0.75 per acre or about

$15 million for our 24 million acres of Iowa crop ground, any water quality actions aren't going to get much public money. In other words it could be many years before we are able to afford any conservation. Can you see how ridiculous and upside down this story is—an unbridled land market essentially free from any obligation to the soil or the water, left entirely to the desires of the landowners; framed against a backdrop where we claim to be doing all we can for water quality and we just need more time and patience for it to work. It appears what we need is not more time, instead, what we need is more common sense and public officials who deserve the title.

Is the River Jealous Land Values Have Jumped?

Well, I see my neighbors made the front page again, big headlines "Iowa farmland values jumped 29% in year." Bully for them. Just the type of headline to make the hearts of all the realtors, auctioneers, and off-farm heirs sitting on mom and dad's inherited acres go aflutter. You might wonder does all this attention make me a little jealous? I guess it kind of does—it is always about the land, and the fat profits and big yields. No one ever talks about me like that—the value of clean water, natural beauty, and scenic river bends, they never jump in price. Of course there are several reasons why. It is not clear that clean water is valued by very many people or if most could even recognize it if they saw it. Certainly the state of Iowa isn't too interested, as they showed when they defunded the IOWATER program providing citizens with the tools and training to monitor local water quality. I guess the theory was why do we want people looking when we know what they will find is bad news. They may start asking questions. Of course some folks do care how clean I am. The public drinking water utilities, like the Des Moines Water Works, are interested because it tells them how much effort it will take to clean me up to meet the federal safe drinking water standards. The public benefits from those actions, but ironically because the public utilities are obligated to only provide safe water, citizens are insulated from the question of how clean I really am. Think how different the debate might be if the Water Works got to send out notices reading, "today drink at your own risk—the water is so bad even we couldn't clean it up! Any questions? Ask a farmer." Boy that might change things! But don't expect it to happen anytime soon, because it's illegal.

The other reason you don't see stories about the value of clean rivers jumping in value is no one really owns me, at least not like the 40-acre fields next to my banks. Well, that's not quite accurate. Someone does own me, all of you, the public owns me and the water flowing through me. The problem is you— the public—seem to have difficulty understanding this type of ownership and its value. This makes me think of the expression how you don't value something until it's gone.

Oh well, maybe it's better no one owns me like they do the farmland. These stories about sharp increases in value really aren't good news no matter what the farm press tries to make people believe. The land knows it's not good news, it just means you will try to farm the land harder to make it pay. The tenant knows it's not good news if it just means next year's rent is going to increase. No, rapid rises in farmland values are only good for one thing, increasing the disruption and the damage done when they come back down.

US FORMS PRODUCTIVITY COALITION

In September 2021 Secretary of Agriculture Vilsack was in Italy to meet with other agricultural leaders from the G-20 nations. While there he announced creation of a new coalition to be led by the United States founded on a commitment to agricultural productivity. One purpose of this new effort was to serve as a counter to the European Union and their commitment to the "farm to fork" initiative, an approach centered on sustainability, organic food, and concern for the environment. It says a great deal about the mindset of American agriculture when the idea of a policy focusing on land, food quality, and sustainability needs to be countered! The Secretary calls our new effort the "Coalition for Productivity Growth" a name that rolls off the tongue! If there is a point here, it is US policy is always going to focus on maximizing crop production with all of the technologies and inputs we can put on to the land. Any efforts to promote conservation, protect water quality, or even address climate issues are going to be add-ons. They will be afterthoughts, programs designed to try to sand down the rough edges of our commitment to productivity, rather than any semblance of an integrated bottoms-up change in our approach.

The underpinning of this American approach is reflected in the politics over whether or not Congress will implement some elements of the Biden administration's "Build Back Better" initiative. From an agricultural perspective the proposals included billions of dollars in new spending for conservation and to initiate climate related programs to focus on how agriculture can help sequester carbon. It appears we are now ready to implement climate related infrastructure, and the Biden administration has proposed bold commitments and promises, such as those made to the UN and at the COP 26 talks. What the US will actually do, no one knows exactly. Big agriculture, and many new private businesses are circling the waters wanting to get their hands on these new climate dollars. In many cases they are essentially asking for money for not doing anything new, as seen in the great clamor to pay "early adopters" for actions they took in the past. Progressives who support these policies believing there is some potential here are left wondering who exactly is going to write the policy, how is it going to be delivered, through what programs, and by which of the agencies now in place? If you consider our progress or lack thereof on other problems, more real, more local, and ones we have actually tried to address, we have little reason to be confident in the success of our new programs. The cleanup of the Chesapeake Bay is not going well nor is our ability to address the hypoxia zone in the Gulf of Mexico, especially when efforts are built on programs like Iowa's failing Nutrient Reduction Strategy. We are professionals at fooling ourselves and expecting the answers to come from somewhere else. We believe the USDA and Congress can swoop in with new programs but we are unwilling to do anything on our own land or on our own farms without receiving new money to do it.

So why are we so willing to fool ourselves and be convinced we are making progress? First, it lets us avoid facing the reality our past efforts are coming up short or of having to confront hard choices, like using regulations or telling people to try harder. Second, it lets us focus our optimism on future results we know will be better, especially if they involve new technology or scientific advancements. And this all works until it doesn't, for example when there is a lack of water in the Colorado River or polluted lakes force us to address threats to our water supplies. In other words, when nature presents real limitations. But even these have been somewhat rare, instead things just gradually get worse and we adjust. The water quality may be deteriorating so we try to get a new source, just don't plan on fishing or swimming in those waters. We change our expectations and over time the public comes to accept the diminished reality. Sure the air in north central Iowa stinks much of the time from the livestock wastes but not all the time. In addition there is never an end point when things are too bad we have to change. There may be exceptions, such as Toledo's famous water pollution, but even then the solutions didn't really change the agricultural pollution happening in the lake's watershed. Instead the new legal policy idea, the "rights of nature" proposed in a Toledo ordinance, was struck down as too extreme and un-American.

You have to give the agricultural groups credit for the success of their public relation campaigns and helping the public believe in the worthiness of their ideas. In September 2021 a new Iowa poll was released showing 80% of Iowans think ethanol is important to the Iowa economy. This seems like an exercise in the obvious, but it gave the ethanol groups something to point to and it sends a warning to the critics and to those promoting alternatives like electric vehicles. Maybe the reaction to stories like this one concerning the importance of ethanol should be this question—if we all believe ethanol is so important then doesn't it make sense we would do a better job caring for the land, soil, and water we need to produce it? Perhaps this is the question to ask in the poll—"given current rates of soil loss and water pollution do you think the present system for raising corn is sustainable?" But we don't seem to go in for these questions. The experts will say the public really doesn't know enough to have an informed opinion on something like that, but then how much does the public really know about ethanol?

Several weeks later another installment of the Iowa poll was released, this one listing which groups have the most trust in society. The poll primarily listed different governmental organizations, but for some reason included the Iowa Farm Bureau. And perhaps it shouldn't surprise us but it ranked above many government institutions, with the exception of the police and the military. 70% of Iowans said they trusted the Iowa Farm Bureau, what a wonderful payoff for the millions of dollars spent on television commercials like their "Farm Bureau Minutes." To invoke Leopold, this may be one of those stones resembling bread. The Farm Bureau is not a government institution. It is a special interest business group spinning its own version of the truth, all with an economic goal wrapped in an anti-government philosophy. Nevertheless nearly the same percent of the public trust them as God and organized religion. And we wonder why the environmental and conservation communities have problems trying to confront the power of the Farm Bureau on water quality and public land issues?

The River Would Like a Little "Freedom to Operate" Too!

January 11, 2022—Well, it is January and it has been cold. Most of my stretches are now covered in ice but I made it out for a little educational excursion. The 2022 Land Expo organized and hosted by Peoples Company, the very successful Iowa farmland company, was being held at the Iowa Events Center. So I bundled up and streamed on down—excuse the pun. I was only able to stay for the first hour or so but that was enough and I got my money's worth! The day started with the obligatory welcome from the Iowa Secretary of Agriculture, who delivered a stack of welcoming platitudes, for example "God made Iowa for agriculture, yes he did" as well as a whopper or two. Such as this doozy, "in 2021 Iowa broke all records for the installation of soil conservation and water quality practices." The source of this nugget is unknown, but the real fear is he actually may believe it is true—but I don't see it. I wish my friend the Back 40 could have joined me because this whole conference focused on him. The agricultural land investment industry growing in the land is changing the very nature of farming!

The first keynote speaker was an old friend, an Iowa farm girl Sarah Wyant, who has grown her agricultural information service and newsletter *Agri-Pulse*, into the nation's leader. Her remarks focused on three issues, the Build Back Better proposal and what is in it for conservation, the planning for the 2023 Farm Bill, and a third topic "freedom to operate." This one piqued my curiosity as I know all of us rivers would enjoy having a bit more freedom to operate—free of the channels, the levees, the tile outlets, and the other insults we face. So I was interested to hear what this idea of freedom to operate means.

Well, I should've seen it coming! It is essentially the Republicans and the Farm Bureau's cagey new way to say keep your stinking rules and regulations off of me! The examples she cited were predictable. California's Proposition 12 rules concerning sow spacing now before the US Supreme Court, which she noted to the approving guffaws of the crowd give California sows more room than most New York City apartments! And of course the rules limiting the use of crop protection chemicals like dicamba. Her focus was on all the things agriculture believes it can't exist without—until it has to. So freedom to operate is essentially a new bottle for old wine—don't regulate or restrict anything agriculture and farmers want to do. It always amazes me how there is never a discussion about why the rules were put in place, or the human and environmental justifications for regulating the conduct or product in question. It is as if all of the rules being opposed did not emerge through lengthy regulatory and administrative processes. Instead, they are apparently cooked up by people who hate agriculture (and eating?) with the purpose being to unfairly restrict agriculture, raise food prices, and force farmers to the wall. Yikes!

You know, though, the story really wasn't that much different in the morning news article in Agri-Pulse concerning US Secretary of Agriculture Vilsack's recent appearance at the American Farm Bureau Federation convention in Atlanta, where he did back flips telling them what they expected—and wanted to hear. Having the agriculture secretary speak at the AFBF annual convention is apparently mandatory or so it seems, though I've never seen the statute requiring it. It even holds true for the Democrats like this year, even though AFBF members widely opposed the election of President Biden, worked full time to carry Trump's big lie banner proudly, and will predictably work to block the Administration's objectives and vote to defeat Democrats at the polls!! I tell you it would be worth being appointed USDA Secretary just to have the opportunity to tell the AFBF to go jump when they invited me to speak to their convention. What would they do—fire me or promise to vote me out of office!

But of course that never happens, and this year the pandering ran to form. The Secretary was sure to tell them it was their President Zippy Duval [not Joe Biden] who had instructed him on what they wanted to hear—and boy did he deliver. When it came time to describe how the department and Administration's efforts relating to agriculture, climate change, and carbon credits will be delivered he told them it will be based on three premises. First they'll be voluntary, second they will be incentive-based, and third there will be no use of regulations! In other words, you don't have to do it if you don't feel like it, if you do anything the public will pay you, and no one will ever require you to do anything. And as frosting on the cake the Secretary said in no way will the USDA's use of CCC money cut into what farmers can expect to be available for their crop insurance and subsidies, aka, farm welfare. And further he promised whatever it is the USDA does will in no way, shape, or form be a carbon bank! This last point effectively cuts the USDA out of playing the critical and needed role as the neutral player creating the marketplace for carbon credits. This means instead the marketplace and prices, will be developed and controlled by folks like Indigo Ag and the other big investment companies, all with booths at the Expo, circling the waters looking for new profits. So you can see how my morning came full circle! Then it was time to go back under the ice, I could feel a January thaw coming on!

WE ARE ALWAYS HEADING WEST

Agriculture has a wonderful willingness to embrace the next thing, the next shiny promising opportunity. Now it is resilient agriculture and the opportunities for agriculture to profit by helping address climate change. We never actually seem to finish addressing the last issue. For example with soil conservation our answer was going to be no till, and for water quality maybe buffer strips, and for soil health using cover crops. And now with climate change we are going to turn carbon into a commodity and build new pipelines so we can continue our all-out corn production and capture the CO_2 emissions to ship them to other states. There is always something new on the horizon, and we never stop and look back at the damages we have done or the promises we left unfulfilled. It is very much like the pioneer spirit of moving west to new lands once these lands got used up or too crowded. The question then is when do we run out of opportunities to head west, and when does it all catch up to us?

Chapter Seven—Politics, Climate, and Carbon—Our Confusing Future

PRINKLES, ETHANOL, AND DELUSIONS

Not being parents we haven't had to deal with the experience of friends whose young kids can have delusions about imaginary threats, like spiders under the bed and venom in the air. Even so, I remember well my own bout with a delusion, an ailment that haunted me for several weeks. I must have been four when I developed a bad case of "prinkles" on the bottom of my feet. They caused so much pain I had to walk or hobble around on the sides of my feet. Try as they did my parents couldn't dissuade me of my belief, even as they explained what I was observing were wrinkles, not prinkles, and everyone has them. I don't remember exactly how long my condition existed and if it ended because I was cured or just got tired of trying to get around on the sides of my feet, but like most childhood delusions I got over them.

My prinkles came to mind in spring 2022 thinking about Iowa's delusional belief in the magical powers of ethanol. The triggering event was the Governor's visit to an Iowa farm, tricked out in her farm girl gingham and jeans, cosplay as one wag described it. She was there to sign one of her main legislative priorities, a bill mandating most Iowa gas stations must carry E-15 a higher blend of ethanol than the existing E-10 available. E-15 is not now widely used or available due in part to the higher equipment costs and resistance from gas station owners. The legislative debate over the E-15 bill was surprisingly fractious, a telling point in a state where ethanol will find its way onto the state seal if supporters have their way. A modified version of the bill eventually passed and the Governor breathtakingly proclaimed it one of the most significant legislative actions of the century, unlocking new riches and opportunities for all Iowans. Mark me down as doubtful.

I am not one to say the Governor is a simpleton, but she and many other Iowa leaders are deeply attached to simplistic thinking when it comes to ethanol. To their minds if ethanol means we use corn to make it, that is a good thing and the more ethanol we can sell the more corn will be used and ultimately we will achieve "Cornvana" or something close to it. To embrace the simple belief ethanol is the magic elixir for Iowa's future you have to overlook a few side effects, namely the conversion of millions of acres of pasture and grasslands to corn production; the increasing pressure to grow corn, even planting "continuous corn" rather than traditional crop rotations; all "fueled" by increased use of nitrogen fertilizer much of which ends up in our rivers and streams. Then there is the soil erosion associated with corn pro-

duction. It's conservatively estimated we lose about 17 pounds of soil for every gallon of ethanol we produce. You can see how taking into consideration complicating factors like these can make the simplistic "more ethanol is great" delusion a little bit more slippery.

Don't worry, this delusion has a first cousin used to help carry the message. Next time you fill up your tank you will see it right there on the gas pump—the label says "made with ethanol—cleaner air for Iowa." You are excused if you haven't recognized this contribution from burning corn-based biofuels. Of course it may be too much to expect ethanol's promoters at IDALS or the corn growers to have added a tagline "and dirtier water too!" Can we at least shake a little salt on the idea more ethanol all the time is better for our state? Are we too simple in our thinking to recognize even good things have limits?

The River on Agriculture's New Found Interest in Climate Change

On the issue of climate change, I am much like my friend from last century, Henry A. Wallace, famous for taking "the long look." I was here long before you arrived and will outlive you if some sad fate befalls your civilization. In other words, the river sees your twists and turns in policy and politics in a different perspective. It's not that human actions are unimportant, it's just that history shows how variable and subject to political whims and economics your actions can be.

I have been watching with interest the escalating discussion about climate change and the proliferation of ideas you are developing to address it. This is the main focus of this chapter, but before you go much further, please let me provide a sober, historic, and river-based perspective on the issue. For the impatient, here is a sneak peek of my conclusion—I doubt if you are sincere or likely to succeed.

First, let's consider how you got here. As a starting point you need to recognize climate change is the cumulative result of hundreds of your actions (or inactions) in recent years. It is essentially a collection of issues you have been unwilling to confront. Consider these examples:

• flooding on the Missouri and Mississippi rivers is made worse by adding more upstream drainage and by farming, in the floodplain;

- soil loss is made worse by relying on a corn and soybean monoculture and farming up to the streambanks;

- land loss is made worse by your commitment to ethanol and keeping your foot on the accelerator of ever expanding production to "feed and fuel the world";

- you didn't pass a carbon tax in 2009 because AFBF and farmers didn't want Congress to " Cap Their Future" or change fuel sources;

- you don't have effective clean water protections and refuse to fund the Iowa natural resources trust fund, because you don't want government to have regulatory power or adequate funding, instead you pretend voluntary self-interest will get you the needed results;

- you didn't improve water quality for Des Moines because you didn't want to give up the freedom to over apply nitrogen, install more drainage tile, and apply animal waste without restraints. In summary, you were unwilling to address the moral hazard of not thinking about those who live downstream.

Second, let's consider the challenges you face in addressing climate change. The key challenge in expecting effective action on climate change is you are expecting the same people and institutions who resisted addressing the smaller issues listed above, to now take actions they have long resisted. To do so now, you expect them to believe in this larger, more abstract issue of climate change. In your desire to act, you won't admit many farmers refuse to believe in, or accept, the scientific basis for climate change.

Do you expect people to give up political power or sovereignty to others they don't trust and who they may even feel are illegitimate? To try and sell yourselves on the need to act, you now argue we have only a ten year window before it is too late. Well, people have been hearing we have "only ten years" to act for generations, on population growth, peak oil, and famines. Do you expect them to believe it now rather than see the argument as an artificial attempt to rush folks to act?

How can you expect people to think beyond themselves for the "planet" on climate change when you can't even get them to think or act in the interest of their neighbors who live in their own watersheds, or for themselves, on more direct and immediate issues like water quality and soil loss? Unless you are willing to examine how you got here, you have little hope of getting out.

I have seen your failure on soil conservation, your inaction on water quality, and your unwillingness to even consider you use too much nitrogen or have too many pigs helping pollute the rivers. I see how you are now resisting opportunities to improve soil health such as expanding the use of cover crops. So now you plan to take a subject most farmers either acknowledge only begrudgingly or don't accept at all, and propose actions with marginal impacts for reducing CO2 or sequestering carbon, all with infinitesimally small contributions to the larger climate debate. Then you argue in good faith agriculture is going to radically or significantly change its behavior for a few dollars and for greater public appreciation! Who is fooling who?

Third, this discussion identifies several key issues you face. How do you get people to agree to act, especially if it is against their short-term economic self-interest? Part of the answer may be to focus on how people's attitudes and awareness of climate change are evolving as more people experience it personally. The wide range of weather and climate related disasters from floods to fires experienced in 2022 had the effect of helping more people consider the issue.

Your main answer is to use a grand plan. First it was the Green New Deal, then it became the Build Back Better plan. Then the ideas merged in the summer of 2022 as an effort to address inflation and fight climate change. Your omnibus approach offers something for everyone. If there is pain, it can be shared or paved over with new alternatives and more money.

A fourth consideration for something as major as addressing climate change, is most citizens will need to see some payoff or result. A critical part of your challenge promoting climate change "solutions" is showing any results or improvements from a personal economic standpoint. If legislation requires people to change their conduct, they will know what it feels like to give up a freedom or pay higher costs. How and when are you going to help them experience the benefits, if in fact there will be benefits or gains? If the answer is we just have to wait a few decades, or worse yet to expect no real personal benefit, then people will find acting very unappealing. This is especially challenging because the arguments in favor of climate action will play out against a backdrop of opposition. The key will be identifying visible deliverables, such as clean energy jobs, cleaner water, or more opportunities to recreate outdoors. For example, the Greater Des Moines Water Trails or ICON project could be pitched as helping address climate change in the Des Moines watershed through improved soil and related water quality efforts.

A key part of the challenge here is you currently have few market incentives for actions producing cleaner water or healthier soil. Plus you have little in the way of effective regulatory structures to require or promote changes on the land. Even private institutional arrangements you might use to help address the issues, such as farm leases, land contracts, and mortgages have no history of including language to value or promote water quality and soil health. From my perspective as the river, if you have any chance to succeed then a real effort will need to be made to identify these positive actions, how to calculate their benefits, and how to integrate the economic value or rewards into your existing relationships. For example, could a farm lease provide tax credits to the landlord if the tenant uses cover crops?

Fifth, because your efforts to address climate change will only happen with political action, the role of politics has to be a focus in any discussion. From a political perspective the Democrats are under considerable pressure to present a grand plan on climate change, in order to respond to their constituencies who expect it. In many ways they are bidding against themselves with few real cards to play, because to make real change, for example reducing reliance on coal, it requires Congressional action and future spending. The question is will voters agree? Will their concerns about the immediacy of the need to act on climate change be sufficient to lead them to support Democrats in future elections? All the while the Republicans will be hammering voters and Democratic candidates with claims about the serious economic harms climate actions will cause, how they will feed inflation, reduce jobs, and increase costs. The uncertainty of any visible results on the climate resulting from unilateral US actions, will be an argument, as will the other "parade of horribles" conservatives associate with these "socialist" ideas. The river can already hear it, "first they came for your lightbulbs now they are coming for your gas powered car!"

This has the potential to be a political disaster if the Democrats overplay the climate issue. This is especially true if all the time, money, and political oxygen spent arguing for climate action, means other equally important issues of healthcare, women's reproductive freedom, poverty, wealth inequality, voter suppression, and immigration, aren't addressed.

Sixth, so is there a way for you to move forward? This is the question your society must answer. From the river's perspective it appears the best way to address climate change is to acknowledge its importance but to address it in the context of other issues, and explain how addressing them is a pathway to cleaner energy and confronting climate change. For example, one way to offer new jobs, higher wages, and address rural poverty, is by greening the economy with solar, wind, and activities to protect natural resources. Better healthcare and health outcomes can come from addressing water quality, air quality, and improved diets.

Rather than climate change needing to, or trying to, be a standalone issue, and political target, it can be integrated into a larger suite of issues, pocketbook issues and questions of fairness more effective in reaching voters. Doing so and articulating the connections between the issues will still offer an outlet for those motivated by the need to address climate change, but by putting your answers into service for the larger common good, you have a greater likelihood to succeed.

WHERE ARE WE ON CLIMATE ACTION?

The river has given us a good deal to think about in examining what we are actually doing on climate issues. While there are positive actions, the results to date are mixed. Consider the backlash to *The New York Times* February 2022 editorial on meeting the people trying to shield agriculture from scrutiny. The responses were very predictable. One side was farmers talking about the actions they take on their farms to illustrate how wrong it was. These farmers may be in the vanguard of new approaches but the truth is they may be among the very few producers acting. If everyone was doing the things they claim then our problems with soil loss, water quality, and declining soil health would disappear. The second branch predictably focused on political dealings in Congress. This involved a kabuki style hearing when the nominee for Under Secretary of USDA. Robert Bonnie, appeared before the House subcommittee on February 8, 2022. Bonnie's confirmation had been held up for months because of his writings about the idea of a carbon bank. So he was already on the ropes defending USDA proposals to use $1 billion in CCC funding to support a new program to produce climate commodities. The attacks from Republicans in Congress included: first, this wasn't an appropriate use of CCC funding; second, the proposals subverted the coming 2023 Farm Bill process; and third, Congress had not been included in developing the ideas. As a kicker, as noted by the River, many in agriculture don't believe in the carbon-climate connection to begin with and don't support any climate efforts by USDA or the Biden administration.

The best political theater was saved for attacks on *The New York Times* editorial including Bonnie being asked for his reaction. He called it "horrible," very disappointing, and added the obligatory "I think farmers, ranchers and forest owners are great stewards of our land." I doubt he believes this is true, largely because the facts on the ground concerning soil losses and water degradation don't back it up! But how could he say anything different in a confirmation hearing before this crowd and expect to leave intact. So there you have it.

Another example questioning our progress was a February 2022 analysis of the various commitments made by corporations in their pledges to reduce CO_2 emissions. The study found their commitments, when analyzed, don't add up to anywhere near the size of reductions they claim. So if the corporations who have both an economic and consumer market driven reason to act on climate, as well as a shareholder corporate regulatory reason for doing so, can't or won't deliver on their promises why should we think the agriculture sector, which doesn't really buy the climate change story and certainly isn't interested in making changes in how it operates, will actually change?

When you boil it down, a skeptic or cynic, take your pick, or someone with a sense of remove and history like the River, can easily conclude this may largely be another exercise in self-delusion. The Biden Administration and the Democrats are happy to propose bold climate initiatives believing in good faith, they will work. But they are unwilling or unable to harness the regulatory tools or financial support for agriculture, to actually achieve changes on the land at any scale. For its part the agricultural sector and the Republicans, much the same, are happy to go along with ideas like the climate smart agricultural legislation and even the USDA's carbon efforts on "climate commodities" as long as they can dictate the terms. These terms include three requirements: it is all voluntary, it is incentive-based (meaning the public will pay), and there will be no regulatory shoe to drop. Remember, this was essentially the message the Secretary gave the American Farm Bureau Federation in January 2022. Given these conditions, climate efforts will become a new source of public money and offer a new justification for why the public needs to continue subsidizing big agriculture. The "we are feeding the world" justification hasn't yet passed its "sell by" date, but the agricultural sector already has its replacement on deck "We are saving the planet." Just like earlier efforts at soil conservation and water quality it will take years, even decades, to know if the efforts to change conditions on the ground are having any effect. What a wonderful insurance policy to have. This means critics or people who argue for more direct actions, like those in Iowa, myself included, who label the Nutrient Reduction Strategy a failure, can be held off and resisted as premature or unreasonable in our expectations. The wonderful mantra of Big Agriculture is we just need to give it more time to work.

The Story of Agriculture, Biofuels, and Chasing Climate Dollars

In Spring 2022 several news stories associated rising food costs with the diversion of food stocks for use in renewable fuels. An NPR story featured bakers having difficulty obtaining vegetable oil and needing to charge more for their cookies. Another story concerned dairy farmers having trouble being able to afford enough corn feed for their dairy herds. Both stories focused on the price increases resulting from using commodities for "renewable" fuels. The stories had the effect of taking the lid off the issue of "food or fuel," a controversy the agricultural sector has long tried to avoid. But now it seems to embrace the issue under the theory we can do it all! Rather than talk about "feeding the world" many in agriculture now describe their function as "feeding and fueling" the world. In one story concerning increasing food costs the commentator said the idea agriculture was designed to produce food was in some ways old-fashioned! Now everything needs to compete with the potential for using food crops to produce renewable fuels.

This new approach seems like it might be a hard sell for the consuming public facing rising food prices. Rather than support policies to develop truly renewable sources of energy such as solar and wind power or develop biofuels based on non-food stock sources such as switchgrass, it seems crazy we have decided to privilege fuel over food. It is also a perfect illustration of how farmers have a historic tendency to be plungers. Plungers in the sense ideas starting with good intentions are often overplayed so they end up being the tail wagging the dog. This certainly is the case today with corn-based ethanol and even soy diesel. The food for fuel debate is not a good one for the agriculture community to embrace. This is especially true if the "environmental" benefits of the "renewable" biofuels products are dubious. Once you look at the embedded costs with corn production such as soil loss, water use, water quality, increased pesticide use, the conversion of marginal land to cropping, and all of the attendant policies associated with our all-out crop production approach, the "value" of biofuels becomes less certain.

So isn't it fitting, perhaps even predictable, the agricultural sector, always "reluctant and resistant" to engaging with environmental issues, is now finding a way to take a new opportunity—demand and need for renewable energy to address climate change—and turn it into another excuse to put more environmental pressure (and damage) on the land and water, all in the name of "environmental stewardship!"

Another dimension of this story is how slow and flat-footed the USDA and other federal actors have been. First, the government starts with several serious limitations or problems. The NRCS is understaffed and demoralized at the local level and the farmer landowner perception of its programs is they are too rigid, rule bound, and complex. Second, the administrative challenges for establishing new programs are steep: a) translating statutory language into regulations and program documents to deliver to farmers and landowners; b) developing field office technical guides to educate and train local staff, who already have full workloads; c) offering new programs but with relatively short dollars for participants; and d) recruiting, hiring, and on-boarding the new conservation staff needed to deliver these programs. The effect is it could take years before the USDA can bring new carbon and climate related programs into effect. It will be almost as complicated as standing up a program like the conservation reserve program in the late 1980s but here the funding for participants is much smaller, making participation less attractive. Unless the USDA is willing to dedicate a crash team of lawyers and conservationists to develop the climate work in a timeframe to get political credit in the next few years, more rapid deployment is unlikely to happen.

All the while those in the private sector, the Carbon Cowboys, as well as the big agricultural funders such as Cargill, will be busy developing their own programs, even competing with the USDA's efforts on payments and signing up producers. This could mean when the USDA finally comes to the field or market with its carbon and climate related initiatives many farmers may have already contracted their land to private companies. This raises its own challenges for whether the USDA can develop programs to complement or coincide with these private efforts, if it needs to.

On the political front you can assume the Republicans in Congress will be throwing up roadblocks such as their delay in confirming Robert Bonnie for his senior USDA position. They will challenge any USDA and Biden administration efforts developing "carbon" markets, banks, or whatever you want to call them. They will also slow walk any funding or other support needed to develop the programs. This was done with an eye on the 2022 elections when they hoped to regain the

House and will be for 2024 when they hope to restore the presidency. The great irony of course is that presidency was premised on the idea climate change is a hoax, meaning there wouldn't be any support of government programs, nationally or internationally, to address it.

THOUGHTS ON THE CO_2 PIPELINES

In 2021 three different companies announced plans to spend billions installing hundreds of miles of pipelines across Iowa to collect the CO_2 now being released at the many ethanol and fertilizers plant operating in the state. The premise is the pipelines are vital to maintaining the market for corn-based ethanol but giving it the status of a low-carbon, greener fuel. To me the proposed CO_2 pipelines are a "solution" that will obstruct real farmer-led efforts to reduce CO_2 and address the climate. Rather than spend billions on a corporate boondoggle designed primarily to profit its backers, the nation needs to invest in farming based efforts like those being led by the Agricultural Outcomes project of the Iowa Soybean Association. The needed answers are to improve soil health, protect water quality, conserve soil, and manage fertilizer application to protect the long-term sustainability and profitability of farmers, while putting money into farmers' pockets. The answer isn't pumping CO_2 into a pipeline, shipping it hundreds of miles away to other states, and then pumping it deep underground in hopes it stays put.

The CO_2 pipeline idea appears to be a classic example of crony capitalism, Iowa style. One effort is being spearheaded by well positioned Republican donors with the former governor along to help. When you examine the financial model it is essentially a house of cards constructed entirely on artificial markets all paid for with public subsidies. For all the political hot air many agricultural groups and conservative politicians spend complaining about the threat of government regulations, the CO_2 pipelines are a direct creation of three regulations. First is the renewable fuel standard, the law and rules requiring petroleum companies to buy and blend 10% ethanol into gasoline. This law is the primary reason there is even a marketplace for ethanol. If the RFS would disappear, as the petroleum sector has sought for years, so will most reasons for ethanol to exist. Second is the idea of premium prices or subsidies provided for low carbon fuels, an approach used in states like California to promote development of cleaner fuels. Pipeline supporters claim sequestering the CO_2 produced will help secure a low carbon fuel rating for ethanol, increasing its value and prolonging its life as a viable fuel. This requires disregarding the potential use of the CO_2 in North Dakota to enhance fracking natural gas and petroleum. The low carbon incentive is also artificially created by supporting state laws which could change. Given that California has announced plans to end production of combustion fuel cars by 2035, the future of "low carbon" fuel incentives may be in jeopardy. The third major source of funding or subsidies to reward operating the pipelines will come from federal tax credits, known as Q45 payments for sequestering the CO_2, worth as much as $85 a ton. The payments are estimated to exceed $20 billion for the proposed pipelines. The existence of these payments is another product of legislation and public funding rather than demand in the private marketplace. So the business premise of the pipeline, a private for-profit venture, is constructed on a foundation of public subsidies and financial incentives all delivered through non-market based regulatory requirements.

To extend this pattern of eating at the public trough, pipeline developers will likely seek federal subsidies to build the pipeline if allowed, under the Administration's efforts to support investments in green infrastructure. If so, it means the pipeline will be partially built with public money and be paid for by additional public subsidies. To complete the public dimensions of this private proposal, growing landowner opposition to signing voluntary easements makes it probable pipeline proponents will ask the Iowa Utility Board to grant them authority to use eminent domain to obtain the right to locate the pipeline on private land. Recent news stories indicate a significant and growing number of landowners in the proposed path are opposed not just to the pipelines but to the idea the companies might be granted eminent domain, forcing them to sell access to their property. This is why the Boards of Supervisors in over 40 of the counties to be crossed by the pipelines have passed resolutions encouraging the IUB to reject any request to use eminent domain. The growing opposition explains why the pipeline companies resisted court orders and requirements by public authorities to release the names of the land owners whose property will be crossed. When you add up all of these plans to dine out on the public nickel it gives a new dimension to the idea of crony capitalism, that is if you can even use capitalism so loosely to describe essentially what is a public investment.

Now think of what the state and the nation could do if we took those same billions and put them to use paying farmers to address CO_2 and other climate related impacts on their farms. Planting cover crops, managing fertilizer use to improve efficiency, better manure handling—these all are the types of practices that can go a long way to limiting the impact of farming on the climate. In a somewhat pathetic move, the pipeline companies are trying to scare farmers by warning them the Sierra Club is behind efforts to block the pipeline. You are getting desperate when you have to create a bogeyman to scare people away from protecting their own land.

If the pipelines don't move forward but instead are recognized as the boondoggles they are, the failure won't be because of the Sierra Club. It will be because Iowans—farmers, landowners, local officials, and citizens alike were smart enough to see through the bill of goods being sold them. Rather than allow the public purse to be used to deliver this pig's ear, the public may realize investing in farmers to improve soil health and to protect the long term fertility and productivity of Iowa's land is a much better use of our money. If there is any lesson we can learn from our expensive flirtation with cellulosic ethanol, perhaps it is the best solutions to improving the health of agriculture are ones we can take on your own back 40s.

The River on the Ethanol Versus Electric Car Debate

I see the forces of Iowa agriculture are gearing up for another political fight they think is vital but may actually be futile and unnecessary. In recent years the growth in electric vehicles in the United States has been remarkable, with every major car company racing to chase the success of Tesla, even setting dates for when they will end the production of liquid fuel vehicles. You knew the cultural zeitgeist had changed when Ford unveiled the electric version of their iconic F-150 pickup.

Khanh with her 2015 Model S

Now you might think a state where wind energy production is burgeoning to the point the state gets over 50% of its energy supply from wind power, making Iowa the nation's leader, would see its way clear to embrace a future of electric vehicles. But then you would not be up to speed on the politics of corn and how it has subverted the traditional common sense of many Iowa politicians. Rather than embrace electric vehicles as the future, Iowa agriculture has staked its future on opposing this inevitable shift, led down this path by the renewable fuel folks, meaning the corn ethanol crowd. Iowa's Republican US senators, always on the lookout for a way to attack the Biden administration policies, have been happy to chime in as has the accidental governor. Their message is electric cars are a dire threat to the future of farming and the health, perhaps even the survival, of Iowa. Irony is not a strong suit of the corn ethanol crew now rallying the agricultural troops to protect the fossil fuel and gasoline sectors to make the state safe for gas guzzlers. I may only be a river but even I can see what a pointless, boneheaded, and eventually ill-fated mission this is. Rather than embrace the electric future, Iowa's leaders even felt it necessary to complain when the Biden administration made over $50 million available to help place electric charging stations along Iowa's interstates. Rather than recognize ethanol's days are inevitably numbered, and begin looking for new alternative uses and markets for corn or corn fields, the agricultural folks want to stand and fight it out—good luck with that.

To help do this they turned to their ready to please friends in the Iowa Legislature to mandate the sale of E-15 blended fuels, an even less efficient fuel most gas stations had no interest in marketing. In fact the gas station owners requested the state provide as much as $200,000 per station to help cover the costs of installing the new tanks and equipment necessary to carry the higher blend of ethanol fuel. It will only be a matter of time before the legislature renews the Governor's past efforts to remove the labels from ethanol pumps all together so consumers won't have a choice or even know what they are putting in their engines.

As this debate was unfolding, my old friend Chris Jones, still gainfully employed at the University of Iowa, at least as of this writing, struck again with a brilliant blog post titled "Iowa is addicted to 'cornography.'" Jones did his usual stellar job of basing his analysis on scientific data to refute the ethanol industry's claim it is a renewable fuel, at least as compared to solar energy. Jones compared the energy produced by converting an acre of corn to ethanol to the energy produced from one acre of solar panels. Leaving aside the environmental costs in water pollution and soil loss associated with corn production and the near absence of any pollution from solar, the real difference is in energy production. An acre of Iowa solar arrays would produce at least 34 times as much energy as an acre of corn. Renewable each year and with no expensive inputs or damage to the land and water, solar would appear to be an investment in the future. Now if you are a seed corn dealer or sell fertilizer, the river can understand why you may not embrace the issue and see the future so clearly. For the rest of Iowa, and for our nation, the answer appears to be much simpler. Rather than embrace foolish boondoggle ideas like CO2 pipelines designed to capture pollution from ethanol and fertilizer plants and ship it to other states, for the purpose of continuing the use of ethanol, putting the same energy and investment into solar energy would be a wiser hedge for our bets. If the state is wise enough to make this type of investment, at some point in the future perhaps the billboards I want to put up near the Raccoon River bridges on the interstates could read, "Raccoon River—cleaned up thanks to solar power in Iowa."

The Des Moines River Land Grant: Land, Water, Technology—and Some Politics

Here is a story involving three of Iowa's most powerful forces: land, water, and technology plus a healthy dose of politics and law. If you think the reference is to ethanol and CO_2 pipelines you need to hold on. Those issues come into the story soon enough but for now the main event is from farther back in Iowa's history. This is the story of the 1846 Des Moines River land grant, which spawned a 40 year legacy of lawsuits, political intrigue, financial misdealing, and clouded land titles. If you can't stand the suspense here is a preview of where the story takes us. Consider these parallels: electric cars are like railroads, ethanol is like a steamboat, and CO_2 pipelines are like navigation improvements on the river.

The story begins on August 8, 1846, just a few months before Iowa is admitted to the Union. That day Congress granted for the purposes of aiding in the improvement of the navigation on the Des Moines River from its mouth "to the Raccoon Fork in said territory, one equal moiety in alternate sections of the public lands remaining unsold and not otherwise disposed of, encumbered, or appropriated, in a strip 5 miles in width on either side of the river" to be selected by representatives of the state. Just picture it, alternating 640-acre sections, 5 miles deep, extending all along both sides of the river. The grant covered more than 300,000 acres of land the state could sell for no less than $1.25 an acre, the proceeds to fund efforts to improve navigation.

Iowa was admitted to the Union by an act of Congress on December 28, 1846, and in early January 1847 the Legislature by joint resolution accepted the land grant. In October 1847 the head of the General Land Office wrote to state officials concerning their need to select the desired lands. In December the state selected the odd numbered sections, vesting title in those lands to the state. In February 1847 the Legislature began the navigation improvements by creating a Board of Public Works to dispose of the land and apply the proceeds as required under the grant for navigation purposes. So far so good, but soon enough the confusion began.

The pivotal plot twist came in February 1848 when the Commissioner of the General Land Office wrote the Iowa Board and included this sentence: "a question has arisen as to the extent of the grant made to Iowa by the act of August 8th, and the opinion of this office has been requested on this point." The letter concluded with this fateful line, "Hence the state is entitled to the alternate sections within 5 miles of the Des Moines River, throughout the whole extent of that River within the limits of Iowa." It is not clear where the question had originated or who had asked for the opinion but the effect of the letter was significant. It added another 900,000 acres to the state's land grant! You can imagine the political intrigue in Washington leading to this beneficial act, an interpretation clearly at odds with the original Congressional action.

The next volley in what would become a decades long litany of political back-and-forth was a September 1848 letter from the Iowa Board of Public Works to the General Land Office questioning a recent Presidential proclamation about federal sales of land along the Des Moines River north of Raccoon Flats. The state argued the notice included lands already granted to Iowa, and noted based on the General Land Office's "very liberal opinion" of February, Iowa had contracted for navigation improvements along 60 miles of the lower Des Moines River.

This comment demonstrated what would be the crux of the fight for the next decades. Iowa had contracted for navigation improvements counting on the land sale revenue from the expanded land grant, and without this revenue it would be unable to meet its obligations and be illegally in debt. In January 1849 the Iowa congressional delegation took up the issue and got a letter in March from the Secretary of Treasury, then in charge of public lands, agreeing with the General Land Office's broad interpretation, noting federal officials had been ordered to reserve from sale any lands north of Raccoon Flats covered by the state's claim. The next twist came in January 1850 when the Secretary of Interior, now in charge of the federal lands, received the list of lands awarded to the various states for internal improvements, including the roughly 900,000 additional acres Iowa was to receive north of Raccoon Flats. In early April 1850 the Secretary of Interior responded to the General Land Office expressing his opinion the grant did not extend north of Raccoon Flats, refusing to approve lands the General Land Office had identified for reservation to Iowa. The Iowa congressional delegation appealed this unwelcome reversal to President Taylor, who ordered his Attorney General to rule on the matter. In July 1850 the Attorney General reversed the Secretary of Interior and ruled the land grant did extend to the northern boundary and the 1848 opinion of the Secretary of Treasury could not be reversed. This view held for a year, until President Taylor died in 1851 and a new cabinet was formed. Then the new Attorney General reversed the state of play, ruling the grant did not extend beyond Raccoon Flats.

At this point the state was in a pickle, two in fact. First it had entered contracts far exceeding the revenue generated by selling the 300,000 acres below Raccoon Flats. This placed the good faith and credit of the state in question, as well as completion of any navigation work. The second pickle, one with dire ramifications for hundreds of settlers, concerned the conflicts now planted between those who had purchased lands in good faith from the General Land Office along the northern river, and subsequent efforts by those, such as the Des Moines River improvement company, who claimed title to the same lands under the state's expanded grant.

For our purposes it is best to pull up now before the risk of confusion becomes even greater and to summarize what happened next. The federal dispute over the meaning of the grant continued until 1861 when Congress issued a joint resolution codified by an 1862 law, extending the grant to the Minnesota border. Congress also ordered the General Land Office to identify 300,000 acres of other federal lands still available in the state, the quantity needed to make up for the "improper sales." Income from these sales was to be used to indemnify claims by settlers impacted by the ruling. As for the hundreds of individual land disputes, cases involving various legal issues concerning preemption and indemnification claims continued to reach the US Supreme Court until the 1890s. For the most part the federal courts ruled against the settlers, siding with the parties claiming title under the Iowa land grant. As for the settlers being thrown off their lands, some lived on for decades, only the wise forbearance of the federal courts averted bloodshed and armed conflicts when writs for eviction were enforced, especially near Fort Dodge.

But what about the River you might be wondering and how in the world does this story relate to our needs today? First, as to the River, efforts to improve navigation of the Des Moines River quickly proved difficult and expensive. Very little came from the funds expended by the board of public works for the purpose. But another even more significant development soon overtook efforts to improve navigation on the Des Moines—the coming of the railroads. By the 1850's railroads were clearly winning any contest to open the nation to development, and were themselves the recipients of generous federal land grants to aid construction.

In other words, the very purposes of the Des Moines River land grant was soon overtaken by a more powerful, efficient, and widely adaptable technology. The litigation and land disputes created by the Des Moines River land grant far outlived any idea of improving navigation on the River. The land didn't go anywhere, instead the fight was over who owned it and where the title had originated. As to society, it moved on to the era of the railroad.

So what is our connection to Iowa today? To my thinking, the connections are clear—using corn to make ethanol is the steamboat navigation of the 1840s. The emergence of electric vehicles is the railroad of today. And efforts to extend the "useful" life of ethanol production, through such devices as constructing CO_2 pipelines, largely paid for with public funds, are our Des Moines River land grants. Not just are the proponents of ethanol willing to bet the public wealth on prolonging a dated and environmentally dubious technology, they hope to organize

agriculture and farmers to resist the nation's move to electric vehicles. Doesn't history tell us it is a foolish step to align farmers with others from our past, the steamboat captains and buggy whip manufacturers, who predictably failed in efforts to fight technological progress?

The River Has a Sense of Humor

Given all the hoopla Iowa's leaders make about the importance of ethanol, it struck me the situation called for a little comic relief. The following "news release" was written at the end of March 2022, to be distributed just before April 1st, a chosen date. After consulting the Professor we decided not to publicize the announcement for fear too many news outlets would print it, believing it was authentic—as had several friends we shared it with! But I can't resist sharing the original text with you.

Headline "Governor requests DOT to develop plan to allow corn planting on Interstate right-of-ways"
Dateline—Des Moines - Friday, April 1, 2022

An unconfirmed report is circling in Iowa agricultural circles to the effect on Friday, April 1st, in a surprise announcement, Iowa's governor Kim Reynolds will order Iowa DOT officials to develop a plan to be implemented by late April to allow corn production on the right-of-ways of Iowa's interstates. Sources close to the governor, who wouldn't go on record in fear for their reputations, indicate she believes this unprecedented step is necessary because of the on-going situation in Ukraine and the unprecedented demand for Iowa corn to "feed and fuel the world." The sources say the governor will exercise her executive authority to order the DOT to allow Iowa corn growers to apply for permits to plant next to the interstates in designated locations. Her actions are believed to be based on her view "tens of thousands of tillable acres are now going to waste being used as Prairie and other natural features." When asked to comment on the governor's proposal, DOT officials said they had no comment on her brilliant idea, but acknowledged there might be logistical challenges implementing it.

Unsubstantiated reports indicate proceeds from the "rent" received by the state will be allocated into three accounts, as determined by DOT staff. The first will be used to pay any damages or liability incurred from the inevitable collisions between motorists and slow moving farm equipment entering the right-of-way. A second portion of the funds will be used to pay for the vehicle damages due to the inevitable increase in collisions between cars and the deer attracted to the roadside food plots. Reported plans for the final 10% of the funds surprised observers with knowledge of the DOT's proposal. Reports indicate the remaining income will be deposited into an account to be used to purchase copies of *The Land Remains*, by emeritus Drake Ag law professor Neil Hamilton and a forthcoming book by Chris Jones. Books are to be provided free to public libraries, high schools, FFA chapters, and local coops.

When asked to comment on the governor's proposal, Griff McGruff, formerly "The Crime Dog," newly hired as public affairs spokesperson for the Iowa Farm Bureau, howled "if these reports are true, our members will be 100% behind the governor's proposal to increase corn production in the state." Mr. McGruff noted Farm Bureau research indicates corn is the most important crop in the history of mankind and may be responsible for employing 60% of Iowa's workforce. When pressed for reaction to the reported plans for use of the rent, McGruff growled and barked "if true, we are opposed to the outrageous proposal to purchase copies of Hamilton and Jones' books! We have reason to believe these books question the wisdom of the voluntary only approach for protecting Iowa soil and water." McGruff sniffed "even though Hamilton was raised on an Adams County farm his record shows a distasteful willingness for independent thought and a lack of support for production agriculture." As for Jones, he noted "that fellow is lucky to still have a job at the University, for now."

When asked about reports of the governor's intentions, William T. Bone, her spokesman, said he could not comment on the news reports but said the governor would be making an important announcement on April 1. When asked about reports the governor told supporters, as shown in a Tik Tok video, since removed from her wall, the idea came to her in a vision after a night enjoying the endless breadsticks and salad bar at Olive Garden, Mr. Bone, known affectionately by colleagues as T-bone, only smiled, noting "she does enjoy her pasta."

When reached at his palatial Dallas County estate Prof. Hamilton said he was surprised by the news and was unaware of plans to plant corn along the interstate highways. He commented the whole proposal seems like some type of outrageous hoax, and fears someone is trying to pull a fast one on Iowa's faithful citizens, not known for having a sense of humor. When provided details of the story Hamilton noted he wasn't sure who might have hatched such an outlandish proposal but whoever it was has a bright future flowing through Iowa politics. More details are expected to be available after the April 1 announcement.

Now, after I see this in print, I almost regret not having pushed the send button, just to know how many "news" outlets might have taken the bait.

Jamie Walters and solar easements in DeKalb County Illinois

Jamie Walter of Whiskey Acres Distillery in DeKalb visited Sunstead during a family visit to the 2021 Des Moines Art Festival. Jamie is the former student who opened the first farm-to-field distillery in the nation—where I selected a barrel of rye we labeled as "Old Prof. H" for my 2019 retirement celebration. Jamie told us about a new 4,000 acre solar array project being built in the DeKalb area in connection with a planned $2 billion Facebook facility. Participating farmers and landowners are being paid $1000 per acre per year for using their property for the solar arrays. This is a unique use of prime farmland, but one many people in agriculture find threatening because it takes the land "out of production," even though it provides significant economic benefits to the landowners. If you take the long view, solar arrays can actually be seen as a form of farmland protection, arguably less destructive than continuing to produce corn for ethanol. At the end of the 30 year contracts the panels and any other facilities can be removed, drainage restored and the land farmed again. This raises an interesting conflict— do you mine the soil now for "renewable" ethanol or do you build solar panels over it for a truly renewable form of energy? Of course passive solar arrays don't result in the same type of downstream economic activity such as buying fertilizer, seed, and equipment or in selling grain or for anyone else who gets a lick off the corn dollar. But if the farmer landowner is making more money with less damage to the land what makes it a bad idea?

In the Iowa water quality debate one constant theme you hear from farmers and local officials is our approach needs to be voluntary, and there is no role for regulation. This premise, essentially an anti-public ideology, is actually written into the Iowa law on water quality. It is one of the main reasons why our current approaches, such as the Nutrient Reduction Strategy, are failing and will continue to, until the state recognizes the necessity of using regulations to establish expected conduct by all citizens, farmers and landowners included. But those in agriculture can be real hypocrites when it comes to regulating other people. An excellent example of this hypocrisy appeared in the June 27, 2021 *Sunday Des Moines Register*. The chair of the Palo Alto County zoning commission wrote on opinion piece about the coming threats of solar arrays. He attacked the idea of using prime agricultural land for solar projects, concerned the activities were not subject to any regulatory controls. His suggestion was to require the developments only be placed on lower quality land so prime farmland could be used to raise corn.

The ironies in the story are many. County officials responsible for protecting vital resources like land, have typically done little to deal with water quality or soil conservation. Like others in agriculture most support "voluntary only" approaches as opposed to regulation. The premise is we need to keep prime land in agricultural production and the belief solar arrays take land out of production. So the suggestion the County may need to use regulations to tell landowners what they can or cannot do with their land when it comes to solar projects is interesting! How does that square with the voluntary only approach and no role for regulations?

THE SAILBOAT

Since this is a book about water and our relation to it, it is appropriate to tell the ill-fated story of our sailboat. If you are a boat owner, or more fortunately, a former boat owner, parts of the tale may be familiar. It all began in the summer of 1984 when I had several occasions to visit a law school friend practicing in New York City. He ran with what, for a Midwestern farm kid, was a fairly rarefied crowd and on several occasions we spent weekends at a Long Island beach house, once even journeying there by seaplane boarded in the East River. Heady, exciting stuff with great people, including many days sailing on his friend's 32 footer. How I enjoyed it, eager to pitch in trimming sails, coiling ropes, and any other task needing done. The next summer found us with the same group for a week on Martha's Vineyard, nude bathing at Gayhead beach, eating lobsters at Menemsha harbor, and of course with more sailing.

When I met my bride to be on June 29, 1985, at a baby shower for a foal I owned, sailing with my friends was still fresh. As a result it was only a matter of time until owning a sailboat was suggested as a great activity for us. She was kind enough or cautious enough at that point in our relationship not to resist, and my proposal for getting started was to book a week long "bareboat" sailing school excursion out of Coral Gables, Florida, for a winter getaway. So off to Florida we went, making our way to the harbor to meet our skipper. It is risky to extrapolate from a sample of one but our experience was interesting. Boiled to its most basic—the process of using your sailboat for week long charter "schools" with tuition paying guests appears to be how old sea salts and hippies afford to pay the bills and have a life on the water far from the reach of authorities. Our first task was making a trip to the nearby grocery store to buy a week's worth of provisions with a list helpfully provided by the skipper. After acquiring a trunk load of food we returned to the boat to store the items. We met the other paying customer also a Midwesterner escaping the winter cold and planned our five days of sailing down the Keys. The week passed quickly without incident, and after 35 years the most vivid memories are being on the water at night under star filled skies. A photo of me at the helm is the one visible reminder in our house it really happened. Unfortunately the experience was not sufficient to satisfy my sailing itch, so on returning home I searched for a used sailboat. No surprise, I soon found one and by spring we were the proud owners of a 21-foot

Bayliner Buccaneer—oh happy days.

We docked the boat at the Red Rock reservoir (created by damming the Des Moines River) near Pella, a 40-mile trip from home. That summer began my life as a skipper and in short it did not go well. To my surprise I learned how different it was being a deckhand on a boat and being the person responsible for the safety of everyone else on board. In reality I never was comfortable in the captain role and it became quickly apparent buying the sailboat was a boneheaded decision. After a year of infrequent use I moved the boat to the Saylorville Reservoir (also created by a flood control dam on the Des Moines—thank you Congressman Neal Smith) north of Des Moines and closer to home, but it really didn't help.

It was there, parked in the lot, my time with the boat reached a breaking point. On a visit to prepare for the upcoming season I noticed the port side main mast stay was kinked near where it clipped to the boat. Without thinking, as will soon become evident, I gripped the stay and undid the clip. At this point the laws of physics and gravity combined with my lack of training and upper body strength took over. While having the fore and aft stays clipped meant the 25 foot mast couldn't fall backwards, it was a different story on the lateral front! Once I popped the clip the mast began falling away to starboard! I grabbed the narrow cable and pulled for dear life but couldn't pull it back to vertical to redo the clip. Now in a standoff with gravity all I could picture was the mast crashing down on the sailboat parked next to me. At that point I began a plaintive scream of "help me, help me!" Thankfully another man working on his nearby boat rushed over, climbed aboard and helped me manhandle the mast and reclip the stay.

It was at this point he said the words that captured my sailing IQ and still ring in my ears "it doesn't look like you thought that one through"—no truer words were spoken in Polk County that day. Suffice it to say we never took the boat out on Saylorville Reservoir and after several years of paying to park it in the boat storage yard—just this side of being abandoned—I gave the boat and all its contents to a friend and former student. I don't remember whether Greg ever sailed the boat or eventually moved it to his nearby acreage to join the other assemblage of cars and equipment as another yard ornament, but I am glad he saved me from the possibility of a watery fate.

He is the same former student with whom I have a unique chainsaw relation. Whenever the urge to buy a chainsaw comes on so does the image of me with a gashed leg. My answer is to buy the chainsaw as a gift for Greg with the promise whenever an Oak tree comes down at Sunstead he will come take care of it. Twenty years, three chainsaws, and eight big trees later the relationship still benefits us both—Greg with ample firewood and me with un-severed limbs.

A few final comments will complete this tale. While Khanh did not object to the sailboat she shed no tears on its departure. If you want to experience owning a sailboat, stand dressed in the shower and tear up hundred dollar bills. In the years since there have been occasions when I have enthusiastically proposed what to her may sound like some new cockamamie scheme—buying a herd of goats for example, and her response will be "it sounds like a sailboat to me." Just enough cold water to snuff a dream—and save a marriage. The old saw most boat owners know is how there are two happy days—the one when you buy it and the one when you sell it or in our case give it away. As I think about it much the same can be said about horses but that is a happier story I'll save for another day.

The River is Putting on a Show

Well, I am putting on quite a show. I have dressed myself up in my fall colors and I'm giving people the opportunity who come out to see the beautiful fall that I can present. The trees along my banks are playing a leading role trading in their green leaves for the colors of fall: copper, russet, red, yellow, and more. As you come around the bend on the river and you see these colors reflected off the water framed by a deep blue sky I dare you to resist saying *wow that is gorgeous!* Then when you throw in some of my high cut banks carved out of sandstone like what you see south of Redfield then you have some of Iowa's river magic. I don't care where you travel or what other of my River friends you may have a chance to float, I will put my "best views" up against them in the gallery of nature's beauty. That is one of my many benefits. If you do come visit me to hike along my banks, fish on my shores, or better yet get out and paddle. Then your reward will be seeing nature at its most basic and timeless form. You may not think of Iowa's rivers as pristine and yes I can't vouch for some of the stuff you let runoff into me, but when it comes to looks we have some fantastic spots. So that's going to be one of my objectives in the months and years ahead— how to get more of you to come out and see the beauty Iowa's rivers and streams have to offer. My hope is by doing so you will come to have a better appreciation and respect for me and for the land along my shores.

Chapter Eight—Looking for Hope and Solutions: Is Local Government the Answer?

The river got some good news on election day 2021

I got some good news in November, 2021, when the voters in Polk County showed just how much they love me. At least that's how I want to read the results of their vote to approve the local property tax bond issue providing $65 million to fund land and water projects. The Polk County Conservation Board had asked the County Board of Supervisors to add the initiative to the ballot just as it had in 2012 with a $50 million bond issue. That one passed with 72% of the vote, well over the needed 60% and the money was put to great use. The $50 million leveraged an additional $42 million from other sources so the impact was almost doubled. This time the request was even larger and with a nice array of potential uses. There wasn't a great deal of attention to the vote until some TV ads ran in the last two weeks, but the conservation folks were very confident polling showed it would pass. And boy did it ever! When the votes were counted it cleared the hurdle at 81% approval. That type of support is almost unheard of for anything, especially a self-imposed property tax increase. Even the local taxpayers association, a group usually opposed to increasing government spending, came out in favor of the proposal. So it is nice to be loved, now I just hope folks use the money wisely and in ways to offer long-term benefits. This strong vote of support for nature might help state legislators consider raising the sales tax to fund the natural resources trust fund so citizens in every county will have money available for use. If that doesn't happen, then voters will need to encourage other counties on the river, like Dallas, to consider their own natural resource bond referenda.

LOCAL GOVERNMENTS: NATURE'S BEST FRIEND NOW

The beautiful fall of 2021 gave people an extra inning to enjoy nature. Visiting a park like Easter Lake or biking one of Iowa's many trails you saw the evidence. If water levels had been higher the Raccoon River would have been full of paddlers, too. The COVID pandemic gave extra value to people being outside and attendance at Polk County parks increased over 30% in 2020 alone.

As the River reported, Polk County residents showed how much they care for nature by voting to approve the Water and Land Legacy bond referendum unlocking another $65 million for conservation. The funding costs about $11 per year for the average homeowner. The new plan allocates $25 million for water projects including $15 million for portions of the ICON water trail system, $20 million for county parks, $10 million for trails, and $10 million for land acquisition. Even those who don't live in Polk County will benefit from the funding. Approving the bonds provides powerful evidence Iowans want more funding for nature. Most readers are aware how in 2010 over 62% of Iowans voted to amend the constitution to create the Natural Resources and Outdoor Recreation Trust Fund—known as Iowa Water and Land Legacy or IWILL. It is to receive the next 3/8 cent increase in the sales tax, but now over a decade later the legislature and state leaders have still not put a penny into the fund! If voters in Polk are any indicator, perhaps politicians will wake up and get the message: Iowans want more natural resource protection and will tax themselves to pay for it.

There is another important story in referendums like this. In our political system we have three branches of government—legislative, executive, and judicial—and three levels of government—federal, state, and local. When it comes to protecting nature, events of recent years show local governments are where the action is as citizens have taken matters into their own hands. Congress finds ways to tie itself in knots over self-inflicted crises like increasing the debt ceiling and keeping government open, dealing with inflation, COVID, and funding the war in Ukraine. At the state level all three branches of Iowa Government seem to have turned their backs on nature. In June 2021 a divided Iowa Supreme Court rejected using the Public Trust Doctrine to hold state officials responsible for protecting rivers like the Raccoon. Frequent manure spills and questionable DNR decisions, like approving Supreme Beef's 11,600 head cattle operation near Bloody Run in northeast Iowa, a protected trout stream, give the impression state officials aren't very concerned about water quality or our environment. The Iowa Legislature went home in 2021 and 2022 without taking any real action on water quality or new funding.

This is why local actions are such a breath of fresh air. Polk County has been leading the way, not just with the natural resources vote. In 2021 the Polk County Soil and Water Conservation District Commission crafted a water quality strategy helping landowners install over fifty saturated buffers in one year. Another important local funding opportunity recently opened, using federal COVID relief funds. In January 2021 local governments in Iowa received more than $1 billion under the American Rescue Plan Act or ARPA—the COVID relief bill pushed through Congress by President Biden. As guidelines for using the funds unfolded, local governments realized they could allocate money for water infrastructure and natural resource related projects. In summer 2022 the Polk County Board of Supervisors allocated over $16 million in ARPA funds for a broad array of water quality and public land related projects, including funds for the ICON water trail, a "batch and build" initiative to construct wetlands to improve water quality, and funding to acquire more flood plain land along the Skunk River in the Chichaqua Bottoms. There the exciting news is the ultimate goal of removing a portion of dike holding back the river, restoring several miles of oxbows and wetlands. Supervisors in other Iowa counties voted to use ARPA funds for nature related projects. The lesson these local leaders embrace is don't give up on nature. Treat it with respect and the citizen reward can be a rich harvest of enjoyment for all.

POLK COUNTY AND JOHN NORWOOD'S SWCD WORK

One of the bright spots in recent years in the Iowa water quality and conservation story has been the impressive projects coming out of Polk County, led by the Soil and Water Conservation District. In 2021 the county carried out a blitz in relation to installing saturated buffer strips and other types of water quality projects on private farmland. Remarkably the county was able to install over 50 saturated buffers in just one year, while the state Department of Agriculture hadn't been able to install that many in ten years. How did this happen? It took many players, but the person most responsible was John Norwood, a Commissioner on the Polk County Soil and Water Conservation

District. It took John, with his background in finance, to bring new thinking and new blood to what in many counties has become a rather moribund soil and water conservation system, more on that in a few pages! John couldn't understand why state and federal officials were pleased with being able to implement conservation practices one farm and one farmer at a time. In his thinking it made more sense to use a "systems approach" to implement the practices at scale by reducing the paperwork burden placed on landowners and by consolidating the funding and contracting. Working with the County to serve as the financial agent to hire a contractor interested in putting in multiple projects rather than just a few, John and the SWCD developed a more aggressive and effective project. Having the staff needed to contact landowners and farmers up and down the selected streams was critical to the project. The result is the state's most urban county, with a soil commission led by a non-traditional, non-farmer advocate, was able to implement one of the state's most effective water quality efforts.

The good news is this approach, now referred to as the "batch and build" method, is being piloted by other counties. As you might expect the project's success led many people to claim responsibility and take credit. One effect was to hip check Norwood to the sidelines and reduce the public recognition for the role he played. As his friend, I know he is sensitive to the fact even though he has lived in Iowa for over 20 years many still treat him as an outsider and reject his ideas as coming from someone who doesn't know the territory. It is the Iowa attitude Meredith Wilson wrote about in *The Music Man,* how our inherent parochialism can lead us to resist new ideas and resent new voices.

The key lessons to take away from the success John and the Polk

County SWCD had are these:

- it takes leadership and vision,
- it takes persistence, and understanding the programs,
- it takes staff capacity to be able to develop and implement plans at scale,
- it takes a context for change, in this situation, continuing concerns from the Des Moines Water Works about water quality issues,
- it is critical to have access to funding, here the money to pay landowners came from the county and state water quality initiative, funds not being used elsewhere.

All these elements created a successful program with very visible results. The truth is a person who some see as a "bothersome outsider" with big ideas was able to help the local SWCD become a successful player and pioneer, using the traditional soil and water conservation system to actually achieve something. Hopefully SWCD commissioners in other counties will be inspired by the success of this approach. Unfortunately my own personal experience serving on the SWCD in neighboring Dallas County shows efforts to expand the work of local SWCD's is harder than one might expect.

BEING A SOIL AND WATER CONSERVATION DISTRICT COMMISSIONER

When you think about the growing role local governments can play in natural resource protection and innovation, one exciting dimension is the opportunity for citizens, readers like you, to become involved. To play a vital role you don't have to be a member of Congress, or change careers to become an NRCS soil technician. Instead all you need to do is step up and volunteer to serve on a local body or seek appointment to a park board. These opportunities are nearby and readily assessable, offering you the chance to help shape events in your backyard. That was my thinking in 2020 when deciding to run as a "write in candidate" for the Soil and Water Conservation District (SWCD) commission in Dallas County.

These locally elected five-member bodies exist in over 3,000 counties in the United States. They are responsible for helping administer the state soil conservation and water quality laws and are the local partner assisting the USDA-NRCS in delivering its myriad of soil and water conservation programs. For over 30 years I taught my agricultural law students about the Iowa soil conservation law and the vital role of the districts, so the opportunity to actually serve on one was exciting. I can now report, after two years on the commission, be mindful of what you get yourself into! To say my experience "serving" as a Commissioner has been eye-opening is an understatement. As an outside observer my impression of the districts was of their broad powers and potential role, a view based on the state law giving districts powerful legal tools to promote conservation and educate farmers and landowners. This perception was buttressed by the Iowa Supreme Court's opinion in *Woodbury County SWCD*, a key 1979 case shielding the district's actions from constitutional challenge. The case illustrates the primary role the SWCDs can play in helping protect the state's soil, declared a vital public resource by the Court.

Unfortunately the rosy view from the outside doesn't mesh with the reality from the inside, and the contradictions are frustrating to those who serve as commissioners and destructive to the state's soil and water resources. The law appears to create a locally elected body with broad authority to help protect our soil and water, but the parts missing from the law make the potential more ephemeral than real. First the districts have no direct funding source, either through state or local appropriations, and they have no ability to levy taxes or to otherwise obtain funds other than by seeking contributions. As a result, any work of the districts depends on the availability of programs funded by the state through the Iowa Department of Agricultural Land Stewardship (IDALS) or the federal government through the USDA-NRCS. Second, the districts have no employees subject to the direction of the commissioners. Instead the employees who work out of the county conservation offices are either selected and paid for by the state or are federal employees of the NRCS who happen to be located in the soil and water conservation district offices. In fact, this isn't true, for while the sign out front may say it is the office of the County Soil and Water Conservation District in reality it is a federal facility, rented and paid for by the USDA.

As a caveat, I admit using my experience and applying it to the broad system of 100 county commissions can be problematic. But conversations with fellow commissioners from across the state reveal my experience and frustration are not just personal but widely shared. The effect of having no budget and no staff render the commissions impotent in many ways, little more than political window dressing. The USDA conservation programs may "require" the local districts to "sign off" on the eligibility of farmers and landowners to participate in various initiatives, but commissioners are not involved in evaluating or selecting the actual participants. Compounding the lack of involvement, the USDA's overly broad interpretation of its privacy rules means commissioners are no longer even allowed access to the maps and plans to see the details of the farms, lands, and practices involved. This creates the absurd result where the locally elected soil commissioners often aren't even aware of the full extent of publicly funded conservation work being conducted in the county, in their name! While the federal employees working in, but not for, the County office may attend the monthly meetings of the commissioners and report on ongoing activities, the commissioners do not direct, supervise, or in any way select this work. The situation is somewhat mixed when state funds and staff are involved for programs delivered through the district, for example to address water quality. Even here the ability of the commissioners to steer the work toward local priorities is limited because the district employees actually work for IDALS. Any project funding is from the state, used for projects selected by state officials based on their priorities. The commission has no funding to direct to locally identified conservation needs or priorities unless it has obtained funds from other sources.

The reality and experience of each district varies, and some commissions do have employees, if they have been able to obtain grants to hire them. The question is who writes the grants? Remember commissioners are unpaid volunteers and experience shows the capacity and motivation to take on the task of grant writing is typically limited. Districts can also seek direct funding from their county boards of supervisors, who can allocate property tax revenues for conservation use as Polk County has done. Experience shows few districts seek or obtain county funding, in large part due to competing demands counties face for property tax revenue. As a result most districts function with limited initiative and SWCD monthly meetings consist of routinely signing off on the NRCS reports as required, and perfunctory compliance with IDALS rules on budgets and reporting. More time may be spent approving the monthly bank statement for the $.28 in interest received, than on conservation priorities in the county. Little gets accomplished, and even worse it appears little is expected of the commissions by anyone else involved in conservation.

I got a firsthand taste of reality serving as a commissioner when invited to speak to the 2022 annual meeting of the Conservation Districts of Iowa (CDI). This group represents the state's 100 SWCD's and the 500 elected commissioners so it is the most important conservation organization in the state, or should be. My task was to provide some much needed "education" for commissioners about their legal authority to enforce Iowa's conservation laws. My remarks were direct and provocative, explaining to them (perhaps for the first time) how under Iowa Code section 161A.61, they have the legal authority to investigate any land they believe is losing soil above established loss limits. My comments were clearly an eye-opener because when asked about this issue fewer than one in ten said they had ever heard they have this power. In fact, several commissioners stopped me later to tell me they had been told they did not have any such authority. Here is a passage from my remarks:

> If you have not heard of it you can be excused because it does not appear many people in Iowa agriculture—perhaps including officials at IDALS are interested in seeing it used. Now I don't mean to offend anyone by saying this but if you want proof—here is a good example. If you have had a soil loss complaint you are familiar with the *Soil and Water Conservation District Policies and Procedures Manual,* an 8-page guide prepared by the Division of Soil Conservation

and Water Quality at IDALS—last updated in September 2018. It provides detailed guidance for how commissions are to investigate and handle complaints under §161A.47 (used when a complaint is filed by a neighboring landowner).

It is interesting the manual never makes reference to Section 161A.61: discretionary inspections by commissioners. As a result it provides no guidance for how they are to be handled. The failure to refer to this important power granted commissioners may be an innocent oversight. Or it could be intentional, you have to ask others.

I explained to the commissioners, my point in focusing on §161A.61 was not to argue it should be widely used. My point was they should know about it and be prepared to use it if necessary. I explained how:

taking formal action to require a landowner to implement soil protections is controversial and can be seen as political, and may not be something you want to do. But as elected commissioners we have a statutory responsibility to the citizens of Iowa. This is not a meeting of the Corn Growers—we are the soil and water conservation commissioners and Iowa law trusts us with an important responsibility to help protect the soil and gives us powerful tools to use if needed. If we do not accept the responsibility then are we living up to the expectation of the law or the state's legacy of conservation leadership?

Will my remarks to the commissioners make any difference? I like to hope so and several stopped to thank me for the explanation, but one talk can't be the basis for a revolution, just a start. The one surprise from the meeting was the lack of attendance. Only 85 of the state's

500 elected commissioners attended, though another 120 sent prox-
ies. Even more telling only one-half of the state's counties were even
represented. I ended my remarks, by suggesting the SWCD's need to
deal with our lack of staff and funds. If the state or the USDA would
provide $10 million dollars each district could have $100,000 to hire
a conservationist and fund a priority watershed project. I ended with
this:

> Don't you think in the great scheme of things when every
> year we pour hundreds of millions (even billions) in public
> funding to support farming in this state—we couldn't find
> the 50 cents an acre needed to fund the work of the soil
> and water conservation districts responsible for helping
> insure the soil remains for us to farm?

Cultural Disintegration in Rural Iowa: Is Poaching a Tree like Polluting a Stream?

In *Tree Thieves: Crimes and Survival in North America's Woods*, Lyndsie
Bourgon offers a detailed explanation of the proliferation of the crime
of tree theft occurring on America's public lands. Her book made me
realize there are interesting cultural parallels in the community attitudes of people who reside near public forests and the trees growing
there, and the relation of rural residents in Iowa to the local lands and
waters. The potential for conflicting attitudes can be especially true
if rural residents feel they are being denied opportunities or access
to what they may see as community resources. Any observer of Iowa
agriculture knows the structure has changed greatly in recent years:
fewer and larger farms, more tenancy and absentee owners, declining
rural populations, and widening economic and wealth divides among

those who remain. She makes the observation how timber poaching and related crimes are rooted in a challenge stretching across North America, "the disintegration of community in the face of economic and cultural change."

Is the disintegration of rural communities a factor in Iowa agriculture, and might it help explain our half-hearted attitudes toward protecting land and water? Consider the changes in attitudes and capacities of the local soil and water conservation districts to "deliver" conservation, the ones encountered speaking to CDI. A number of factors influence a reduction in the ability of the districts to reach farmers:

- farms are much larger so the reach of programs is more limited, for example an acreage cap on funding to support cover crops means larger farms have less incentive to apply;
- more farmland is under short-term lease, so there is much less interest or incentive for tenants to install conservation practices,
- conservation districts and NRCS are challenged in being able to communicate with the non-operator landowners, and may not even know who they are or where they live; and
- fewer farmers are serving on SWCD's, leading to cultural changes in the makeup of commissions.

Historically SWCD commissioners were well-known, established farmers, respected among their farming contemporaries and embedded in the local social fabric. Today in some counties the identity of the commissioners has changed significantly. Consider the Dallas County commission. None of our members are traditional farmers, most of us know few, if anyone, who is a farmer in the county. Conversely most farmers do not know any of the commissioners or have any connection with us. Given these shifts it is clear how this impacts our ability to reach farmers or why they might have little trust in our work. When you add to this the limited staff capacity and the relative youth and inexperience of many newly hired NRCS conservation field staff, there is little community of culture for conservation shared between the SWCD and the farming community.

If the question is switched to what are the alternatives to the traditional voluntary approach where farmers came to the conservation district office for answers and to participate in programs, the possibilities are uncertain. One approach could be to move to a regulatory system using mandates and a set of expected standards to measure farmers' conduct. But there are many reasons why this approach might not work including farmer resistance and the lack of political will on the part of conservation officials to actually enforce such standards. Would it be a better system than where we are now, or just another source of frustration and cultural divide? The larger and better question may be how do we go about re-claiming and rekindling a culture of care for conservation among farmers and landowners? This is a challenge when many people involved in farming believe things are just fine and there is no real need to change anything they are doing in relation to the land or soil. One of the many ironies in this situation is how the "resources" being lost or devalued by soil erosion and poor farming are the property of the farmers and landowners, their land and soil.

One problem, or opportunity, in this situation is the need for better information and better data as to the costs of the erosion. Would farmers care more if they knew how their land values and productivity were being negatively affected by their current practices? Would it make farmers and landowners more willing to consider changing practices, such as avoiding fall tillage? What if a poster or information was made available by the state or the USDA to the effect, "do you know a typical Iowa farm loses X dollars in fertility and soil quality from soil losses, for every 1 inch of rain fall?"

Another example of how cultural disintegration may be happening in rural Iowa concerns the effect larger land holdings and farming by tenants may have in removing these operations from the local community. For example the Dallas County commission has no idea what percent of the county is being farmed under lease, or how much is owned by non-operator landowners, or the amount of land being rented to operators from other counties, so there is no real knowledge of their operations.

In many counties in southern Iowa a significant amount of land has been acquired by out-of-staters solely to maintain hunting camps, primarily for white tail deer and turkey. In some ways this trend in locking up land from "use" by neighbors and locals has a parallel to the experiences Bourgon notes concerning how local people feel being shut out from using lands preserved as national forests or parks. This trend creates incentives for locals to engage in poaching. Certainly there are similar cultural divides in attitudes toward land owned by out-of-state investors in many rural counties. Potential resentment is ingrained in anything revealing the wealth divide in land ownership, and how it corrodes the idea land is a shared community resource, even when it is privately owned.

One part of the tree theft story concerns the public officials who want to create parks and forests. Their efforts are often opposed by local residents who see them as outsiders working to take away employment opportunities. This same local resentment is evident in Iowa debates over acquiring public lands and protecting private lands, such as the conservation easement activities of the Iowa Natural Heritage Foundation. The divide is often between local farmers who see these lands as potential farms being "locked up" by those they characterize as outsiders who want to protect and use the rivers and lands for recreation but expect locals to limit their own private activities. Is poaching a tree from public land on a par with poaching the ability of citizens to

use and enjoy the river with manure spills or running cows in the stream? The parallel may be in how we have come to treat the river as a commons. Farmers and adjacent landowners may view the river as a natural disposal  site. In many ways this is a consumptive use of a public resource, while the public wants to use the rivers and public lands for recreation, or nature-based non-consumptive uses.

TURNING EFFORTS AT HISTORIC PRESERVATION INTO POLITICAL FIGHTS

An October 2021 *The New York Times* article detailed how an innocent effort in Montana to designate a national heritage area had been turned into a major political controversy by local anti-government actors. A local activist had made a series of false claims about the initiative, wrapped around the now predictable arguments it was somehow a federal land grab and would greatly limit the ability of farmers and landowners to make traditional uses of their property. The tale involved all of the usual suspects: the state Farm Bureau, ultra conservative political groups, Republican politicians including the governor, and of course featured bitter local community hearings. Efforts to generate the local cost-share and support for the initiative had been underway for many years, pursued as a tourism and economic development initiative. Then the conspiracy nuts and the "wowsers" came out of the woodwork, basing their attacks on wild claims relating to property rights, land grabs, and taking of land.

Naturally the person who became the local figurehead for the opposition used the episode to run for office, attracting interest by other Republican leaders. The effort led the state legislature to pass a law saying no federal heritage area designations will be allowed in Montana, though it is unclear such a law is even enforceable. Predictably, the episode was also used to launch an effort in Congress to not renew the federal statute authorizing heritage designations. Unfortunately the dispute in Montana was not a solitary event. In May 2021 the *Midwest News* reported a similar attack against the proposed Willa Cather historic district near the author's home town of Red Cloud, Nebraska. The activists opposing the initiative had whipped up the locals, describing the designation as an oppressive federal land-grab. The lesson is when you combine the issue of property rights with the combustible political environment found in many rural quarters today, results like those in Nebraska and Montana appear like clockwork.

There are a number of questions to ask about these situations as well as possible lessons to consider. One question is how do we expect to develop reasonable public policy if these types of attacks on even innocent historic designations can be expected? A second is how do these examples illustrate the larger Trumpian inspired and unleashed dumbing down of the public square? There are many explanations for these developments, including the willingness of people to believe in fictions, and the power of conspiracy beliefs to make the holders feel special with inside knowledge. Typically, the opposition is strongest among those who are poorly educated, marginalized, and resentful of not being listened to—an anger often focused on people like the author, and likely, readers like you. This is the cultural disintegration Bourgon wrote of in *Tree Thieves*.

Another factor may be a concern efforts to promote local tourism-based economic development could potentially place restraints on extractive activities and threaten land freedom! This certainly helps explain why the local Farm Bureaus are often involved, joined by the mineral sector, builders, and other extractive industries. These groups may know the local opposition is phony and they may not even support the craziest of the conspirators. But they are certainly willing to let them do the political work opposing government action and appear willing to accept what may be long term, harmful social and cultural impacts coming from such conflicts, such as corrosion of trust or support for the public good, as a price to pay for their personal economic goals.

DING DARLING AND IOWA TODAY

I have been thinking of Ding Darling, Iowa's famous conservationist and what he might think about Iowa in 2022. There are several events Darling would have found appalling. First was an announcement by the Iowa DNR any state park rangers and forest service employees residing in houses located in the parks and state forests needed to move and find new places to live. The policy change would have affected over two-dozen state employees residing on the properties they help manage, where they help safeguard the health of citizens using them. The justification was the state could not afford the perhaps as much as $2 million required to maintain the houses and bring them up to code. Even though employees have resided there for decades, officials noted providing housing was never part of their employment. So rather than have state park rangers live at the facilities they are responsible for, they would be required to find housing nearby. Naturally, there was to be no change in their duties or responsibilities, it would just make it harder and longer for them to respond to anything happening at the parks.

There is little doubt Darling would have found this idea stupid. In fact he would probably have argued if the DNR director had any integrity the person would resign rather than carry out such a maneuver. The uproar greeting the DNR's announcement led the legislature to back off the idea and "find" the funds needed to allow continued use of the residences for now.

The second Iowa development was legislation introduced in the General Assembly to essentially make it impossible for the DNR or the County conservation boards to acquire new land for public use as parks and other purposes. The idea was to limit the amount governments could pay for land to 70% of the fair market value, meaning acquisitions could happen only if sellers were willing to sell at a steep discount. The proposal was just one of the ideas forwarded by the Farm Bureau and other organizations who oppose any expansion of public land. Supporters of the legislation were unwilling to admit their real justification and instead were happy to hide behind the smokescreen of claiming by preventing public agencies from buying property at market value, they were preserving opportunities for new and young farmers to purchase these lands. Of course, the legislation had no provisions to somehow make that possibility more likely, but it did offer political cover for essentially an anti-public, and more significantly, an anti-property rights development. The hypocrisy of proposals like this is how the Farm Bureau has long held itself out as the main defender of private property and the rights of landowners. Here the real burden was on landowners who would not be able to voluntarily sell land to public agencies. If Darling were alive and using his pen and political cartoons to illustrate the illogic of proposals like this, the idea would have been on the front page of the newspaper and the hypocrisy exposed. Thankfully it didn't require resurrecting Darling to generate sufficient opposition to prevent this bad idea from moving in the 2022 legislature, although it may well rear its head in the future.

Darling also came to mind with a national controversy, a dispute in 2021 involving the duck stamp program administered by the Department of Interior. It appears then Sec. of Interior Zinke, before being forced to resign over ethics scandals, had changed the rules for the duck stamp competition to require the artwork include images of hunting. As a result duck stamp submissions needed to include such things as duck calls, boxes of shells, decoys, or other active indicia of hunting. This had never been a requirement previously, and the new rules led to significant controversy and resistance by both the artists who submit images for the competition and among the many non-hunters in the community of birdwatchers, who collect duck stamps. The episode was a perfect example of the willingness of the Trump administration to make anything into a wedge issue if possible and to create another political litmus test. Trying to highlight the importance of hunting at the cost of other potential supporters of the duck stamp program, was just one more attempt to, as they like to say, "own the liberals." The goal wasn't so much promoting hunting, as it was the politics of winning. Darling would have been dumbfounded by how small-minded and mean-spirited his Republican Party had become. One of the many positive developments from ending the Trump administration's control over federal programs was in August 2021 the Biden administration and the new Department of Interior reversed the rules, returning the duck stamp to its more traditional purpose. Now in September, 2023 when the Duck Stamp unveiling takes place at Drake University it will be free of this taint.

Where Are My Visitors?

Why don't more people visit me? I am right here and the number of places and ways to get out on me, to kayak, canoe, fish, bird watch are increasing. Maybe I have an image problem. The old expression "river rat" marked the type of person who enjoyed the river, fishing with diddy poles, drinking, and shooting guns. Being on the river had a bit of a "white trashy" dimension to it. If you start there and then add other worries— who you might encounter on the river or what might be in the water—livestock wastes, *E. coli*, and nitrites, you create a whole new fear dimension. When you consider the costs of buying a canoe, the logistics of getting on the water, the shuttling of vehicles to drop-off and pickup, which can add an hour on both ends, the reality is getting out on the water can be costly in money and time.

It makes me think of a conversation the professor had with his paddling buddy John. As they floated by one of my towering bluffs, John asked "out of a thousand Iowans how many do you think have ever spent time paddling on one of our rivers?" The professor thought about it and said probably no more than ten percent or maybe even fewer, perhaps one in 100. To which John said he thought it was probably closer to one in 1,000. There you have it—whether the answer is one in 100 or one in 1,000 (and I tend to agree with John) the point is most people have never been on the river. Driving over and looking down from a bridge is as close as most people get to me. Or even worse their experience may have been their property being damaged by a flood. Think of my last doozy, the great '93 flood that inundated much of Des Moines including knocking the Water Works off line for over a week, or the 2008 flood on the Cedar that devastated downtown Cedar Rapids. More people may have been "in" the river than "on" the river, and being displaced or damaged by a flood is not a recipe for learning to love me. This may answer my own question, why I don't have more visitors. We are going to have to work on how to change this dynamic! The good news, as we have learned, is many local governments are working to expand the ability of citizens to connect with the rivers, and I say it is about time!

WHAT IS IOWA'S PLAN FOR PROTECTING NATURE

The good news we can draw from the stories of local actions to protect nature is how they show what is possible with leadership, initiative, and good opportunities. The insights we can draw from the opposition to land and nature protections—both at the state and sometimes local level, is perhaps we are just in a period of political division where effective actions can be blocked, hopefully a period that might soften with time. The two "sides" to these stories illustrate some of the divisions in society, divisions nature might be able to help us heal. The puzzling aspect of the debate is how on the one hand you have many reasons to support natural resource protection. These include strong public interest in outdoor recreation such as bike trail use, boating, camping, and sharp increases in use of the state parks. We also have significant public support for improving clean water and for establishing permanent funding for natural resource protection as evidenced in the local bonding votes and passage of the Natural Resources Trust Fund. Plus there are significant economic development opportunities from natural resource enhancement as reflected by the new cafés and bars in small towns on bike trails and the growing number of paddling outfitters. The business community knows quality of life is greatly enhanced by the availability of outdoor recreation opportunities and are key to attracting employees and growing businesses. This is one reason why the Des Moines business community has dedicated millions to ICON, the central Iowa water trails initiative.

On the other side of the ledger, reasons for support get weighed against the opposition to park funding, public land acquisition, and natural resource protection in general. What is the opposition really based on? Is it we can't afford to care for our parks due to shortfalls in the DNR budget the Legislature resists expanding? A second reason to oppose natural resource protection is we can't afford to raise income taxes to do so, but isn't this more evidence why public support for raising the sales tax should be harnessed? Or is the real reason because the Farm Bureau opposes adding more public lands or new trails? Increasing the rural urban interface raises fears farming practices may be exposed to public scrutiny, so to avoid questions, expanding public recreation is opposed. Are these reasons enough to explain why the state is hesitant to protect nature? Perhaps. If so, the question is what happened to the Ding Darling Republicans, the outdoors people and

nature lovers? How did protecting nature devolve into a partisan issue? Republicans fish and hunt, canoe and enjoy the outdoors, just
like Democrats and Independents. To help understand our divisions
and to see if there are places where the power of the natural resource
opportunities have allowed us to act, I visited two locations offering
examples for how we can move forward—the Iowa Great Lakes and
the Upper Iowa River.

VISITING OKOBOJI

On a summer trip I headed northwest to visit our famous Iowa Great
Lakes and Lake Okoboji. The visit gave me the opportunity to spend
time with Joe McGovern from the Iowa Natural Heritage Foundation
to talk about the many Lakes projects we have completed and to learn
more about what is being done. We had a great paddle along Angler's
Bay in Big Spirit Lake, two hours gliding through the bulrushes, fishing on the eastern shore of this beautiful lake with water clear 4 to 5
feet down. This was the water side of a major land project the Foundation protected when we led the efforts to purchase Anglers Bay for $6.2
million. In the late 1990's $1 million was raised to put into the project
and the Iowa general assembly made a special appropriation for another $4.5 million, allowing the DNR to buy the stretch of shoreline.
During my visit in 2021 the DNR was busy removing many of the trees
growing on the bank because they were shading out and killing the
shoreline bulrushes so critically important to the natural fish hatchery.
Without INHF stepping in to spear head fund raising for the Angler's
Bay project, this long stretch of shoreline would today look just like
the adjoining land, wall-to-wall housing with trailers and lengthy boat
docks crowding the shoreline, the reality found on either side. In the

future few people on the lake will realize the shore land is protected and fewer still will know or even think about how the bulrushes came to be protected. That is the essence of what INHF does. Our work and partnerships with state and local agencies are valuable for the future of the state even if difficult for people to see or appreciate. Thankfully we have donors who own land and people who have wealth willing to support our work. Just as important are the opportunities to work with local partners, citizen groups, and governments.

It is interesting to see how the situation at Lake Okoboji and the Great Lakes contrasts to much of the rest of Iowa in recognizing the value of nature and the opportunities clean water and protecting open space can bring. If local residents there can value the lakes so much they are willing to spend private and public funds to protect them why can't this be true in the rest of Iowa? Perhaps the answer is we do provide protections but just don't recognize it. Don't the whitewater courses in Charles City, Elkader, and Manchester reflect an appreciation for nature and all it brings? Isn't Lake Red Rock an economic driver for Pella, and Lake Rathbun one for Chariton, Albia, and Centerville? For that matter consider the economic activity and attention the Whiterock Conservancy brings to Coon Rapids? But do Iowa officials have a good handle on the economic development activity flowing from these natural features? If we did, couldn't this help dissolve or thaw some of the opposition? The reality is there are opportunities all across Iowa where funding, personal wealth, people who support natural resource protection and forward-looking public officials can combine to create a brighter future.

My Visit to the Upper Iowa River.

August 2021 also brought an opportunity to paddle on the Upper Iowa River, again with my friend Joe McGovern. Our plan was to paddle a stretch of the river past several properties INHF has been involved in protecting. In some ways, I have a long history with the Upper Iowa River, beginning in the summer of 1974 as a research assistant for ISU's Department of Forestry. The assignment was a research project in Northeast Iowa and Southwest Wisconsin studying how local rivers can create recreational potential to support local economies. Our reception was a bit chilly because this was shortly after federal officials had promoted listing the Upper Iowa under the new national Wild and Scenic River Act. Their goal was to "protect" a long stretch of the Upper Iowa, the only Iowa river eligible for consideration. It probably comes as no surprise to readers to learn the mere suggestion of "federal intervention" generated a significant amount of vocal and, at times, almost violent, local opposition. As a result the idea of the Upper Iowa being named a nationally protected river died. Today, 40 years later, the story is much different, one reason I was excited to be on the Upper Iowa with Joe.

As we paddled down the river we passed long stretches of properties the INHF has helped protect over the last 30 years. Today, over 50% of the corridor of the Upper Iowa, primarily the most scenic stretches flowing north west of Decorah is protected in some way. So what changed in the last thirty years to make this level of protection possible?

- First, the river didn't go away, it is resilient, and just had to wait until society caught up, offering better ideas for protection.

- Second, a critical ingredient was having an organization like the INHF willing to work on the ground with landowners, free from the fear the federal government or state was going to take the river. The Foundation's approach is less threatening to local landowners because the organization will listen to their concerns and work with them to overcome their objections.

- Third, in some ways the landowners have changed, both in their motivations and in recognizing the value of the river. Even the identity of many landowners has changed as the next generation of new owners appreciate the value of protecting the views from the river.

- Fourth, the local community's recognition that the value of the river have evolved, and today it is now seen as an important regional resource to protect and promote as vital to the "Driftless Region."

- Fifth, the legal tools available for protection are much more refined. Rather than simply buying up large stretches of property, INHF and local partners have focused on keeping development off the ridgelines and protecting bottomlands next to the river. By using conservation easements in connection with private ownership it has been possible to show how protection is possible without having to make land owned by the public.

If you have the chance to travel the Upper Iowa River, you will discover how it is, without question, one of the most beautiful and scenic stretches of river, not just in Iowa, but anywhere in the Midwest. As we paddled it was truly remarkable to consider what protecting the corridor has to teach us. It illustrates how patience, versatility, and a willingness to meet landowners where they are can be critical to protecting natural areas, whether a river, lake, or prairie. Having a range of different types of protection to fit landowner's needs is also vital. Our seven mile journey passed properties subject to as many as five different forms of protection. There are some properties actually owned by the state DNR with full public ownership. There are other properties INHF owns as a private foundation and others where we hold a conservation easement but the land remains in private ownership. There are some properties owned by the US Fish and Wildlife Service, and others have been acquired by the County Conservation Board as county parks. A majority of the protected land is still in private ownership but subject to some form of conservation easement protecting the river and its values. The key is all of these various arrangements and land transactions have been voluntary, reflecting decisions made by the owners. Collectively the goal of these owners and the public and private partners has been to protect the beauty and character of the river and the adjacent land so all users—today and in the future—will be able to enjoy it. This example of cooperation has created a recipe for success, one offering not just a bright future for the Upper Iowa but potentially applicable across Iowa.

Meeting Up with Project AWARE

In mid-July 2021 the annual installment of Project AWARE happened on me! Project AWARE is a week-long citizen led river cleanup program now in its 25th year. Sponsored by the Iowa DNR and other groups, it is a way to engage people of all ages in river cleanups. It had originally been scheduled for 2020 on the Raccoon but was delayed because of the pandemic. I was amazed by the size of the crowd who showed up at Whiterock Conservancy near Coon Rapids to register for the activities— over 340 people planned to participate! The AWARE part of the label stands for "a watershed awareness river expedition" and it is a little bit like taking Iowa's famous RAGBRAI bike event but putting it on to the river. You can only imagine what a scene it makes to find over 300 people in canoes spending a week paddling along stretches of my branches hauling out trash, trying to clean up the riverbanks. All this while learning about water quality, making new friends, and recreating with nature. People came from all over the state and many nearby to participate and the amount of trash and debris they pulled out of me was impressive. It kind of felt like going to the spa!

I couldn't help thinking wouldn't it be nice if we could get 300 of the farmers and landowners living and farming adjacent to me to show the same level of interest in doing something to help keep me clean. That would make a nice river adventure and something farm groups and 4-H clubs could collaborate on. I'm not sure if they would call it Project AWARE for Farmers. More likely it would be Project FEAR—Farmers Eventually Accepting Responsibility, worried if they don't act someone might make them!

On the same Sunday Project AWARE started the *Des Moines Register* carried a long story about how increasing river recreation is helping drive concerns about water quality and agriculture's role. Interestingly, the story contained no comments from anyone involved in agriculture, a surprise as you might think this would be a big issue for farmers. Perhaps the reality is the agriculture sector recognizes it is better to ignore the question rather than engage discussing it. They are confident if the policy choice is between more pigs and bigger corn crops or you "playing" in the river—pigs, corn, and agriculture will win every time! As I see it, they really don't need to engage on the issue, the deck is stacked and they deal the cards. Little stands as a restraint on agriculture's "ability" to pollute, i.e., use me to carry away their wastes. So why would they engage? Who is going to stand up and say "screw you" to the public and those working for healthier, safer water, even if this is the message of their actions? They don't have to speak or act in part because state officials are doing their dirty work for them. Excuse my venting, I just wish every week was Project AWARE and every river in the state got to experience how citizens care. Now that would give me hope.

Seth and cows.

Chapter Nine—Three Things Iowa Needs: More Truth Tellers, More Hope, and More Imagination

WHERE ARE THE TRUTH TELLERS?

On Feb. 2nd, 2022, Thomas Friedman had a column in *The New York Times* praising Neil Young and Liz Cheney. Neil Young was being called out for standing up against Spotify for promoting misinformation on COVID vaccinations, and Liz Cheney was commended for her willingness to challenge Trump and the Republican Party's willingness to adopt the big lie of a stolen election. The column was premised on environmental issues and climate change, and their parallels to democracy and civil society. Both have been resilient historically, in part because they had systems of buffers and redundancies in place to withstand shocks. For the environment the buffers are the atmosphere, the Arctic, the oceans, the rain forests, and resources able to absorb and withstand the impact of human action. Democracy had its buffers too—truth and trust in institutions shared by a large enough portion of the population democracies could survive challenges by demagogues and social unrest. Friedman's point was both the environment and democracy are being challenged by current events, which may indicate the buffers are weakening and our resilience is under threat.

Truth tellers like Neil Young and Liz Cheney are vitally important for being willing to push back against misinformation. They can lead and inspire others to do the same. Reading Friedman's analysis made clear the parallels we face in attitudes toward water quality and soil loss. As this book has tried to demonstrate, large segments of our modern agriculture system are willing to either ignore the problems being caused and wish them away or alternatively are satisfied making false and empty claims of progress. The claims are often only possible by ignoring real indicators, such as declining soil health, and instead focusing on other measures, such as the number of farmer meetings held, or reports about what producers say they plan to do, all of some value but without merit as measures of actual progress. This is why having truth tellers in the agricultural water and land debate is so important.

In his book *1000 Years of Joys and Sorrow*, Ai Wei Wei explained how he used his power in challenging the Chinese state. Nicole Hannah-Jones did the same in the *1619 Project*, discomfiting America in the accounting of our history of racism. You don't have to agree with them or accept their views to acknowledge their impact and value in helping change our conversations. It is time for America and for Iowa agriculture, and our use of nature writ large, to be confronted with the reality of history. This is where the work of people like Chris Jones, Art Cullen, and others as truth tellers takes on great importance. Their goal is not to criticize or to tear down, but to challenge us to do better and to use the truth to lead to reflection and change. In his new book *This America of Ours: Bernard and Avis DeVoto and the Forgotten Fight to Save the Wild*, Nate Schweber tells the powerful story of the role the couple played in the post-war years stopping an attempt to remove hundreds of millions of acres of western forest and grazing land from federal control and transfer it to the states and private owners. His series of blockbuster articles in *Harpers* brought the clandestine plans of the western stockmen and Senator McCarran to national attention in time for them to be blocked. Later articles helped prevent the construction of dams in Dinosaur National Park, a plan that if successful would have jeopardized the integrity of every national park in America. The DeVoto's work proved the power and value of truth tellers and the need for voices willing to stand up and protect the public lands. These voices and truth tellers are just as valuable and needed today.

It is easy to understand why agriculture enjoys the status quo and is troubled by those who dare challenge their assumptions. If you start from the position agriculture is blameless in causing challenges to water quality, soil health, climate change, or even rural decline, and instead expect praise and deference as well as compensation for any action you take, then criticism is most unwelcome. Agriculture's fear is these doubters, people who they label incorrectly as hating farmers, might actually be reaching people, causing them to stop and question what may really be causing our problems. Worse if that happens and the number of concerned citizens grows, the public might come to not trust agriculture's claims and even expect it to own up to its impacts. Heaven forbid, this could even lead to the public embracing the utility of regulation or conditioning access to public subsidies, such as for crop insurance or farm supports, on farmers taking active steps to protect water quality and improve soil health. It might mean the public will expect the agribusiness sector to accept responsibility for the central role it plays in creating the economic system locking farmers into their practices. This is what made the video op-ed released by *The New York Times* in February 2021 so important, not just because it visually captured the reality of the current situation but also because *The New York Times* has significant reach through their audience and their role in society.

The River Sees Regulations like Leopold's Stones

By now you know the professor is very taken with the idea regulations are a valuable tool we can use to protect me and water quality. He means well but I don't necessarily share his optimism about your ability to use regulations. My view comes from experience and what I see about how you humans are able to adopt regulations and then find ways to avoid them. For example, you love to set numerical limits in your regulations such as no manure disposal within so many feet of an occupied house, or setting the requirements to have a permit for a livestock facility at some number, let's say 2,400 head of pigs. Then isn't it always interesting how the new design for a hog facility is based on holding 2,390 pigs, a convenient number allowing it to escape the regulation. Of course that's not how it's seen by the person building the operation, their argument is they are in compliance with the law. They just happen to be of a size where the regulations don't apply. My experience is rather than simply substituting numbers for common sense, people need to find ways to take a more holistic view for how you protect the soil and water. It might even start with some idea of morality or as Aldo Leopold liked to say a land ethic—thinking about your impact on land and water in the first place.

Leopold is a good source for this issue because one of his most powerful metaphors was "When the logic of history calls out for bread and all we have are stones, we are at great pains to describe how much the stones resemble bread." Don't your numeric rules of 2,400 pigs resemble a stone more than bread? Rather than regulate livestock operations on their potential environmental impacts you set arbitrary numbers to determine when the rules apply. But do you think the manure from 2,390 pigs smells much different than from 2,400 or the risks to water quality are less? Let alone who goes into the facility to count the number of pigs to determine if a few more head might have slipped in? Your approach makes me wonder if many of your "regulations" are really more for show than good faith attempts to limit and address potential issues.

MEETING WITH MARY SKOPEC AT THE LAKESIDE LAB

To test my belief there are other truth tellers working on water quality I headed to the Iowa Great Lakes to interview someone in a position to know, Mary Skopec head of the Lakeside Lab. I enjoyed our long conversation about the history of the Lakeside Lab and about her personal story. Several years ago Mary left the Department of Natural Resources for her current position with the University of Iowa. She essentially got out when the getting was good, after the department eliminated the $200,000 funding for the IOWATER monitoring program she managed. This citizen science effort engaged hundreds of Iowans in monitoring water quality and trained more each year. Perhaps it's obvious why the program fell in the cross hairs of DNR's "new leadership," one more willing to dance to the tune set by agricultural interests who were concerned all these "citizens" were finding out just how bad Iowa's water quality was. She said it was clear leaders didn't want to know, hear, or say anything about what was truly going on with water quality and in particular the impacts of agriculture. Mary's comments were echoed in a long interview with Alan Bonini who also recently left the DNR after a dozen years in leadership. He believes similar experiences are shared by other senior DNR staff, typically committed environmentalists, who were either forced out or left in disgust.

Mary said we are now in a situation where the young Iowa-born students coming through her classes at the Lakeside Lab can't wait to get out of Iowa. They are anxious to go to Colorado or Oregon or some other place with more nature and a better attitude toward it. I asked how we can change that perspective and how long it might take to do so. This is a question without an easy answer. Our conclusion was, we didn't get into this fix overnight and we won't reverse it quickly, particularly now when the political tide is running against change and with relatively few good ideas as to how, or when it could change. The Iowa Supreme Court's 2021 decision against using the public trust doctrine to protect the Raccoon River, the Bloody Run feedlot permit, and other actions of the general assembly do not point in a hopeful direction. When you throw in increasing land values and the efforts to maintain a commitment to ethanol at all costs, you have a recipe for continued degradation of our soil and water. These are reasons why we must next turn to finding hope!

Finding Hope from Those Who Have Made the Change

Seth Watkins is a farmer, cattleman, environmentalist, and family man. From his Pinhook Farm (pictured on pg. 222) in southwest Iowa near Clarinda, Seth has forged a national following for his clear-eyed explanations about the power of regenerative agriculture. It is a message he delivers in frequent appearances at food and farming conferences and in a well viewed Ted Talk. If you have the good fortune to listen to Seth you will be struck by what motivated him to change his approach toward agriculture. There were several factors but the most important one for he and his wife Christie was concern the serious health issues affecting two of their children were somehow tied to his agricultural practices. Seth found himself asking why am I working against Mother Nature, using all these chemicals? Then during the middle of an Iowa spring blizzard when he found himself faced with trying to save new borne calves, not unlike my father Ham so many years ago, Seth had an "a-ha moment." It was an Epiphany, the time when minds can change, and it changed how Seth will farm for the rest of his life. Not did Seth just switch the timing of when he breeds his cows so they calf in April, he began rethinking his whole operation. Today he would say his main joy is farming with nature, seeing the birds and wildlife in his prairie strips and developing ecologically sound and profitable farming practices, like converting his hilly crop ground back to grass to graze his cows. These are what give him pleasure and hope.

The issue of how and when minds may change takes several ingredients. First, it requires people being willing to change, to think or see things differently, or to be confronted with an existential crisis. Second, you need to consider the obstacles people face in making a change, notably confronting the dogma, the happy talk, the opinions of peers, and the criticism associated when questioning an agricultural practice. One of the main goals of the agricultural dogma is to prevent people like Seth from having this opportunity, to keep folks thinking and walking the party line. The risk is if farmers see a better way then you may lose them. They may consider joining a "radical group" like the Practical Farmers of Iowa, or foregoing the confinement factory route to raise pigs for Niman Ranch, or doing what Seth did by taking a different path for his farming operation. This is one reason why having information about alternatives is so important, so people can have choices, so they might hear different perspectives. Giving voice to other views isn't somehow being disloyal or intentionally confrontational. It is to serve as a truth teller of perspectives other than what the dominant forces, the hegemony, will provide.

The River Hopes you Won't Treat It Like a Roadside Zoo or Puppy Mill

For several years the Iowa Supreme Court dealt with a controversy involving Happy Hollow, a roadside "zoo" and litigation by animal rights organizations to have it closed. Recently the Court ruled the zoo needed to close, and held the owners in contempt and responsible for paying damages, due to the disappearance of many animals after issuance of the close order and their unwillingness to cooperate in identifying where the animals were moved. As sad and disturbing as the case was, a key in the controversy was the apparent failures by USDA inspectors, in renewing the zoo's license even after problems had been identified. Similarly, Iowa Department of Agriculture inspectors involved in the matter seemed to "slow walk" the complaints lodged against the zoo and appeared to run interference for the owners in the legal action. Several common factors are reflected in their attitudes:

• lack of concern for the animals or their welfare,

• failure to carry out administrative responsibilities, as most citizens would interpret them, and

• bias toward the "farmers" and feeling the complainant's demands to protect the animals were the real problem.

Callousness and disregard for the welfare of the animals is bad enough coming from the owners, but even harder to stomach coming from public employees charged with responsibility for ensuring the care and welfare of the animals being ill-housed and cared for in the zoo.

Unfortunately the situation is not unique. The *Des Moines Register* has carried many stories about notorious puppy mills operating in Iowa. One story from October 2021 concerned a federal judge finally stepping in to act against one of Iowa's most notorious and problematic puppy mills. There was a similar vein to the story and the zoo episode. The USDA inspectors had been slow in performing their duties inspecting the operation, even given its long history of problems. Many readers may not realize Iowa has a reputation as one of the worst puppy mill states in the nation. Of course there is an agricultural angle to the story. Over the years when legislative proposals have been introduced to strengthen Iowa's laws to protect animals, regulate puppy mills, and increase penalties for people who abuse animals, agricultural groups have resisted and watered down any legislative changes. Their fears, seemingly as poorly grounded as concerns about other environmental rules, are enhancing animal welfare laws will somehow create potential liability for farmers raising livestock. The opposition is not just mistaken but maliciously immoral in the willingness to place the welfare of innocent animals in the hands of those who prey on them for profit, as in the case of the puppy mills, without consistent and compassionate oversight by regulators.

So the good news is the Iowa courts had the common sense and decency to step in and protect the animals when the owners wouldn't and when the responsible government employees were either unwilling, afraid, or just indifferent. You may wonder why a river is talking about these animals and their care? The reason is simple, the same indifference some people are happy to show their animals is no different than the way many people treat me. Dump in your waste, cave in my banks, channelize me if you need to! How different are these actions than the mistreatment of animals, whether in a roadside zoo or one of Iowa's many puppy mills? The attitudes and actions of many government officials "responsible" for protecting me show the same indifference.

Observations from Afar: What Can We Learn from James Rebanks?

One way to gain new perspectives on a current reality is to consider how similar issues are dealt with in other countries. In that regard, one very insightful voice addressing the challenges faced by farmers using more sustainable and regenerative practices to support their families, is the British hill farmer James Rebanks. He vaulted to international acclaim in 2015 with his best-seller *The Shepherd's Life*, detailing his family and their farm in the Lake District, a portrait heralded as one of the top ten books of the year. In 2020 he followed up with *Pastoral Song: A Farmer's Journey*, a richly woven tale exploring the history of changes in British agriculture and the challenges his family faces bringing more hope and ecological balance to their farm. Reading his book found me underlining many passages and reflecting on how powerful and applicable his observations are to what we face in the US and in Iowa. For example, he states "there is almost no acceptance in farming or in the political sphere that the insatiable pursuit of industrial efficiency on the land might itself be the problem." This amplifies the point made here on several occasions, industrial agriculture believes nothing it ever does is wrong, that is until maybe at some later time when the truth can't be denied, but by then we are typically off to the next shiny distraction.

He reflects on how his father followed the agriculture tradition of adopting new technology and products in the hope of staying profitable, but laments how "there were profoundly important questions about the potential effects of each new technology that it was nobody's job to ask or answer." This is so true about our fascination and attachment with new technologies, our love of can kicking described in Chapter Six. We don't question the potential impacts, and even if we might think about them it's not clear where to ask our questions or who would answer. Our system is the glorious product of free enterprise and a deregulated economy with no precautionary principle.

He explains there is danger in looking at agriculture as a morality tale with good guys or bad guys, when really what we have is people trying to get by with the tools they have available. A good example might be the different perspectives of farmers raising pigs for Niman Ranch and those who dominate Iowa pork production on using gestation crates to confine breeding sows. Niman growers view the practice as inherently inhumane. They supported the California law regulating crates and banning importing pork not conforming to California's rules, in the October 2022 case before the US Supreme Court. On the other hand the Iowa and National pork groups challenged the California law, with the support from the US Department of Justice, arguing it goes too far in regulating how pigs are raised in other states. There are good reasons to believe gestation crates are cruel and inhumane, even if more "efficient" in the number of baby pigs produced. But what danger and damage do we do reducing arguments simply to good and bad? Do we aim our anger at the wrong people, should we direct it at the packing plants and swine integrators rather than the growers? Regardless of your view, Rebanks reminds us "the enduring truth is we all are and always will be complicit (directly or indirectly) in killing for our food, regardless of what we eat." This is a powerful idea, sobering but true, we all—eaters and farmers alike—need to be reminded of, if for no other reason than to dampen our hubris. We need to avoid simplistic, reductionist answers and instead see nature and farming as a system.

Simply abandoning farming doesn't necessarily mean a wild natural system will replace it. Rebanks comments how the Enlightenment suggests most of us have "escaped" from agriculture, and can just "enjoy" nature. But to believe this is true means ignoring the reality others are doing the dirty work for us. He says, "such utopianism speaks to our better selves, but there is a thin line between idealism and bull shit." The truth is we need to put farming and nature back together, not drive them further apart. Unfortunately, as he sees it, the current politics of agriculture and food really fail to address the structural problems of our food system. All the power and profits are taken by larger corporations that care little for the health of people, farms, or ecosystems. Instead, politicians in the UK, just as in the US, focus on subsidies and environmental programs trying to pave over the worst of our problems.

Rebanks is candid in talking about how his type of Hill farming may not be the most productive or efficient even though it is much better for the land, nature, and his family. He acknowledges the farm may not win many prizes or make much money, and "it won't feed the world." His comment on this last point is worth the price of the book, describing it as "the proud boast of the least sustainable farming system." To conclude, Rebanks is optimistic about how farming has changed with more farmers shifting back to their old ways and using more ecological approaches, noting "the fertilizer, medicine, pesticides, fuels, feed, tractors, and machinery we once bought that made our farm lose money have turned out to be the very things that did all of the damage." At several points in talking about how agriculture in the United Kingdom has changed for the worse he equates the experience to ours, saying "the tragedy is we are becoming a second rate version of the broken American Midwest." Observations like this are difficult to read, when our self-image is one of bounty and productivity not as an example of a failing environmentally destructive model. The point is what one sees depends on where you look. There is value in looking at your work from another perspective and through the eyes of others.

NICK OFFERMAN AND FARMING

One of life's great surprises is learning you have new friends and fellow travelers in unlikely places. I had this discovery in December 2021 when I picked up a copy of Nick Offerman's book *Where the Deer and Antelope Play*. I wasn't very familiar with him or a fan, as we didn't watch his hit TV show *Parks and Rec*, but my respect for him changed reading his book and others he has written. He writes largely about his love and respect for the land, quoting at length from people like Wendell Berry and Aldo Leopold who have influenced him. How can you not like someone when you share many of the same heroes? I didn't expect to find these themes, at least not given the book's title, but I suppose his publisher resisted a more accurate one, like *Nick Offerman reflects on sustainable agriculture and the land ethic!*

In fact the connections between his thinking and mine are even stronger, as he writes at length about how he found James Rebanks the British farmer you just met. The difference in our experience is Rebanks' writings have moved me from afar. Offerman's experience has been much different. He has taken the opportunity to visit the Rebanks farm while filming in the United Kingdom and has developed a strong friendship and bond with him and his family. He has gone so far as to own some of the beautiful belted Galloway cattle grazing on Rebanks Hill farm. If you are looking for an entertaining read filled with sharp political observations I encourage you to check out any of the Offerman oeuvre.

Offerman has a funny, off kilter way of describing things, but if his politics align with yours you will be rewarded. His working class, farm boy, Midwestern sensibilities are refracted through his own financial success and fame, providing an interesting point of contrast to what he sees happening in US politics and popular culture. His book *Gumption* is a series of chapters about people he sees as important to our history, in many ways his heroes. Of course it includes descriptions of Aldo Leopold and Wendell Berry as well as other political figures. I was most struck learning about Frederick Douglass. Consider this quotation from Douglas:

> If there is no struggle, there is no progress. Those who profess to favor freedom and yet depreciate agitation, are men who want crops without plowing the ground. They want rain without thunder and lightning. They want the ocean without the awful roar of its waters. This struggle may be a moral one; or it may be a physical one; or it may be both moral and physical; but it must be a struggle. Power concedes nothing without a demand. It never did and it never will.

Clearly, Frederick Douglass's statement about what is involved in the struggle is applicable to our debates about protecting the rivers, soil, and the land. Here is another important Frederick Douglass quote:

> In thinking of America, I sometimes find myself admiring her blue sky, her grand old woods, her fertile fields, her beautiful rivers, her mighty lands, and star crowned mountains. But my rapture is soon checked, my joy is soon turned to mourning when I remember that all is cursed with infernal actions of slaveholding, robbery, and wrong; when I remember that with the waters of her noblest riv-

ers, the tears of my brethren are borne to the ocean, disregarded and forgotten, and that her most fertile fields drank daily of the warm blood of my outraged sisters; I am filled with un-alterable loathing.

I am not ashamed to owe a debt to Nick Offerman for opening my eyes to Fredrick Douglas. We must never be too old to learn, regardless of the source.

The River on Why We Need Bridges

If you get a chance to see me it's most likely as you pass over on a bridge. You might even sit up and strain to look over the guardrails to see if I have much water or character. If you are a paddler you know how important bridges can be, they serve as way markers so you know where you are to judge your progress, and they serve as logical places for putting in or taking out. I've been thinking about bridges lately and their importance in connecting us across a divide. It may be physical but it can be mental, a thought that's difficult to accept. New land, new opportunities, and new ideas might exist if we can cross to the other side.

The image of a bridge is a helpful way to envision a challenge you face shaping the future of agricultural policy and how you will use the billions in public money you spend subsidizing agriculture. On the side where you are now, the money goes for things like crop insurance, price support payments, trade war compensation, and even disaster assistance for floods and droughts. These dollars and programs help lock you into your "all corn and soybean" diet with your foot always on the accelerator for more yields, more productivity, and more acres. The resulting demand for more fertilizer, more pesticides, bigger fields and higher rents, are washed out as a guzzle of ethanol, coated with a frosting layer of hog manure. This is the system society is increasingly recognizing as destructive of the soil, water, estuaries, rivers, and wildlife. This is the farming system you seem locked into, and like most prisoners, whether voluntary or involuntary, it can be hard to break the lock, or loosen the chains to find a way out to try something new.

On the other side of the divide, on the far bank there are promises of new opportunities—for income, for the environment, and for your own enjoyment, welfare, and peace of mind. The challenge of climate change makes it vital you consider how farming can change to be better for the land, the environment, for public good, and the climate and of course for yourselves. Some changes are relatively easy to make—planting cover crops so fields don't lay bare after harvest, using growing plants to absorb the excess nitrogen available in the soil. The exciting news is more farmers are taking these steps and each fall after harvest more fields are blanketed with cover crops. Small changes like this are like the first steps out onto the bridge. When the steps don't cause you to fall in, and even prove of value, it makes the next steps easier. Other steps may be more costly, like retiring marginal land from cropping to plant prairie strips, and some new tools may still be evolving like our understanding how soil health and carbon work together. Like any bridge this one has to be built one beam and one girder at a time all in line with a design, hopefully one to support its weight, stand the test of time, and get people to the other side. This is where you may be with your agricultural policy, an inflection point when new opportunities beckon testing the inertia of the status quo.

You see the need for a bridge in part because the side of the riverbank you are standing on is beginning to erode. You will always have a farm policy where growing corn and beans will play important roles, but you recognize more is needed. You recognize bridges will be critical to mitigate and stabilize the changes you are experiencing from the changing climate. You hope by taking steps now you can promote the longevity of farming and the productivity of your land.

You realize the vital role the public has played, today and over history, supporting agriculture and the institutional structure you used to build your system—the farm programs, crop insurance, land-grant universities, and public research. But you know these systems are under stress and the public expects its money will be used wisely to address evolving public needs. All these are reasons to consider how to cross to the other side, how to build your bridge. Any new journey or effort is difficult to begin even when you recognize the need to start. Once you begin you may find the distance you have to bridge isn't that great from a practical or policy viewpoint. Much of the structure may already be in place, your conservation programs, options for working lands like the conservation security program, and new soil health efforts of the USDA. Even the initial forays into considering carbon as a commodity are important steps on the bridge. All provide a structure to step out onto, to test and see what weight they hold, and to gauge what new decking can be put down to extend their reach.

When it comes to policy, a generation of researchers have labored under the banner of sustainable agriculture and their efforts are bearing fruit. Planting prairie strips to improve water quality, using data analytics to identify the unproductive fields that can be put to natural uses, and improved nitrogen management to reduce water pollution, are all being proven up. Intellectually, a new generation of progressive farmers and researchers are rallying under the banner of regenerative agriculture and focusing on soil health as a lens to see a different and better future. These are the people already on the other side of the bridge beckoning you to join them. They are building their part of the bridge and reaching back across for you and others to join in this project of change.

Iowa Needs More Imagination and Big Ideas

As we think about our future, one important ingredient will be identifying projects and activities with the scale to improve our water and land situation and with the excitement to inspire and engage large numbers of citizens. As I see it Iowa needs more imagination for how we can use our natural resources, our creativity, and our wisdom to use and improve our rivers and lands. Part of seeking imagination has to deal with scale, with big ideas, ones that can be transformative, helping inspire and motivate others to act, whether as communities, individuals, or organizations. Iowa has a number of examples of these big ideas, ones by their creativity and impact going beyond the normal range of our activities.

The Greater Des Moines River Trail network project, now known as ICON, is a perfect example of a big idea, one showing what is possible when leadership, funding, and local governments can be harnessed together. This $120 million project is designed to improve the opportunities for people to recreate and connect with the rivers and streams flowing in the greater Des Moines region. The effort has been spearheaded by local businesses, most notably by Rick Tollackson and Hubbell Homes. Over $80 million of private contributions and federal, state, and local grants have already been secured to implement a range of activities. Most notable are the significant changes planned for the dams on the Des Moines River in the center of the city. The goal is to open the river for recreation by creating a white water course to engage water enthusiasts of all ages and skills. These large-scale improvements on the Raccoon and the Des Moines rivers will make it possible for citizens of all ages to see and use the rivers as welcoming recreational opportunities and as natural resources to enjoy. The

ICON project is weaving together the work of businesses, organizations, and local governments to implement a larger collective vision for connecting citizens to the rivers.

Another example of a big idea is what the Garst family has created on their lands near Coon Rapids. Over 5,000 acres have been transferred to the Whiterock Conservancy, the largest family created land trust in the state. Whiterock is involved in protecting miles of the Raccoon River flowing through its valleys, hundreds of acres of oak savannas, and other natural features, as well as active farmland being stewarded with state-of-the-art resilient agriculture practices. Miles of recreation trails for bikers, hikers, riders, and four wheelers, are woven throughout the property, blended with campsites, historic cabins, and other opportunities for people to enjoy one of the largest and most pristine pieces of privately owned land in the state. The Garst family, long known for their historic role in Iowa agriculture, recently pioneered another creative method to protect the land. In the fall of 2021 when the decision was made to sell almost 2,000 acres of family owned crop ground, the Garst family worked with lawyers and advisors to develop a conservation easement tied to the land being sold, designed to project into the future the soil health and land protection practices they have implemented. By doing so, the Garst's demonstrated how a long-term commitment to protecting land can be achieved, even if it does mean the land may not sell for the highest price as if unencumbered. Their decision to implement the conservation easement illustrates a level of commitment to land stewardship that should inspire other Iowans interested in the future of this land.

The Garst activity at Whiterock is not the only example of how an Iowa family has used their history on the land and their personal resources to create an inspiring and long lasting component of Iowa's land legacy. Two miles south of Dallas Center the 250-acre Brenton Arboretum is a beautifully landscaped tract of former crop ground now planted with hundreds of species of trees from across the globe. What began with the activities of Buzz Brenton, patriarch of the well-known central Iowa family most famous for banking, has evolved over the

years into a widely known and well-loved feature of the central Iowa landscape. When he began, his goal was to plant a variety of trees. But as with many things,  planting a few tree species led to planting a few more. And planting more led to recognizing the need to develop a master plan for how the rolling hills and streams could be designed into a living educational classroom for the generations who follow. Now 25 years into this exercise, the Brentons have created an invaluable and unique example of natural systems of trees, prairie, wetlands, ponds, and streams. The Arboretum is somewhat incongruent, nestled among miles of corn, but it gives those who walk its trails and see the diversity of the trees, insight into what nature holds and inspiration for thinking about the future of their own land holdings, large or small.

Big ideas don't only come with individual projects located on designated patches of land, big ideas can be found in new ways of thinking and approaches to how we can enhance our efforts to protect land and water and improve our agricultural systems. The Iowa Soybean Association has accomplished just this idea, by developing the Agricultural Outcomes project. This initiative is working with hundreds of individual farmers and landowners to improve the management of their land to improve soil health, protect water quality, reduce fertilizer use, and to sequester carbon. Participating farmers receive per acre payments based on the practices they implement. Funding is provided by participating corporations, such as Cargill and PepsiCo, interested in supporting improved and regenerative agricultural practices as a way to reduce the CO_2 emissions related to their own business activities. Local governments like the city of Cedar Rapids with its interest in controlling flooding on the upstream rivers, and the state of Iowa with its interest in water quality, have also provided funding. The national significance of the effort is reflected in the decision by USDA in September 2022 to award almost $100 million to expand the work of the Ag Outcomes fund into other Midwestern states. By illustrating how private industry, farm organizations, communities, and farmers can work together to promote the adoption of improved farming practices, the Ag Outcomes fund is helping illuminate an innovative alternative to using regulatory-based government programs which carry their own political risks and friction. By engaging farmers through voluntary, economic incentive-based efforts the Ag Outcomes fund is showing how better farming practices can be implemented at scale if there is a vision and plan.

BIG IDEAS IOWANS CAN CONSIDER

The examples above are real and underway, raising hopes for their success. But what about the future—what other "big ideas" could the state consider, ones to help transform current efforts and transcend some of our divisions? I make no claim to being a visionary or to the ability to foretell the future—but like many of you, I do like to dream, to think about new ideas and projects. The following are examples of two "Big Ideas" I believe Iowans should embrace.

After visiting the Upper Iowa River near Decorah in spring 2022, I traveled to far Southwest Iowa along the Missouri River. My goal was to visit Waubonsie State Park, another wonderful example how the INHF helped expand Iowa's public lands. Several years ago the Boy Scouts decided to decommission Camp Washita, adjacent to the Waubonsie. They worked with the foundation and the state to add roughly 1,000 acres to the existing park. My reason for visiting was because Waubonsie sits at the southern end of the Loess Hills and walking the front ridgeline trail means you can overlook the wide Missouri River Valley.

The Loess Hills are Iowa's most unique geological landform, a roughly 200-mile-long range of hills and bluffs rising up to 400 feet above the flood plain, constructed from stacked soil particles windblown from the bed of a vast lake. Loess Hills appear in only two places: in western Iowa and along the Yellow River in China. The Loess Hills have presented an intriguing opportunity for Iowans for decades and many ideas for protecting and preserving them have been suggested. The state has acquired many parcels now managed as parts of the Loess Hills State Forest. In addition, several state parks are located there, including Preparation Canyon, used as a staging ground by the Mormons in their trek West in the late 1840s, and Stone State Park on the northern edge of Sioux City. Thankfully several counties located in the hills have acquired and protected portions as county parks, especially on the west facing ridgeline.

Even with these examples, the larger idea of protecting the entire Loess Hills landform has been predictably controversial, but that hasn't stopped people from trying. In the late 1990s the *Des Moines*

Register campaigned to protect them. In the 1990's the National Park Service conducted a planning initiative to identify whether or not the region was suited for designation as an extensive multi-unit National Park. The results were National Park status was not possible, largely due to the high percentage of private land ownership in the area, over 90% in most places. Most landowners and county governments were uniformly opposed to any national park designation. The opposition, partly based on fears the federal government was going to engage in a land grab, taking land away from owners, foreshadowed the opposition many park and public land proposals face today. The local resistance in the Loess Hills was not unlike the experience along the Upper Iowa River, and the potential scenic river designation in the 1970's. Both episodes fit Iowa's history of missing significant resource protection opportunities, notably the failed effort to create the Hawkeye National Forest in southeast Iowa at the end of the Depression.

Even with the backdrop of local opposition to more extensive preservation, the reality on the ground is many landowners, residents, and local governments appreciate the unique significance of the Loess Hills. The reality is—the Loess Hills are resilient—and unless we allow them to be mined as fill dirt for housing developments, or otherwise destroyed, such as past proposals to use the canyons as landfills, they will continue to exist. The hundreds of landowners with historic and sentimental ties to the hills are an important factor helping ensure their existence.

The opportunity that attracted my visit was the idea of creating a linear trail along the ridgeline of the bluffs. A LoHi trail which could run from the southern end, starting in Waubonsie State Park and proceed almost 200 miles north to Sioux City where Stone State Park could serve as a northern terminus. The LoHi trail could be Iowa's version of the Appalachian Trail. A linear park could weave together the various pieces of public land, already in state and county parks, along with privately owned but protected land, such as parcels under easements to the INHF and the Nature Conservancy.

Such a long distance trail is not just an intriguing opportunity, a trail may be more acceptable to local residents. It is certainly more feasible and less costly than large-scale public acquisition. Several factors make a LoHi trail the type of big idea Iowa should pursue:

1) The Loess Hills are one of Iowa's and the nation's most unique natural features, and

2) Are geographically contained and identifiable, only 200 miles long in a corridor roughly 5 to 10 miles wide, above the Missouri Valley floodplain. Many existing pieces, already in public ownership or protected, can serve as pearls on the potential necklace of a linear trail, and recognition of the unique value of the hills is reflected in county conservation boards acquiring properties along the ridgeline, and developing segments of a trail system,

3) The history of resistance to large-scale protection efforts creates a context to develop a more acceptable vision for a relatively low impact, low cost trail system, using a narrow trail corridor, only a few yards wide, combining public land and easements on private land,

4) The success and economic development of existing bike trails like the Wabash Trace at the southern end of the Loess Hills, and of other long-distance national trails most notably the Appalachian Trail, show the potential for local communities and residents, and

5) The project would involve an identifiable number of property owners and public bodies, making a project more achievable and creating the opportunity to use alternative routes such as secondary roads to complete a project.

The great idea behind the LoHi trail is it represents a big vision, the type of big idea and big dream Iowa needs to pursue. In fall 2022 the opportunity to expand efforts to create a LoHi trail got a significant boost when the Boy Scouts announced they entered an agreement with the INHF to sell the 1,800 acre Little Sioux Scout Ranch. Sale of the camp, perhaps the largest contiguous tract of privately owned forest in the Loess Hills, to the INHF means the property will be preserved, rather than parceled for development. It will be open to the public, possibly by a transfer to the State, as an addition to the surrounding Loess Hills State Forest. Twenty-six miles of trail now transect the camp, making the Little Sioux Scout Ranch one more pearl on the necklace, bringing the LoHi trail a step closer to reality.

PLANNING A SUMMIT ON NATURE IN IOWA

I have spent much of the last three years writing and thinking about Iowa's water and land, traveling the state to see it and talking to many Iowans about what we need for our future. The key questions are how can we energize new action and awareness about our wealth of nature and what can we do to enhance and protect it? My experiences leave me in awe of the breadth and richness of Iowa's natural world and by the multitude of individuals and organizations working to improve our opportunities. Given their scale and energy it is surprising how slow our progress is and how demoralized many people appear. The "Big Idea" emerging from this is to imagine what might be possible if we bring all the elements of Iowa's nature, individuals and organizations alike, together in an Iowa Nature Summit? Participants can share their work, identify our challenges, develop common efforts, and set a plan for the future, a plan underpinned by concrete commitments of action participants will take in the months and years ahead.

Just picture it—a two-day Iowa Nature Summit held in late Fall 2023, bringing together hundreds of citizens from across the state, all working with nature in some way. The breadth of topics is exciting and surprising—prairie enthusiasts and bird watchers, county conservation boards and local tourism officials, as well as hikers, bikers, and paddlers will all be there. As will those working to protect and restore our rivers, lakes, wetlands, and forests. Connections with nature will be reflected through the arts, culture, history, and faith, as will the fundamental roles of farming, food, land, soil, and health. Those working on environmental policy and land protection, the land trusts like Iowa Natural Heritage Foundation and environmental groups like the Ikes and the Iowa Environmental Council, will all be at the Summit. The public bodies responsible to nature, the water works, the conservation boards, and the state DNR will all play a role. As will the education sector, college and university professors, student environmental and wildlife clubs, and youth involved in 4-H, FFA, and scouting interested in Iowa's natural world. The call to participate will be open and ecumenical, the only requirement being a commitment to work in good faith to protect and enhance Iowa's nature.

A gathering of this type and scale has not happened in my lifetime, and perhaps never in our state but that does not mean a Summit on Nature in Iowa is not possible. What might come from it you ask? That is hard to predict until it is planned and takes place, but how could the results and outcomes detract from our work? If participants come in good spirit, ready to share, to learn, and to think creatively and optimistically about Iowa's nature and what we can do to protect and enhance it, the potential is unlimited.

Such a Summit will help us realize the breadth and depth of our collective work. It will help illuminate the connections between many nature issues, ones we may think are unrelated. It will demonstrate to politicians and the public not just that Iowa is rich in nature, but that Iowans care passionately about it. A Summit can only serve to increase our awareness, open new lines of communication and cooperation among participants, and inspire even stronger, collaborative efforts. If individuals and organizations desiring to participate are willing to make specific and concrete commitments about their future work, real and measurable actions should result. The acres of land protected, the new wetlands constructed, the prairies restored, the miles of trail built and marked, are all just examples of the actions many participants now take. The Summit could serve as a milepost and lay down a marker for our progress in the years ahead.

If Iowans want to enjoy a more beautiful, healthy, and sustainable natural world, we need to move on from our current reality, the doldrums seeming to slow our pace and sap our energy. Our status quo for nature can not be worrying about the next shoe to drop or bad idea or law coming from those who do not share our values and respect for nature. Instead of fearing the next problem, we need to lace up our boots, renew our commitments, reflect on our state's legacy of leadership in conservation and stewardship, and then chart the new course. Clearly, one meeting—call it a Summit, a Congress, or whatever—won't by itself achieve our goals but I have no doubt it is a good place to start.

Exploring the ICON water trail. Murray Hill Scenic Overlook

Chapter Ten—What Does the River Know?

CONNECTING WITH THE RIVER

In many ways our journey began on the river, paddling on the Raccoon looking for inspiration and even enlightenment. The river has been a faithful companion sharing its insights and perspectives, giving us another way to approach these issues. As our time together draws to a close it seemed only fitting to return to the river—this time the Mississippi. In early October 2022 I traveled to LeClaire just north of Davenport, and boarded the Riverboat Twilight (pictured on pg. 182) for a two-day excursion north. The first day was 83 miles upriver with the evening spent in Dubuque's Grand Harbor Hotel, returning south the next day. It was a fascinating trip and one anyone interested in the river and nature should consider taking. The 120 of us on the excursion enjoyed hours of riverside scenery on two cool sunlit days, as well as a fascinating and educational narration from the owner-captain, and surprisingly delicious food. The tree lined bluffs were beginning their extravagant turn to fall colors and the pelicans, eagles, coots, and other birds were regular companions.

River travel may tempt one toward profundity, something writers should avoid, but let me claim these two exemptions. First, spend an hour on the Mississippi and you will be impressed by the vital role it plays in the nation's economy. Riverside factories producing an array of goods from molasses to scotch tape, barge fleets laden with newly harvested grain headed toward the Gulf, history filled river towns like Clinton, once the nation's center for lumber milling and minting new millionaires, are all just part of the hum of commerce passing by. Second, on the Upper Mississippi, citizens are connected to the river in ways not possible on the lower reaches. In his entrancing new book *Life on the Mississippi,* Rinker Buck tells the story of building a flatboat and launching it on a journey down the Ohio to Cairo and then a thousand miles south on the Mississippi to New Orleans. His richly told adventure, a water-based follow up to his 2014 *Oregon Trail,* is filled with history and encounters but one observation was surprisingly poignant. He notes how on the lower Mississippi below St. Louis, citizens and communities are essentially walled off from any connections to the river. The height of the riverside dikes, towering 90 feet in some places, and the Army Corp's success in channelizing and controlling the river to harness it for navigation render it largely inaccessible for recreation and enjoying nature. No quaint riverside towns like LeClaire or Bellevue, or cities like Dubuque welcoming boats to tie up in downtown harbors near the center of town. No regular traffic of fishermen and pleasure boaters greeted Buck on his journey south. The priority the Corps gives to barges and flood control is understandable, but it has come with many costs, not the least of which is severing the people from the river. The river knows this separation, this estrangement, contributes to us viewing the river guardedly as a flooding threat, rather than welcoming it as a friend and warehouse of nature.

The River Finds A Friend

I know the river needs friends and it would be hard to find a better one than Mike Delaney. Not just does he own a stretch of land along my banks south of Minden, land he is restoring to Prairie, he also founded the Raccoon River Watershed Association back in 2005. This volunteer nonprofit group brings together neighbors, conservationists, local officials, and anyone interested in the health, history, and future of the North Raccoon River to learn, to share, and to advocate for me. Now that is what I mean by having friends.

Mike left, with author, and Ty Smedes right

You know it didn't have to be like this for Mike, now retired after a long career teaching sociology at DMACC. He grew up fishing and spending time at his family's lake cabin in Northeast Indiana and had become an avid paddler. Over 30 years ago when he and his wife Dell began thinking of buying their own piece of Iowa as a nature retreat, friends took them to Decorah with all it has to offer. But they concluded it was too far away for a real connection, so instead they drew a circle 100 miles around Des Moines and set out looking for land. In a matter of weeks a realtor in nearby Dallas Center called about a 30-acre tract split by a river, you guessed it, me!

The rest is history as the saying goes. Working to restore the prairie, planting an orchard, eventually building a cabin for weekend visits, their lives took on a pattern familiar to anyone who has followed their dream of "having a place in the country." A few years later when the adjoining 30-acre farm field became available they bought it and were able to plant it to create a first class prairie. During these decades they fell in love with their land and with me. While people like to think you are the ones making the decisions, "we bought that field in..." Who knows, maybe the process really works the other way around. Rather than you buying the land, could it be the land selects you! I certainly like to think the river played a major role in Mike Delaney's decision to "buy" me and what an investment he has been! He is showing through his deeds what a true friend is. As creator of the SPARKS, the group of elders working to influence Iowans on the environment, as a leader in the Izaak Walton League working to revitalize this historic group with new ideas and new members, and as a frequent public voice, Mike Delaney is just the type of friend the river needs. My hope is his work and that of his colleagues can inspire more of you to pick up the fight for my future, as well as your own.

WHAT IF WE HAD A NATIONAL SOIL LAW?

A former law student recently returned to Iowa for a visit from her current residence in the European Union. She has been away for almost ten years working on a series of environmental and agriculture projects in several European countries. As we talked she explained her work for an international journal on the subject of soil law and policy. I asked her whether there was a comma between soil and law and she said no the subject is actually "soil law." I told her this was an interesting terminology, one I had never heard used in the context of United States law. While we have soil conservation laws and other laws dealing with soil we never frame the discussion in the context of "soil law." One challenge under American law is soil is not treated the same as air and water. It is not considered a public resource, but instead is treated as part of real property. Real property law is a question of state law in the US and there is no federal law directly applicable to soil. What might be different if we had a soil law?

If we treated soil like the water, as a form of *res publica* rather than as private property and just one dimension of land ownership, a number of things might change. One effect of considering soil as property is we essentially treat it like coal or timber, an extractive resource. You can sell it by the truckload for fill or you can let it erode away, and no one can do anything about it. That is unless they can prove you are somehow harming their property. Under Iowa soil conservation law, if you silt in the neighbor's waterway they may bring an action. Under nuisance law if you remove the lateral support so a building's foundation is endangered that may be actionable, just as are questions of altering the drainage, or filling in a road ditch. But if you simply silt in a river or a reservoir there is no real legal cause of action available. Even if there were, the questions would shift to identifying whose soil caused the problem and how to hold them responsible? Soil is treated much like a form of nonpoint source water pollution, a legal distinction without much scientific basis but of great legal significance in shielding those who lose soil or pollute water from any consequences. Think how things might change if we considered soil a public resource as opposed to just a form of private property.

In Pinker's book on the *Enlightenment*, the chapter on reason addresses how society uses reasoning to make advances. One valuable aspect of reasoning is being able to make predictions as a way to test science and evaluate our actions. He writes, "the acid test of empirical rationality is prediction. Science proceeds by testing the predictions of hypotheses." This is an interesting idea to consider as it applies in the agriculture and water quality context for at least two reasons. First, what can we predict will be the outcome of the policies we adopt, and second how do the predicted problems and other ill effects politicians often make about environmental programs, hold up to scrutiny, such as labeling voluntary conservation programs as "land grabs?"

One value of considering what results are predictable from the policies we enact is how it helps explain our relative lack of progress on water quality issues. When we begin by making compliance with the law entirely voluntary should we be surprised if people don't change their behavior? The following is what the river thinks about this issue of our predictable results.

The River Wonders, Are You Really Serious?

Based on your history of progress, or lack thereof, in protecting the quality of the water flowing through me and in addressing soil conservation, I need to ask a very fundamental question, are you really serious, or are you just going through the motions and fooling yourselves? Here are several reasons why it appears to me you may not be serious:

First, you employ approaches predictably ineffective at any scale, ones based more on faith and "magical thinking" or spurious non-scientific distinctions like treating "nonpoint source pollution" differently than point sources, even when much of your "nonpoint" pollution comes out of pipes, like tile outlets.

Second, you reject using regulatory authority, even though

it is your society's most common and effective tool to change behavior. Instead you say the best approach is to rely on voluntary action by individuals, even when economic incentives and peer group pressures are against acting.

Third, you do not promote adopting the best scientific approaches or using tools to limit the impact on environmental resources, like improved fertilizer management and reduced tillage, meaning you don't even use what you know works.

Fourth, you fail to provide adequate staff or funding for the soil and water conservation programs you do make available, forcing applicants to compete for funding rather than working with everyone who volunteers!

Fifth, you make no effort to establish timelines, goals, or set priorities, for when your efforts will be successful, or even provide a distilled vision of what success might look like. In effect, no one can even say how society might benefit if your programs work.

Finally, rather than evaluate how well your programs work, and recalibrate the efforts if they are falling short, or try new technologies or alternatives, you instead most often either double down on what isn't working, or move on to new issues and distractions. I can see this happening now in the rapid shift of attention and funding to addressing climate change and sequestering carbon, while long-term soil conservation goals remain unfulfilled. Based on this litany, the fatigue and frustration I can see setting in among the public and those most concerned about environmental issues, are predictable.

LEADERSHIP AND PAUL JOHNSON

A critical issue in Iowa's land and water story is our need for leadership, as well as our need for vision and priorities. These needs have come into sharper focus in recent years with a number of developments, two from the summer of 2021. The first was the Iowa Supreme Court's rejection of the public trust doctrine to review the DNR's lack of rules to protect the Raccoon River, a decision discussed previously. The second concerned the DNR permit for the cattle feedlot near Bloody Run Creek. The question in summer 2021 was a petition asking the DNR director to review the agency decision, but she rejected the petition on the grounds she had no power or discretion to review or reverse decisions made by her staff

These results made me think about how differently the matters might have been resolved if a law the legislature passed in 1989 had gone into effect. The law was authored by Representative Paul Johnson, a well-known environmental advocate and Leopoldian from the Decorah area. It was designed to create an independent office of the environmental advocate who could serve as an intervener in legal proceedings to represent the interests of natural resources such as our soil, land, and water. The law was one of the most progressive at the time on the concept of the rights of nature. No surprise, it was not well received by conservatives and those who feared the progression of environmental protections. Then governor Terry Branstad, vetoed the legislation, saying it was unnecessary, in part because Iowa's environmental laws were adequate. He said a cops and robbers approach to environmental protection was not something the state needed. The 30 years since show both how wrong he was concerning the adequacy of our laws or our willingness to enforce them, and how valuable such an office would be to our state. An environmental advocate would no doubt have been involved in the public trust doctrine case, or more likely would have worked with the Department of Natural Resources to ensure water quality protections had been enacted for the Raccoon, as opposed to leaving them to the voluntary desires of landowners and others who live along the river. Similarly the office of the environmental advocate would have been available to represent the interests of Bloody Run Creek. Instead, Iowa has an agency head who claims she is powerless to review what many believe were egregious rule violations in approving the cattle feedlot permit, and we have a state Supreme Court unwilling to intervene on behalf of the river.

Paul Johnson died in 2021 and in a remembrance of him for the Iowa Natural Heritage Foundation, I noted his importance to Iowa's natural resource history. In his role as a legislator he understood the power of law to establish guidelines for society. He was the driving force behind the 1987 groundwater protection act which among other things created the Leopold Center for Sustainable Agriculture at Iowa State University. He was responsible for developing REAP, the resource enhancement and protection program that has put several hundred million dollars to work in thousands of projects all across the state connecting citizens with nature. Paul's life and work show the incredible value one voice and one person can have when speaking for nature. His record contrasts starkly to the governor who vetoed the environmental advocate law, a record showing little regard for the state's natural resources. The lesson for us today is our message can't just be a litany of "woe is me what might have been." Instead the message should be "it's not too late, we still have work to do." His life and accomplishments show what is possible and prove there is room for new Paul Johnsons.

The good news is his friends and family have formed an organization to forward his legacy, in particular his belief in a private lands conservation initiative. In October 2022 they organized a conference to expand on Paul's ideas. Former Senator Tom Harkin and Secretary of Agriculture Tom Vilsack were there to honor Paul and to speak to his role in land stewardship. Over one hundred friends, family, and admirers were there to consider what might be possible. While the effort is a work in progress, it was exciting to learn one of the first actions has been to provide funding for several students pursuing careers in natural resource policy. Paul knew, as should we all, our time here is limited and the future will only be bright if we empower the next generation of leaders to continue this work.

THOUGHTS ON WHAT *THE RIVER KNOWS*

Given the title, one question to answer is what exactly does the river know? There are many ways to answer the question but here is a list of six things I believe the river knows. Then we will hear how the river answers the same question.

First, the river knows it has friends but it needs many more to develop and implement the programs needed to protect it and to realize its potential. There is only so much the river can do by itself, it can flow and persevere, but much of the rest is up to us.

Second, the river believes we are in a period of confusion, we say we love the land, the soil, and water, but do little to show our love in any active sense. Now with the climate challenge before us we seem most interested in using it as an opportunity for new income, rather than actually doing something for the water or land.

Third, the river knows we seem to have no limits—on the number of pigs, the acres of corn, or using more fertilizer, and we don't expect—or respect—anyone to suggest there are any limits to modern farming. We have hitched our fates to intensive farming practices and technologies ultimately unhealthy for us and the river: ethanol, fall tillage, neonic seed coatings, increased pesticide reliance, and unlimited livestock expansion.

Fourth, the river is heartened by the number of farmers coming to value soil health, water management, and resilient agriculture, but it knows their numbers are limited and growing too slowly. It is glad for private efforts like the Iowa Soybean Association's Agricultural Outcomes fund, helping farmers improve soil and water, and showing how progress can be made. Their example proves more can be achieved if we have the will.

Fifth, the river sees the institutions who should be its friends hamstrung by structural limits, like the soil and water conservation districts, by political restraints as with the Department of Natural Resources, or by a lack of vision as with the drainage districts, making it unclear who the river can look to for help.

Sixth and finally, the river is encouraged by how local governments, city councils, county conservation boards, boards of supervisors, and voters are willing to step up. By allocating American Rescue Plan Act dollars to nature and by passing local bond issues to fund conservation, local officials and citizens are showing the way, even while the state and federal governments seem increasingly impotent, strangled by political division and anti-public ideologies.

What Does the River Really Know?

A hat tip to the Professor for suggesting a list of what I know. He has captured much truth but his ideas don't focus on action. That is what I need—action! I need the type of force a good flood can bring, to wash away bad habits and patterns of thought. Here is what I know:

First, Iowa needs clearer thinking and a better plan for nature and for farming. Many of the things Professor Waller wrote about 30 years ago are true today, just as are the images drawn by Ding Darling in the 1930's. Your view of domination—of riding and working the land and water as if we were horses in your stable—is at the root of your problems. The issues and answers always begin with you and never me or the land.

Second, Iowa needs more imagination and bigger ideas to inspire people and improve their lives while at the same time respecting the land and water. The ideas are out there and many examples were detailed in the previous chapter. I won't belabor them here other than to note how they illuminate what can be done, how the opportunities before you are not limited to only growing more corn and beans, your century-long infatuation, but go much broader and deeper into your relation with nature. Years ago the Professor taught a class "Rural Lands and Rural Livelihoods," noting how you could weave a whole new set of nature-based economic activities into your rural agricultural structure, if you had the vision.

Third, Iowa needs to seize the opportunity of new attention to the climate to reclaim your legacy of leadership in soil and water stewardship. The opportunities before you have the potential to be transformative if you focus on homegrown solutions designed to distribute the benefits and actions across the landscape, engaging every farm if possible. Don't let the opportunity devolve into a dollar chase, where political debates over how to value and market carbon credits, overwhelms both the scientific understanding of how soils work and the practical benefits of caring for the land.

Fourth, you need to quit fooling yourself with false claims of progress and consider the realities of what is happening to the land and water. Your self-image as good stewards and claims of progress can blind you to the real opportunities. You are smarter than you are showing. Only by accepting reality will you recognize the need for action and the true scale of your challenges. Then the value of new opportunities will be crystallized.

Fifth, Iowa needs to welcome new people to continue your history of immigration that made you strong. Whether it is the surge in Hispanic families giving new life to Perry, Storm Lake, and Denison or the legions fleeing conflicts in the Balkans or unrest in Africa, these new Iowans share invaluable traits and strengths you need. A strong work ethic, a desire to build better lives for their families, an entrepreneurial spirit, and a generational commitment—these traits are common with Iowa's new immigrants and part of your heritage. I recently learned about a new initiative In Harmony Farm located only a few miles from my banks near Earlham in Dallas County. It is designed as an incubator farm for new immigrant families who completed a training period on smaller urban farms but are now ready to move to larger operations. The exciting project was made possible through the philanthropy of a local couple. As a river, I am excited to hear new voices and have these families out on the land. From my perspective, it is just as rewarding to hear a family from Burundi as they tend the crops and feed their families as it was 150 years ago to hear the Danish of the Professor's ancestors. There really is no difference or shouldn't be, unless you think the color of their skin or continent of their origin is significant. The river knows these don't matter as does the land. It is well past time more Iowans realized it too.

Sixth, regardless what label you use, Iowa needs a set of accepted guidelines or regulations for stewarding the land and water, otherwise you will always start from zero. One of the farming community's greatest successes and perhaps its most dangerous action for rivers and society is the "no role for regulation" mantra it repeats at every turn. Politicians appear happy to kneel at this alter, even elevating it into state law. But it is a fool's errand, explaining why your efforts like the Nutrient Reduction Strategy can never succeed. Without any ability to say no, to limit the use of harmful practices, fall tillage for example, your progress will always be measured by the actions of those who care the least, not the good stewards who care the most. Worse yet your failure to establish basic minimal expectations for protecting the water and land mean whenever local conservation officials propose a new project, such as constructing a wetland, they first must convince landowners they even need to act, usually facilitated with public funds. But if any action is voluntary little can be done to "require" participation if landowners still say no. As a result, local watershed coordinators and conservationists must always start at zero. Think how different the communications would be if the landowner's choice was not whether to act but instead a need to act, with the decision being which conservation option to choose.

Reflecting on current policy debates it seems like we are in a period of calm or even stagnation. One bright spot might be how it appears an increasing number of citizens share a growing concern about our lack of progress and inaction. Might this lead us to some type of inflection point or is it just a function of frustration? Is it possible a growing awareness of our need to take a different approach will increase the public and eventually political support for getting serious about what we're doing? If so, this raises several questions. What might be the catalyst for such a change? Will it be a significant piece of future legislation? Could the upcoming 2023 Farm Bill deliberations give Congress the opportunity to replicate and expand the revolutionary programs in the 1985 conservation title? Might books like *The River Knows* and

The Land Remains play a role in educating the public and fueling the debates? Perhaps the carbon, climate, and soil health issues and the new attention they bring will be the catalyst, or at least a reason for new thinking.

What could the state's agenda be? Here are six things Iowa can do now to help bring about a brighter future:

First we can increase the sales tax and fund the natural resources trust fund to generate the amounts of funding needed for large-scale actions and to empower local activities.

Second we need to realize the continuing expansion of livestock production and manure handling impact water quality, and look for improvements such as digitizing land records for manure management plans to prevent over-application and limiting the location of new confined feeding operations.

Third we need to acknowledge the Nutrient Reduction Strategy as written is insufficient, and understand it will take reasonable stewardship regulations to serve as a baseline of protections to achieve any significant improvement.

Fourth we need to encourage Congress to rationalize the federal farm support programs, so we don't fund illogical activities, like the 400,000 acres of land Iowans farm in the two-year floodplain, and to reform conservation programs and crop insurance.

Fifth our focus on climate and carbon efforts need to focus on changing how we manage the land, soil, and water, increasing the use of cover crops, decreasing the reliance on tillage, and improving fertilizer management. Farm-based approaches will be more effective and more distributive than CO_2 pipelines.

Sixth we need to utilize the HUC12 watershed boundary system, as well as the soil and water conservation districts and the drainage districts as institutional tools to help develop, refine, and deliver water quality plans and engage and empower local actors. All these steps require a vision for the future of Iowa's water, land, and agriculture and a plan for how to achieve the vision. To think about how you can be part of the vision, the River has these suggestions.

What Do I, the River, Need You To Do?

I have already told you the river needs more friends but this begs the question how you can become a friend of the river. Here are some ideas for you to consider:

First, think about me, see me as you drive by and consider the role rivers play in your life. Consider what the river does for your community and the values I provide: natural beauty, a place to rest, a home for nature, a source of water and perhaps power, a source of recreation, boating, fishing, or a whitewater park; perhaps even the very reason your town exists, as a "river city."

Second, get out on the river if possible or at least walk my banks and enjoy the opportunities all rivers provide for connecting with nature.

Third, be aware how the river is being impacted, whether through flood control, water withdrawn for irrigation, and how it's impacted by drought.

Fourth, join an organization focused on the values of the river and water, such as Iowa Rivers Revival. Participate in a river cleanup such as the annual Project AWARE, or others run by River Keeper organizations. There is no better way to connect with me than by getting your feet wet and helping protect my health!

Fifth, talk about me with your family and friends, share your experiences so they don't take me for granted.

Sixth, make sure local officials and politicians know how you feel about rivers and how you hope they will act to protect me.

The key is thinking about the river now and what I can mean to you. This creates an opportunity for you to think about what it might mean if something tragic happens and I am gone, effectively unavailable for your use. It is true we often don't know what we have until we lose it—so the key is for you to recognize my value, to use me, love me, and protect me now. If you do these things, I promise your rewards will be real, all rivers know when we make new friends.

CONCLUSION: WHAT IS NATURE'S PLACE IN IOWA AND CAN JUSTICE HELP US DEFINE IT?

As we come to the conclusion of our time with the river, new opportunities are opening. The idea of an Iowa Nature Summit proposed in Chapter Nine is going to happen late in 2023. A central question and focus at the Iowa Nature Summit, one that shapes the health and future of the river, will be what is nature's place in Iowa? Readers will have their own answers but here are some to consider:

- it is the very foundation, the canvas on which we live and work,
- it is the land we farm, air we breathe, water we drink, and wildlife we see,
- it is the playground where we recreate and find peace,
- it is the outdoor classroom where we learn and teach children about science and life,
- it is the lakes, rivers, forests, grasslands, and geography shaping our physical surroundings, and
- it is the weather, climate, and atmosphere giving us rain,

snow, storms, sunny days and the seasons. Nature is all these and more.

If we tried to "calculate" the dollar value of these natural services how great would be that sum? But how do we even begin to value a sunny day, or a Lakeside hike, or a morel hunt in the woods? All these "natural services" are ones we take largely for granted, assuming they will continue to be present, but is our assumption valid? Do we have in place the rules and the ethics to protect nature? When we think about "protecting" nature it is often in the context of potential conflicts. Most often these involve consumptive uses, economic actions using nature, typically degrading it in some way. Converting farmland to houses and server farms, bulldozing an oak savanna or plowing a grassland hill to plant corn, or constructing a new CAFO with the accompanying odors. All these we do, promising to comply with any applicable rules, assuming this will minimize the impact on neighbors, water, air, and nature. These rules and laws are how we protect nature.

If that is true then the question becomes where do we place nature in these decisions, or do we consider it at all? Do we begin by asking how a planned action will impact nature and calculate if the benefits are worth the costs? Or do we treat our impact on nature as cost-free and ask only how will the individual or landowners benefit, not weighing the cost to nature? When you think about the laws and rules we like to call environmental protections, our safeguards for nature, the truth is they really operate not as protections but as licenses to use the environment or nature, often in negative ways. A "clean water permit" tells you how much pollution you can add to a river. A manure management plan tells you how and where you can use the land to dispose of animal wastes. Of course the goal of these laws is to minimize the

risks or damage to nature, to balance its needs with the economic desires of individuals. Are we confident this balancing is really done with
an eye toward nature? This "balancing" is even worse when activities
are free of regulations, then the need to balance or even consider nature is nonexistent. No permit is needed to bulldoze a grove of trees, to
plow a Prairie, to tile a field, or to limit what we call "nonpoint sources"
of water pollution, the primary source of Iowa's poor water quality. In
these cases the place of nature is to yield to our economic desires. Not
much balancing there.

So, to return to the beginning—to the question of what is the place
of nature in Iowa, we appear to have three answers:

- First, it is fundamental, perhaps the single most critical
  factor in the strength of the economy, in the quality of life,
  and in our own health.

- Second, even given this importance the place of nature
  in our decisions is not addressed with much intention, instead we assume whatever we might choose given the circumstances will promote nature. Some choices are more
  positive than others but still it is a choice.

- Third, the truth may be, as sad as it is to admit, for many
  of our actions and for many people the choice is at best to
  treat nature as an afterthought, if it is considered at all. That
  is why it is critical we focus on this topic. Not just to ask
  what is nature's place in Iowa, but to consider what should
  be nature's place in how we Iowans conduct our lives.

This is why our focus can't just be on what is nature's place but also
on how the goal of justice should shape our answers. What does justice mean for nature?

- First it means we must recognize nature as having a stake in our actions. It is not just a blank canvas waiting for us to decide its fate, instead nature must be included in our thinking and decision-making on how our actions impact it.

- Second, we must recognize since nature can't act or speak for itself we have the obligation and responsibility to act and speak for it, to articulate its needs and to weigh and balance them with other needs.

- Third, identifying who or how we speak for nature is critical, if we don't then the interests of nature will not be considered and only the perceived needs of humans will drive our actions.

- Fourth, giving nature a voice means allowing those who speak for it, or those given this role, are allowed to speak, to participate and to be heard, not just the powerful economic and political voices with the most to gain by using nature.

- Fifth, this means ensuring the interests of the public, neighbors, communities, and future generations, not just individual actors, are heard. It means public officials responsible for nature, for protecting and stewarding its future, perform their duties wisely and well.

- Sixth, justice for nature requires us to recognize how broadly its benefits are shared, not just in our consumptive uses but in all the nonconsumptive values it offers, in clean water, pure air, public lands, and open spaces. It means recognizing nature has many living components other than humans, respecting the role of wildlife, healthy soils, and biodiversity to broaden our thinking about nature.

Using justice as a lens to examine the place of nature in our lives offers many benefits. It brings attention to the role of law and policy in shaping our affairs. Justice, like nature, is non-political meaning they should both be common, shared values. Few people will say they are opposed to nature, even fewer will defend actions that are unjust. This does not mean there are not differences in how we might view and weigh these values in any given situation. Therein is perhaps the most important benefit to be gained by turning our focus to nature and justice. Doing so requires us to focus on people and our actions, on how our decisions shape the future. If we do this, the river is optimistic we will find new ways to appreciate it and to discover what the river knows.

IOWA NATURE SUMMIT

NOV. 16-17, 2023 DRAKE UNIVERSITY

Acknowledgments

Writing a book involves many supporting hands. A number of individuals deserve acknowledgment and thanks for their role in helping shape this narrative. A disclaimer though, the fact an individual is listed isn't a basis for ascribing them any responsibility for the opinions and views expressed by the author or the river. The members of what we affectionately call Harry's Book Club provided reactions to an early draft and offered many helpful comments. They include Jim Autry, Harry Bookey, Bob Riley, Dr. Dick Deming, Jeff Chungath, Jeff Fleming, and Mike Schaefer. I want to thank the members of the SPARKS, a group of elders who have been holding weekly calls for the last two years to discuss Iowa's environmental issues. Many themes reflected here were first proposed and discussed among the SPARKS, in particular the big ideas reflected in Chapter Nine. Members who deserve a particular shout out include Christine Curry, Mike Delaney, and Pat Boddy for their helpful insights. A number of my agricultural law colleagues also shared insights on the book, including Jennie Zwagerman, my successor at Drake, and other trusted friends and colleagues like Susan Schneider at the University of Arkansas and Anthony Schutz at the University of Nebraska Lincoln. I benefited from the support and encouragement of several other friends and authors, notably Sarah Vogel whose outstanding book *The Farmers Lawyer* tells the poignant tale of the 1980's farm crisis, and Beth Hoffman author of *Bet the Farm* who has added so much to the Iowa food and farming scene.

As noted in the dedication, my friends and colleagues at the Iowa Natural Heritage Foundation deserve great credit for the work they are doing all across our state helping landowners and local officials protect unique lands and waters. It is been a great personal honor to be involved with the Foundation board now for over 30 years. A special thank you to Joe McGovern the president of INHF for his support and friendship. A number of colleagues, either former employees of the Iowa DNR such as Mary Skopec and Alan Bonini, or current employees like Iowa's number one paddler Nate Hoogeveen shared insights as to the current Iowa water situation. Roger Wolf from the Iowa Soybean Association kindly agreed to be interviewed for the book. I benefited from the comments and insights provided by several other friends who read drafts including Julie Ghrist, Jerry Anderson, Amy Goldman Fowler, Larry Stone, Paul Willis, and Luke Hoffman. Several Iowa environmental leaders deserve thanks for their support as well including Mark Ackelson, Ray Harding, Seth Watkins, Matt Russell, and Chris Jones. As you will read in the first chapters, the book was influenced by my opportunity to spend time on the Raccoon River, so a special thank you to my friend and paddling buddy John Norwood for his support and encouragement the many times we ventured out on the river. I also want to thank my colleagues on the Dallas County Soil and Water Conservation Commission, and the hundreds of fellow commissioners all across the state fighting to protect the soil and water we depend on for our future.

Our good friends Susan and Bill Knapp deserve special thanks for providing a winter getaway at their home on Siesta Key, the perfect place to write and develop the themes for this book. Any book about Iowa nature stands on the work of other authors, and no one has played a more leading role than Connie Mutel at the University of Iowa for her nature writing. Steve Semken at Ice Cube Press deserves special thanks for having faith in my writing and for creating the opportunity to share these views with readers. This book and *The Land Remains* would not exist without his great work. Finally, any project like this one spanning over two years is only possible with the support of a loving family. In my situation, this means my wife Khanh, my partner at Sunstead, where we enjoy raising food for friends, sharing the bounty, and caring for our large herd of cats. They no doubt indirectly influenced this writing as well. For more information about many of the organizations mentioned and for information about the Iowa Nature Summit planned for later in 2023, please see the reading list and resource guide. Thank you for your interest in the river and I hope to see you sometime on Iowa's rivers and streams, perhaps even on our friend and narrator the Raccoon.

Suggested Reading List

Mark Arax, *The Dreamt Land: Chasing Water and Dust Across California*, Alfred A Knopf, 2019

John M. Barry, *Rising Tide: The Great Mississippi Flood of 1927 and How It Changed America*, Simon and Schuster, 1997

Guilio Boccaletti, *Water: A Biography*, Pantheon Books, 2021

Lyndsie Bourgon, *Tree Thieves: Crime and Survival in North America's Woods*, Little, Brown Spark, 2022

Douglas Brinkley, *The Silent Spring Revolution: John F. Kennedy, Rachel Carson, Lyndon Johnson, Richard Nixon and the Great Environmental Awakening*, Harper Collins, 2022

Rinker Buck, *Life on the Mississippi: An Epic American Adventure*, Avid Reader Press, 2022

Ivan Doig, *This House of Sky: Landscapes of the Western Mind*, Harcourt Inc., 1978

Martin Doyle, *The Source: How Rivers Made America and America Remade Its Rivers*, WW Norton and Company, 2018

Dan Egan, *The Death and Life of the Great Lakes*, WW Norton Company, 2017

Dan Egan, *The Devil's Element: Phosphorus and a World Out of Balance*, WW Norton and Company, 2023

Beth Hoffman, *Bet the Farm: the Dollars and Cents of Growing Food in America*, Island Press, 2021

Tyler Kelley, *Holding Back the River: The Struggle Against Nature on America's Waterways*, Avid Reader Press, 2021

Ezra Klein, *Why We're Polarized*, Avid Reader Press, 2020

Kristen Kobes Du Mez, *Jesus and John Wayne: How White Evangelicals Corrupted a Faith and Fractured a Nation*, Liveright, 2020

Aldo Leopold, *A Sand County Almanac and Sketches Here and There*, Oxford University Press, 1949

Cornelia F. Mutel, *The Emerald Horizon: the History of Nature in Iowa*, University of Iowa Press, 2008

Cornelia F. Mutel, ed., *Tending Iowa's Land: Pathways to a Sustainable Future*, University of Iowa Press, 2022

Nick Offerman, *Gumption: Relighting the Torch of Freedom with America's Gutsiest Troublemakers*, Dutton, 2015

Nick Offerman, *Where the Deer and the Antelope Play: the Pastoral Observations of One Ignorant American Who Loves to Walk Outside*, Dutton, 2021

David Owen, *Where the Water Goes: Life and Death Along the Colorado River*, Riverhead Books, 2017

Steven Pinker, *Enlightenment Now: The Case for Reason, Science, Humanism, and Progress*, Viking, 2018

Annie Proulx, *Fen, Bog, and Swamp: A Short History of Peatland Destruction and Its Role in the Climate Crisis*, Scribner, 2022

James Rebanks, *A Shepherd's Life*, 2015

James Rebanks, *Pastoral Song: A Farmer's Journey*, Custom House, 2020

Marc Reisner, *Cadillac Desert: The American West and Its Disappearing Water*, Penguin Books, 1986

Paul Schneider, *Old Man River: the Mississippi River in North American History*, Henry Holt and Company, 2013

Nate Schweber, *This America of Ours: Bernard and Avis DeVoto and the Forgotten Fight to Save the Wild*, Mariner Books, 2022

Lawrence C Smith, *Rivers of Power: How a Natural Force Raised Kingdoms, Destroyed Civilizations and Shapes Our World*, Little, Brown Spark, 2020

John Steinbeck, *The Grapes of Wrath*, Viking, 1939

Katherine Stewart, *The Power Worshippers: Inside the Dangerous Rise of Religious Nationalism*, Bloomsbury, 2020

Maya K. Van Rossum, *The Green Amendment: the People's Fight for a Clean, Safe, and Healthy Environment*, Disruption Books, 2022

Robert James Waller, *Just Beyond the Firelight: stories and essays*, Iowa State Press, 1988

Robert James Waller, *Iowa: perspectives on today and tomorrow*, Iowa State Press, 1991

Ai Wei Wei, *1000 Years of Joys and Sorrows: a Memoir*, Crown, 2021

Gary White and Matt Damon, *The Worth of Water: Our Story of Chasing Solutions to the World's Greatest Challenge*, Penguin, 2022

Nate Hoogeveen, *Paddling Iowa: 128 Outstanding Journeys by Canoe and Kayak*, Otter Run Media, 2012

Wallace Stegner, *Beyond the Hundredth Meridian: John Wesley Powell and the Second Opening of the West*, Houghton Mifflin Co, 1954

OTHER RESOURCES

America's Rivers – www.americanrivers.org/rivers/
Iowa Natural Heritage Foundation – www.inhf.org
Iowa Rivers Revival – www.iowarivers.org
Iowa Nature Summit – www.iowanature.org
Niman Ranch – www.nimanranch.com

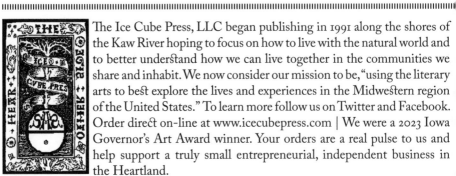

The Ice Cube Press, LLC began publishing in 1991 along the shores of the Kaw River hoping to focus on how to live with the natural world and to better understand how we can live together in the communities we share and inhabit. We now consider our mission to be, "using the literary arts to best explore the lives and experiences in the Midwestern region of the United States." To learn more follow us on Twitter and Facebook. Order direct on-line at www.icecubepress.com | We were a 2023 Iowa Governor's Art Award winner. Your orders are a real pulse to us and help support a truly small entrepreneurial, independent business in the Heartland.